SHANKAR GOYAL
MARCHING WITH HISTORY

Professor Shankar Goyal delivering the Presidential Address to the XXXVII Annual Congress of the Epigraphical Society of India, held at Baroda, 2012.

Shankar Goyal
Marching with History

Foreword by
KUMKUM ROY

Edited with an Introduction by
RADHIKA SESHAN

ADITYA PRAKASHAN
New Delhi

First Edition, 2021

ISBN 978-81-950961-3-8
Rs. 900

Published by Aditya Prakashan, 2/18, Ansari Road, New Delhi – 110 002.

Email: contact@adityaprakashan.com
Website: www.adityaprakashan.com

Printed in India at Thomson Press (India) Limited

Dedicated to Professor Shankar Goyal's **Piddu**,
his faithful canine companion until just before frution,
by the editor and contributors.

Editorial

These volumes are a festschrift to Professor Shankar Goyal, a historian of international repute. The planning for the festschrift began in 2018, about a year before Professor Goyal retired from his official position as Professor in the Department of History, Jai Narain Vyas University, Jodhpur, and we are very glad to see the volumes out in print now. The word 'official' has been deliberately used here, for while Professor Goyal is no longer in office, he continues to be involved in his work to the same extent.

The original idea was to put together a single volume, with papers by different scholars on the various areas of Shankar Goyal's own research. While planning that, we also received a number of articles on his own writings, rather than just on his areas of research, and thus, the publication gradually developed, to become two volumes. Each volume is complete in itself, but at the same time, are also companion volumes. We believe that the volumes, individually and jointly, will contribute significantly to the academic world, by bringing together a range of papers on the themes with which Professor Goyal has been consistently engaged.

This first volume, containing scholarly papers by Mahesh Vikram Singh, Vibha Upadhyaya, T.S. Ravishankar, J.K. Sharma, L.S. Rathore, A. Chandrasekaran, Nagendra Singh Bhati, and Sharad Rajimwale, focusses on Professor Shankar Goyal's own writings. Radhika Seshan has written an initial detailed paper on Professor Goyal's work, which lists his works and includes comments on them by eminent historians. The other contributors in this volume, who have been engaged with both Professor Goyal and his work, have discussed in their respective papers his approach to the discipline and contributions to historical studies in general and also to the specific areas on which he has worked. The volume will, we are sure, be of tremendous value to all the serious students of ancient Indian history, bringing together as it does, the work of Professor Shankar Goyal on history and historiography.

The companion volume titled *Situating Indian History for Shankar Goyal* brings together the work of scholars such as Nayanjot Lahiri, Udai Prakash Arora, Shireen Moosvi, Susmita Basu Majumdar, Romila Thapar, Kumkum Roy, Suchandra Ghosh, R. Champakalakshmi, P. Shanmugam, R. Mahalakshmi, Radhika Seshan, Irfan Habib, Saiyid Zaheer Husain Jafri, Ishrat Alam and Bhairabi Prasad Sahu, and many others. All these scholars have engaged with different aspects of Professor Shankar Goyal's work, so that, where the first volume is on his own writing, the second reflects his wide-ranging interests in the fields of history and historiography.

Finally, a last word on the dedication of the volume to Professor Shankar Goyal's canine companion Piddu, who was present at the beginning of the journey toward this festschrift, and who participated in his own way in all the discussions, but who passed away before their publication.

December 12, 2020

Radhika Seshan
Professor of History
Savitribai Phule Pune University, Pune

Foreword

Born in 1959, Shankar Goyal, son of the famous historian S.R. Goyal and Kusum Goyal, has contributed significantly to our understanding of early and early medieval history. The contributors to this volume have presented and discussed his voluminous work in detail and at length.

Shankar Goyal's publications, focusing on issues of historiography in general, the period of Harshavardhana in particular, and Rajasthan, where he has lived and worked for decades, have been prolific. Apart from his long-standing engagement with the history of Harsha, Goyal has also investigated other major dynasties such as the Guptas and the Vākāṭakas. Many of the volumes that he has edited contain contributions from scholars representing diverse points of view. In combining and collating these, Goyal has demonstrated his diligence, empathy and understanding, standing for an open-ended tradition of scholarship that is valuable in situations where academic discourse occasionally tends to be unnecessarily and fruitlessly polarized.

As important, Shankar Goyal has demonstrated a commitment toward developing a detailed understanding of a wide range of themes and issues, scrutinizing sources with care and throughness. He displays an ability to analyze a range of textual, inscriptional and numismatic material and combine these to arrive at his conclusions. This is a distinctive hallmark of his scholarship that is particularly valuable in a situation where we often tend to jump to rapid conclusions, and lack the patience required for painstaking investigations. Further, methodologically, Goyal consistently contextualizes his discussion on political events, processes, personalities and institutions in terms of the wider political, economic and cultural worlds within which these are located.

In the present volume, Radhika Seshan provides a detailed and annotated bibliographical survey of the publications of Shankar Goyal and their reception by contemporary scholars. Also included is a list of his ever-growing publications. This would be valuable for those who are interested in a bird's eye view of his work, and who may wish to follow up any of the themes.

The volume includes two essays by Mahesh Vikram Singh. In the first, he discusses Shankar Goyal's analysis of the historiography on ancient India in general, while the second focuses on Goyal's investigations on his favourite subject, Harshavardhana. In the first of these essays, Singh contextualizes Goyal's contribution by comparing it with other attempts at providing historiographical surveys. He also provides summaries of Goyal's work. As in the case of Seshan's contribution, this will enable the curious reader to find her/ his way through Goyal's prolific scholarship.

The grounds on which Shankar Goyal agrees or disagrees with earlier scholars have also been documented carefully. These include an evaluation of the chronology of sources such as the Vedas and Purāṇas, about which there is unlikely to be any consensus. For later periods, textual traditions are juxtaposed with inscriptional and numismatic evidence, and, to a lesser extent, archaeological sources as well.

Singh highlights both the areas where Shankar Goyal engages with contemporary scholarship as well as those on which he touches lightly or not at all. Once again, this is useful in order to contextualize Goyal's work. Goyal distinguishes between historical studies on the basis of their perspectives as well as their chronology, using 1947 as a marker. While this works reasonably well in most cases, not all scholarship fits in neatly within this framework. Also, while the dynastic framework works reasonably well, there is much in recent scholarship that moves beyond this understanding of the political. Given Goyal's indefatigable intellectual curiosity and energy, I am sure that he will take these into consideration in future.

Singh's second essay focuses on Shankar Goyal's fascination with Harsha, which has been a constant feature for decades. Singh traces the trajectory of this involvement, as well as the different facets of Harsha and his times that Goyal has painstakingly drawn attention to. It is an excellent example of the kinds of results that can be achieved through intensive and constant engagement with a theme. Indeed, one of the points Singh elaborates and reiterates is the way in which Goyal revisits and teases apart the standard sources, the *Harshacharita* of Bāṇabhaṭṭa and the Chinese pilgrim Yuan Chwang's account, examining these critically, drawing attention to the perspectives and preoccupations of the authors, and utilizing them with care. What is also significant, as Singh highlights, is that Goyal attempts to contextualize Harsha in terms of contemporary political, economic, cultural and religious contexts, moving away from a bald narrative of political events and dynastic changes.

Vibha Upadhyaya draws attention to Shankar Goyal's discussion on Marxist historiography, which is a running strand through several of his books and articles. She points out how Goyal advocates a critical approach, recognizing the importance of contextualizing historical developments in terms of economic processes, but also acknowledging the importance of other spheres in shaping historical events. Here, it may be noted that Marxist historiography has not been monolithic—in fact there have been lively and sometimes heated debates amongst Marxist historians, and these have often been fruitful. This is an area where perhaps a more nuanced engagement is both possible and desirable.

The next essay, by T. S. Ravishankar, examines how Shankar Goyal has used both epigraphic and numismatic evidence in his research. The author draws attention to the Goyal's analysis of Gupta and Vākāṭaka inscriptions in particular. These studies range from the intricacies of dynastic history, to an investigation of the possible economic milieu of the time. The author also notes Goyal's study of Aśokan inscriptions. And, given Goyal's abiding preoccupation with Harsha, Ravishankar mentions his treatment of the king's inscriptions as well. Also, Goyal's interest in historiographical matters extends to numismatics, where he has provided insights on numismatic studies by evaluating the contributions of eminent scholars.

J.K. Sharma focuses on Shankar Goyal's discussion on the Gupta age. Here, as in the case of other themes, there is a concern with historiographical trends as well as the interpretation of a range of sources—textual, epigraphic, and numismatic. Assessing the significance of the Gupta age has been a contentious issue. However, as Sharma points out, Goyal steers through these controversies and attempts an independent evaluation of economic, political, religious and cultural developments.

Although Shankar Goyal's primary focus has been on the political history of north India, he has also given attention to the Deccan and South India. The significance of these endeavours has been highlighted by A. Chandrasekaran. The author draws attention to Goyal's perceptive studies on the Vākāṭakas. Further south, Goyal has explored the rich Tamil *bhakti* tradition. And, expectedly, given his abiding interest in historiographical issues, he has attempted to critically evaluate the trends in studies of south Indian history as well.

In a brief essay, Nagendra Singh Bhati returns to one of Shankar Goyal's central concerns—the declining popularity of studies on political theory and political history. In illustrating this, Bhati draws on Goyal's engagement with the works of P.S. Bhati.

The final contribution, by Sharad Rajimwale, traces the ways in which orientalist and nationalist ideas have emerged, and been modified over the last two centuries, as well as Shankar Goyal's response to these ideas. Rajimwale's engagement is at once critical and incisive.

All in all, the volume provides a map and a guide for readers who may be interested in making their way through the extensive and intensive investigations that have been the hallmark of Shankar Goyal's scholarship. What is valuable is his willingness to engage with, understand as well as present diverse strands of thought. Also valuable is his commitment to and appreciation of the minute details of sources — textual, epigraphic, and numismatic. It is to be hoped that his attention to these details, as well as his scholarly pursuits will enrich the discipline in the years ahead.

November 30, 2020

Kumkum Roy
Centre for Historical Studies
Jawaharlal Nehru University, New Delhi

Introduction

Shankar Goyal: A Life in History and Historiography

This volume is a tribute to a prolific writer and a serious scholar of history, whose contribution to the discipline is truly remarkable. His many years of research and writing — and, of course, teaching — have influenced many researchers, young and old, and his works will continue to carry great weight among future generations of researchers as well.

Shankar Goyal retired in 2019 from his position as Professor of the Department of History, Jai Narain Vyas University, Jodhpur. An alumnus of the Deccan College, Pune, his work has primarily focussed on early Indian history, and on the early medieval period of India's past. His works on Harsha are seminal and will undoubtedly be the standard reference point for many years to come.

However, what I think is particularly important, is that Shankar Goyal places the study of history in the context of time and space as well as of historiography. The relevance of historiography, and the need to have a thorough grounding in the works of earlier scholars and of the sources, is something that underpins everything that he has written. History, well studied, requires a clear and objective understanding not only of the time being studied, but also the later time in which an earlier period is being written about. Historiography, as he has constantly said, is the base of understanding processes of historical continuity and change. It is this aspect that this volume seeks to highlight, through studies of what Shankar Goyal has written. This volume is therefore both, a study of the historiography of Shankar Goyal, and the relevance of such writing to the study of history as a whole.

It is necessary to emphasise here that Shankar Goyal also exemplifies the ability to change ideas, and to accept different ideas and approaches over time. History and its study is about broadening the scope of one's own understanding, and it is this aspect that one can trace if one takes all of Shankar Goyal's works in chronological order. Initially, his writings and thoughts were much influenced by his father, the late Professor S.R. Goyal, who had himself been a major proponent of the integral approach. Following his father, Shankar Goyal too had this approach to the study of history. His writings have always underlined the need to understand the *how* and the *why* rather than just the *what* and the *when* of history. Conventionally, it has been said that political history has always been about the *what*, but Shankar Goyal has shown how, through political history also, questions of the *how* and *why* can also be raised and answered.

In his later writings, one can see the influence of the Marxist approach. Shankar Goyal himself states that he has been considerably influenced by Professor Romila Thapar and by the late Professor R.S. Sharma. The latter's writings on the Kali age and on feudalism, for example, have led to Shankar Goyal's own more recent writings on feudalism. His work on the Vākāṭaka economy, for example, has traced the feudal elements in that period. Further researches in this direction are to be seen in his recent works on the age of Harsha and on Yuan Chwang. However, it must be pointed out that while Shankar Goyal's research into the question of feudalism was inspired by R.S. Sharma, his work is in no way a mere repetition; rather, he has taken the entire debate on feudalism further ahead.

As part of this new research, one of the most important aspects has been his work on placing the age of Harsha as clearly marking the transition to the 'medieval' age. This age, as marking the end of the classical age and the rise of feudalism, and the changes that took place in social, economic and political life from the Gupta age to the age of Harsha, have all identified markers of change.

Shankar Goyal's most recent work, on Yuan Chwang, is yet another seminal contribution to the field of history. In recent times, he is the only historian to have examined Yuan Chwang's writings again; but what to me is the most important feature, is that he has studied Yuan Chwang not just as a 'foreign travellers' account', but as one that throws greater light on the processes of change, and the ways in which this traveller identified change. These details, Shankar Goyal has placed within his broader discussion on feudal processes. Given the importance of his work, it is not surprising that Chinese translations of both, Shankar Goyal's work on Harsha and on Yuan Chwang, are in the pipeline, and should be published shortly.

Thus, any researcher on the issue of transitions, on feudalism, on culture, or on defining moments in history, would do well to study the writings of Shankar Goyal in greater detail. It is, I think, necessary to reiterate here that Shankar Goyal's corpus of writings have placed before the scholarly community a standard of historical work that emphasises critique and questioning. History is about continuity and change, about time and space, and about the context of both the age and the writing about that age. It is also about understanding why, in a particular time, certain kinds of writings dominated, and the ways in which such thinking and writing began to be questioned. In his own work, Shankar Goyal has demonstrated that no one can be static in approach. His work has enriched our understanding of all these aspects of writing, researching, and thinking about history.

The volume begins with a study of Shankar Goyal's works. This is a chronological account of his writings and has included some of the important reviews of the work. (On a very personal note, I must say that until the bibliography for this paper was put together, I had not consciously realised just how much work he has done, and how much I have used his work in my classes!).

The volume then goes on to Mahesh Vikram Singh's paper entitled 'Shankar Goyal on Modern Historiography of Ancient India'. Shankar Goyal's *Recent Historiography of Ancient India*, published in 1997, is the starting point of this paper, for in this book, he has provided detailed analyses of both, recent writings (recent of course used in the context of the year of publication) on the period, as well as analyses of earlier works of the historiography of the period. Thus, this book in itself is of tremendous value for students and scholars of history. Singh has pointed out that the distinctive feature of Shankar Goyal's writing is that he has tried to bring out both the contributions and the limitations of the works that he has studied in this book. The paper has been divided into several sections, each dealing with a specific aspect of the historiography studied by Shankar Goyal.

Chapter six of the volume has also been contributed by Mahesh Vikram Singh, and deals with 'Situating Harsha in the History of Early India by Shankar Goyal'. Singh has here analysed the work of Shankar Goyal within the framework that the latter has used, of locating political history against the "backdrop of whole social, economic, demographic and anthropological settings." Singh has also drawn attention to Shankar Goyal's work on *The Significance of Yuan Chwang in the Context of the Seventh Century: A Critical Assessment*, and the stand that Goyal has taken on this traveller, in comparison with other historians on the subject. Singh has therefore provided a good overview of the trends in history and historiography, something that is particularly relevant in a tribute to a scholar who has always foregrounded historiography.

Vibha Upadhyaya's paper entitled 'Shankar Goyal's Studies on the Marxist Interpretations of Ancient India' (chapter three) takes up one aspect of interpretation. She has therefore examined one work of Goyal's in particular, his *Marxist Interpretation of Ancient Indian History* (Bhandarkar Oriental Research Institute, Pune, 2002). In this work, as Upadhyaya has pointed out, Shankar Goyal has examined the contribution of scholars using the Marxist methodology and approach in their writings on ancient India. Shankar Goyal has here taken a broad sweep, for he deals with the writings of Marxist scholars from S.A. Dange onwards, through D.D. Kosambi, R.S. Sharma, Romila Thapar, D.N. Jha, G.M. Bongard-Levin, H.P. Ray, and many others.

Shankar Goyal has also contributed tremendously to the fields of epigraphic and numismatic studies, the focus of the next paper in this volume. T.S. Ravishankar, in his 'Shankar Goyal's Probings in Epigraphical and Numismatic Studies' (chapter four), has drawn attention to his immense contribution in this field. Shankar Goyal's epigraphical studies have brought to light much more evidence on the Vākāṭaka age. As Ravishankar has pointed out, Shankar Goyal's contribution here is extremely significant, bringing to light, as it does, the nature of Vākāṭaka economy, and, as always, a review of the earlier writings on this important dynasty. Equally important, in Ravishankar's view, has been Shankar Goyal's paper in the book jointly edited by Munish Chandra Joshi, S.K. Gupta and Shankar Goyal, entitled *King Chandra and the Meharauli Pillar* (Meerut, 1989). In the field of numismatics, Shankar Goyal's contributions are no less significant.

The Gupta age is one that has been of great importance to scholars. This is the focus of the next chapter in this volume, the contribution of J.K. Sharma, on 'Shankar Goyal on the Gupta Age'. As Sharma has pointed out, Shankar Goyal has underlined the "changing perceptions of the Gupta period due mainly to the alternative interpretations of literary, numismatic and epigraphical (including archaeology) sources." Sharma has here provided an exhaustive survey of Shankar Goyal's writings on the Gupta age.

L.S. Rathore takes us into another of Shankar Goyal's key concerns, in chapter seven of the book entitled 'Shankar Goyal's Contribution to Medieval/Modern History and Historiography of Rajasthan'. Three significant works have been brought out by Shankar Goyal on this question, which cover different aspects of the sources of the history of Rajasthan. As always, Shankar Goyal has, in these books, also discussed historiography in great detail. Rathore has drawn the attention of the reader to Shankar Goyal's chapter on Tod's *Annals and Antiquities of Rajasthan* in particular, for, as he says, Shankar Goyal has described both the contributions of Tod to the study of region, and the broader historical focus on chronological histories.

Another dimension of Shankar Goyal's research has been on the Deccan and South India, the focus of the next chapter in the book. A.

Chandrasekaran, in his chapter entitled 'Shankar Goyal's Studies on the History of Deccan and South India', has drawn our attention to this aspect. Mention has been made earlier of Shankar Goyal's contribution to the study of the Vākāṭaka dynasty. As Chandrasekaran points out, this is far from the sum total of Shankar Goyal's contribution to the history of the south of India. His analysis of the Bhakti movement, and particularly on the Nāyanārs and Āḷvārs, is something that Chandrasekaran has particularly highlighted. Once again, historiography remains a key area for Shankar Goyal, seen here in his studies of the works of S. Krishnaswami Aiyangar, K.A. Nilakanta Sastri and T.V. Mahalingam. Shankar Goyal has also discussed the spread of Buddhism in the Tamil land.

Chapter nine of the book, by Nagendra Singh Bhati, entitled 'Shankar Goyal on the Problems of the Decline of Political Theory and Political History', has drawn our attention to Shankar Goyal's discussions on political theory. As Bhati says, Shankar Goyal has made a comparison between the state of studies on political theory and political history in the West and in India, pointing out that, in the former, such studies are making a comeback, which does not appear to be the case here. Bhati particularly draws our attention to Shankar Goyal's critical examaination of the decline and revival of normative political theory.

The final chapter in the book, 'India as a Multicultural Society: Shankar Goyal's View', by Sharad Rajimwale, has examined the ways in which Shankar Goyal has analysed the emergence of multiculturalism in the Indian context. Shankar Goyal has focussed on the Western research, and the tropes that were utilised by Western scholars to study India, and has then moved on to discuss the issue of India's growth as a 'nation'. Rajimwale has studied the many dimensions that Shankar Goyal has put forward, and analysed them in the context of history and historiography.

In sum, this volume brings together the multifarious nature of Shankar Goyal's work. In keeping with Shankar Goyal's own maxims, the contributors to this volume have been both critical and appreciative of the work that this historian has done, in the course of a long and fruitful career. We believe that this book will help the community of scholars and students of history to understand the ways in which, through his own work, Shankar Goyal has consistently sought to highlight time, space, and the contextuality of history writing.

December 12, 2020

Radhika Seshan
Professor of History
Savitribai Phule Pune University, Pune

Contents

Chapter One

Shankar Goyal's Intellectual Odyssey

RADHIKA SESHAN
Professor of History
Savitribai Phule Pune University

I. ACADEMIC JOURNEY SO FAR

An *alumnus* of the prestigious Deccan College, Pune, Shankar Goyal is Professor of History, Jai Narain Vyas University, Jodhpur (Rajasthan). He is the son of late Professor S.R. Goyal, a renowned historian, who had been Professor and Head, Department of History, Jai Narain Vyas University, Jodhpur. Born in the year 1959, Shankar Goyal did his graduation from the University of Rajasthan, Jaipur, postgraduation from the Deccan College, Pune, and earned his doctoral degree on *Main Trends in Indian Historiography Since Independence*, and D. Litt. degree on *Political History as an Integral Study of Political Life and Institutions : A Multidisciplinary Approach to Harsha and His Times* both from Jai Narain Vyas University, Jodhpur.

Apart from publishing over 150 research articles in reputed national and foreign journals and standard works, Professor Goyal has also authored and edited / co-edited about forty research works so far, dealing with some aspects of ancient Indian history and the historiography of medieval/modern Rajasthan. These include twenty one books authored by him, namely, 1. *History and Historiography of the Age of Harsha* (1992), 2. *Aspects of Ancient Indian History and Historiography* (1993), 3. *History Writing of Early India* (1996), 4. *The Image of Classical India* (1997), 5. *Recent Historiography of Ancient India* (his Ph.D. work, 1997), 6. *Ancient Indian Numismatics* (1998), 7. *Marxist Interpretation of Ancient

Indian History (2000), 8. *Prāchīna Bhāratīya Itihāsa aura Saṁskṛti* (2001), 9. *Problems of Ancient Indian History* (2001), 10. *Contemporary Interpreters of Ancient India* (2003), 11. *Harsha : A Multidisciplinary Political Study* (his D.Litt. thesis, 2006), 12. *Ancient India : A Multidisciplinary Approach* (2006), 13. *175 Years of Vākāṭaka History and Historiography* (2009), 14. *Probings in Indian History* (2009), 15. *Studies in the History of Deccan and South India* (2009), 16. *The 'Medieval' Factor and the Age of Harsha: A Cultural Study* (2016), 17. *Origin and Growth of History Writing in Rajasthan*, Volume I : *Khyats and Allied Works of Historical Genre* (2017), 18. *Origin and Growth of History Writing in Rajasthan*, Volume II : *Historians and Historiography in Modern Rajasthan* (2018), 19. *Harsha Revisited : A Re-interpretation of Existing Data* (2018), 20. *The Significance of Yuan Chwang in the Context of the Seventh Century : A Critical Assessment* (2018), and 21. *The Classical Age : A Study in Feudalization* (2021, to be published shortly). His edited/co-edited works include : 22. *King Chandra and the Meharauli Pillar* (with Munish Chandra Joshi and S.K. Gupta,1989), 23. *Political History in a Changing World* (with G.C. Pande and S.K. Gupta,1992), 24. *Reappraising Gupta History for S.R. Goyal* (with B.Ch. Chhabra et al,1992), 25. *S. R. Goyal : His Multidimensional Historiography* (with Jagannath Agrawal,1992), 26. *Spectrum of Nehru's Thought* (with Sobhag Mathur,1994), 27. *Bhāratīya Itihāsa ko Rajasthan kā Avadāna* (with Sobhag Mathur,1995), 28. *Bhāratīya Saṁskṛti ko Rajasthan kā Avadāna* (with Sobhag Mathur,1995), 29. *Indian Art of the Gupta Age* (with S.R. Goyal, 2000), 30. *Prāchīna Bhārata kā Ādhunika Itihāsa-Lekhana* (2000), 31. *Reconstructing Indian History for S.R. Goyal*, Volume I : *Professor S. R. Goyal : The Profile of a Historian* (2003), 32. *Reconstructing Indian History for S.R. Goyal*, Volume II : *India's Ancient Past* (2003), 33. *Reconstructing Indian History for S. R. Goyal*, Volume III : *India's Medieval and Modern Past* (2003), 34. *Reconstructing Indian History for S.R. Goyal*, Volume IV : *Rajasthan: From Prehistory to the Independence Era* (2003), 35. *Investigating Indian Society* (2013), 36. *Indian Society : The Regional Contours* (2013), 37. *Reinterpreting Indian History* (2014), 38. *History and Politics* (2015), 39. *Early India: Historical Probings* (2015), and 40. *Origin and Growth of History Writing in Rajasthan*, Volume III : *Historians and Historiography in Contemporary Rajasthan* (2019). Professor Goyal's books and many articles brought him encomium from scholars, such as, Professors R. N. Dandekar, G.C. Pande, R. S. Sharma, Irfan Habib, Romila Thapar, R. Champakalakshmi, Shireen Moosvi, Kumkum Roy, A. M. Shastri, Bardwell L. Smith (Minnesota, U.S.A.), Walter M. Spink (Michigan, U.S.A.), Maurizio Taddei (Napoli, Italy), P. K. Mitra (Rajshahi, Bangladesh) and many others.

Committed to the dissemination of scientific and secular history through the teaching and writing of history, Professor Shankar Goyal has been General President of the Epigraphical Society of India (2012) and Sectional President of the South Indian History Congress (2009), Tamilnadu History Congress (2016) and Indian History Congress (2017). He has travelled widely in China (2012), Australia (2013), the United States (2014), Canada (2014), Europe (2019) and Egypt (2019). He was also invited by the Organising Committee of the 16th World Sanskrit Conference, 2015, Silpakorn University, Bangkok, Thailand, to participate in the deliberations of their Epigraphy Section to promote Indian epigraphical studies on the world forum. He has also delivered many prestigious endowment lectures in various universities of India.

II. BOOKS

The first research paper of Shankar Goyal was published in the year 1974 and the first book in 1992. Since then he has been working ceaselessly and silently, and the outcome is his voluminous contribution bearing at every inch a stamp of high quality and original thinking. The main areas of his interest have been political history, especially of the age of Harsha, historiography, cultural history, epigraphy, numismatics and art but he has written a lot—and that too authoritatively—on various other branches of Indological studies. The standard of the researches of a scholar is known by the general opinion about his scholarship in the academic world, by the reviews of his works in learned national and international journals, by the views expressed on them by eminent scholars of the subject, and by the notices his works receive in standard works of others. From this point of view the research works of Shankar Goyal may be regarded as of a very high order. They have been greatly appreciated and praised in their reviews published not only in the Indian journals, including *Journal of Indian History*, *The Indian Historial Review*, *Annals of the Bhandarkar Oriental Research Institute*, *Quarterly Review of Historial Studies*, *History Today*, *Bhāratī*, *Vishveshvaranand Indological Journal*, *Journal of the Epigraphical Society of India*, *Journal of the Numismatic Society of India*, etc., newspapers, like, *National Herald*, *The Hindustan Times*, *Indian Express*, *The Hindu*, etc., but also in reputed foreign journals, such as, *East and West* (Italy), *Journal of the Royal Asiatic Society* (London), *Journal of the American Oriental Society* (New Haven), *Estudios de Asia y Africa* (Mexico), *Journal of the Asiatic Society of Bangladesh* (Dacca), etc. Shankar Goyal's works are also found discussed at scores of places in standard works, like, *The Vākāṭakas : An Essay in Hindu Iconology* (by Hans T. Bakker, Egbert Frosten, Groningen, The Netherlands, 1997), *A*

Peep into Socio-Political Dynamics of Early Indian History (by Mahesh Vikram Singh, Mahatma Gandhi Kashi Vidyapith, Varanasi, 2002), *Prārambhika Bhārata kā Parichaya* (by R.S. Sharma, Orient Longman, New Delhi, 2004), *The Vākāṭaka Heritage : Indian Culture at the Crossroads* (ed. by Hans T. Bakker, Egbert Forsten, Groningen, The Netherlands, 2004), *India Rediscovered: A New Vision of History and Call of the Age* (by Mahesh Vikram Singh, Northern Book Centre, New Delhi, 2006), *Rajasthan Itihāsa ke Abhigyāna Rūpa* (by G.S.L. Devra, Rajasthan Hindi Grantha Academy, Jaipur, 2010), *Ideas and Movements in the Age of the Mauryas* (by S.N. Dube, Indian Institute of Advanced Study, Rashtrapati Nivas, Shimla, 2012), and *The Past Before Us : Historical Traditions of Early North India* (by Romila Thapar, Permanent Black, New Delhi, 2013). Many papers/chapters have also been written on Shankar Goyal's suggestions, e.g., S.V. Sohoni, 'In Defence of Mayūra and Bāṇa', in *Bulletin of the Deccan College Post-Graduate and Research Institute*, Vol. 53, 1993, pp. 351-55; Manorama Upadhyaya, 'Harsha aura Rajasthan', in *Rajasthan Bhāratī*, Volume I : *Bhāratīya Itihāsa ko Rajasthan kā Avadāna*, eds. Sobhag Mathur and Shankar Goyal, Jodhpur, 1995, pp. II, 21-26; W.R. Antarkar, 'The Era of King Harṣa (-vardhana) of Kanoj', in *Annals of the Bhandarkar Oriental Research Institute*, Vol. LXXVIII, 1997, pp. 223-31; and Pradip Meshram, 'Vākāṭaka Coins : Not Myth, A Reality', in *The Journal of the Numismatic Society of India*, Vol. LXXII, Part I, 2010, pp. 34-41; etc. Other scholars who take note of Shankar Goyal's suggestions and theories include Hermann Kulke, Ellen M. Raven, Ashvini Agrawal, Chandrashekhar Gupta, J.K. Sharma, Rajwant Rao, Manmohan Kumar, Nandini Sinha Kapur, etc. It is not possible to enumerate all of them.

For me it is indeed a matter of great privilege and pleasure to compile the extracts from the reviews of Shankar Goyal's works published in various journals, national and international, well known newspapers, and also from the views expressed on them by eminent historians. For this I have consulted his records and files and taken oral help from him. For the benefit of my readers I am also providing an introductory note on his each books, making the readers familiar with the extensive range and variety of his works, sometimes brought out in multiple volumes, and his contribution to historical studies. A list of his select research articles is also given at the end. But here let me first discuss his own works :

1. History and Historiography of the Age of Harsha (Kusumanjali Prakashan, Jodhpur, 1992) : Shankar Goyal's *History and Historiography of the Age of Harsha*, his first research work, is divided into four parts, the whole being arranged in fourteen consecutive chapters. Unlike other monographs on Harsha which simply concentrate on narrating history of the age of Harsha, Goyal devotes first four chapters of part one, covering nearly a hundred pages, to a critical examination of the historiographical approaches of different scholars who have written on this monarch—specially, R.C. Majumdar, V.S. Pathak, B.N. Sharma, D. Devahuti, K.K. Thaplyal and S.R. Goyal—pointing out to the limitations and ideological conditioning of each of them, before dealing with the sources of Harsha. In contrast to the old-fashioned historiographical tradition based on the assumption that literary texts are 'innocent', this work adopts a more critical approach. Here Goyal reappraised the reliability of Yuan Chwang, specially his testimony on religious matters and his tendency to enlarge exceedingly his own role in his relations with Harsha and Bhāskaravarman. Similarly, he has tried to show that Bāṇa's testimony also is not so reliable as it is generally assumed to be. In an appendix to this part he has also tried to show that there is some doubt regarding Harsha's authorship of the three plays attributed to him.

Part two of Goyal's work includes seven chapters (5-11) on the political background of the rise of the Pushyabhūti dynasty, their early history, Rājyavardhana II, early reign of Harsha, his wars and conquests, the extent of Harsha's empire, the sphere of his influence and his relations with China and Iran. Here it may be pointed out that Goyal's approach to the history of Harsha is basically different, for in his study he has not merely been concerned with 'what' and 'when' questions but 'how' and 'why' questions as well regarding the political events of the period. It is indeed an exercise in putting into practice the concept of 'new political history' which has now gradually become popular in India. In this view political history means an integrated study of society, economy, religion, and polity as well as their interrelatedness in producing and shaping political events.

Part three of Goyal's work comprises chapters 12 and 13. Here Goyal looks upon the culture of the period (c. 550-750 A.D.) not only as an aggregate of the data found in the works of Bāṇa and other contemporary writers, but as the cultural situation which marked the end of the 'classicism' of the Gupta age and the beginning of early 'medievalism'. This part also deals with the emergence of feudalism and its impact on the *zeitgeist*, the regionalism and insularity in economic, political and cultural life.

The final part of Goyal's work consists of a single chapter that evaluates Harsha's life and deeds. In this chapter, among other things, he has tried to show that Harsha did never adopt Buddhism as his *personal* religion. Here, he has also raised the all important question of why Harsha failed to impart stability to his empire and has tried to offer a cogent answer. After giving consideration to all the available data he has come to the conclusion that Harsha was a child of his age, and not it maker.

EXTRACTS FROM SOME VIEWS AND REVIEWS

'All in all, a solid piece of work.'

***Journal of the American Oriental Society*, New Haven.**

'Generally speaking, Shankar Goyal's appraisal of Harsha's reign is balanced and convincing, A sovereign who had perhaps until not so long ago been overrated on account of the many surviving sources favourable to him is here cut down to more modest properties and takes on what is perhaps his rightful place in the historical context.'

***East and West*, Rome.**

'The book clearly manifests the author's familiarity with the sources and works dealing with the age of Harsha. It provides a good introduction to the main problems of the period as well as to the works that discuss them. ... In his interpretations the author presents a valuable assessment of them. ... The author is certainly knowledgeable about the subject and the reader will be rewarded by a thorough reading.'

***Journal of the Royal Asiatic Society*, London.**

'Here is a most courageous attempt to rescue history from myth-making. This fiercely objective book of history and historiography presents the most satisfying of all the accounts of king Harsha so far written.'

***Journal of the Asiatic Society of Bangladesh*, Dacca.**

'The work reflects thorough research and objective analysis.'

***Journal of Indian History*, Trivandrum.**

'The book with its noble perspective and analytical acumen should undoubtedly be welcome to students and scholars.'

***The Indian Historical Review*, New Delhi.**

'The entire book is written in a frank and straightforward manner. ... It is not merely data collection but an attempt to find out the 'how' and 'why' of events in the life and times of Harsha.'

***Indica*, Bombay.**

'The present monograph is an excellent piece of analytical research and bears full testimony to Shankar Goyal's exhaustive collection of the material and its critical examination.'

***Bhāratī*, Varanasi.**

'...the book under review deserves credit for opening new vista of research in this field and is, therefore, a great contribution to the discipline of history. ... Shankar Goyal's claim of dealing with 'how' and 'why' questions of Harsha's age and his search for a harmonious pattern may be considered to have been well established in most of the cases.'

***Quarterly Review of Historical Studies*, Calcutta.**

'Shankar Goyal analyses controversies with good common sense and a healthy dose of skepticism. ... On the most of the major questions his judgements seem reasonable and fair.'

***Estudios de Asia y Africa*, Mexico.**

'The book will be useful. ... the author has given a good account of the documentary evidence for Harsha's reign.'

***Annals of the Bhandarkar Oriental Research Institute*, Poona.**

'...a valuable contribution towards solving the problems of history writing in ancient India. ... the author has succeeded in applying his analytical approach to the problems of history writing of Harsha's period. ... It is also beyond doubt that the students and researchers of Harsha and his times will widely welcome this work.'

***Vishveshvaranand Indological Journal*, Hoshiarpur.**

'It is an elaborate research work which takes a critical look at the subject and in the process stimulates the appetite.'

***National Herald*, New Delhi.**

'The monograph is a detailed and critical examination of various phases and trends through which the historiography of the age of Harsha has passed. ... Certainly it sheds new light on this ancient Indian monarch and his age.'

***The Hindu*, Chennai.**

'Shankar Goyal's *History and Historiography of the Age of Harsha* is an impressive work which brings this important ruler and his times to life. It is comprehensive in its coverage, and not only most informative but most interesting to read. The author not only writes extremely well, but argues with commendable objectivity, guiding the reader through the fascinating complexity of this important period. One could only wish that all of our books were written with such commitment and intelligence.'

Professor Walter M. Spink, Michigan, U.S.A.

'Shankar Goyal's work is indeed the most comprehensive and exhaustive treatise on the history of Harshan India. Incorporating the best features of modern scholarship this work is likely to stand unsurpassed for many years.'

Professor Priti Kumar Mitra, Hawaii, Honolulu, U.S.A.

'You have produced a valuable piece of research.'

Professor R.S. Sharma, Patna.

'...the author shows his awareness of the functions of politics within society. In his compilation of references he includes not only monographs but also some important essays from other works. The narrative of the dynasty touches on various questions which have been raised in the past and attempts to give some answers. The coverage is uptodate.'

Professor Romila Thapar, New Delhi.

'The work is well-done. ...'

Professor G.C. Pande, Allahabad.

'It is an excellent piece of work. ... though Harsha's history has received continual attention in Indian historiography, the present attempt seems to be the most illuminating, both in terms of the historiographical perceptions of Goyal and the factual/ interpretative components of the analysis.'

Professor Upendra Thakur, Bodh-Gaya.

'The book is profoundly thought-provoking and its presentation is lucid and analytical. It will become indispensable for all students of the history of Harsha.'

Professor Lallanji Gopal, Varanasi.

'The book is a testimony of Shankar Goyal's scholarship and the high standard of his researches. It will remain a standard work on the subject for many years to come.'

Professor G.N. Sharma, Udaipur.

'Shankar Goyal has put in hard labour in preparing the monograph entitled *History and Historiography of the Age of Harsha* which is an exhaustive as well as a critical research work of great merit on the subject.'

Professor S.N. Dube, Jaipur.

'Your recent work is really very useful as the latest critical book on the subject. ... I congratulate you for this beautiful work which surpasses and replaces all the earlier works on the theme.'

Professor A.M. Shastri, Nagpur.

'You have treated the age of Harsha in a very comprehensive manner and with detail of every aspect of the problem.'

Professor V.N. Misra, Poona.

'It is an excellent work. ...'

Professor K.T.M. Hegde, Baroda.

'The book bespeaks of the hard work you have put in to prepare it. It is quite comprehensive and uptodate.'

Professor Devendra Handa, Chandigarh.

'...a very useful contribution.'

Professor S.V. Sohoni, Poona.

'Yours is that type of work which should be done in all spheres of Indological studies.'

Professor N.N. Bhattacharyya, Calcutta.

2. Aspects of Ancient Indian History and Historiography (Harman Publishing House, New Delhi, 1993) : The present work is a collection of Shankar Goyal's studies in various aspects of ancient Indian history and historiography. In the essays given in Part I he explains the nature of 'new archaeology' and 'new political history', several problems concerning the history of Buddhism and some concerning numismatics, Gupta art, dynastic history and administrative organisation. He also provides a fresh insight into the Vākāṭaka-Gupta relations and the political ideology of the imperial Guptas. His long article on the formation of the middle ages in India is regarded by R.S. Sharma as one of the best which has ever appeared from the pen of any scholar on this subject. In Part II some articles of historiographical interest are given. They deal with the nature of early Buddhist historiography, recent historiography of the Gupta age, main trends in Vākāṭaka historiography, V.S. Pathak's interpretation of the *charita kāvyas* and recent historiogaphy of the post-Gupta age. In a separate chapter he has examined S.R. Goyal's approach to history.

EXTRACTS FROM SOME VIEWS AND REVIEWS

'Your *Aspects of Ancient Indian History and Historiography* brings together in a handy volume your occasional writings on a variety of problems agitating serious students of ancient Indian history. ... I congratulate you for this work of your scattered writings not easily accessible to interested readers.'

Professor A.M. Shastri, Nagpur.

'*Aspects of Ancient Indian History and Historiography* is a collection of twenty-three essays by Shankar Goyal. ... Such a range of topics reflects the wide spectrum of the author's knowledge and research. ...The author deserves to be congratulated on publishing such as the present monograph which is definitely thought-provoking and readable contribution.'

Professor Ashvini Agrawal, Chandigrah.

3. History Writing of Early India : New Discoveries and Approaches (Kusumanjali Prakashan, Jodhpur, 1996) : The history of early India, from the earliest times to the end of the Maurya dynasty, has attracted the attention of modern scholars from the beginning of the Indological studies. The period incorporates what is generally described as 'traditional' history and also the age of the warring *janapadas* and of the Nanda-Maurya empire. For this vast span of time the sources available to historians are usually of uncertain date, diverse in nature, quite often contradictory in import and usually difficult to be reconciled with each other. Further, it was in this period that Indian polity saw the transition from tribal or lineage society to state and from state to empire.

The attitudes and approaches of modern historians to the chronology, relative importance and significance of sources available to them as well as to what each of them thinks should be the questions he should pose before himself for investigation, have greatly differed. The present monograph makes an indepth study of these changing dimensions of the history writing of early India. It is a pioneer work on the subject—at least no other work dealing so exhaustively with the new discoveries and the changing attitudes and approaches of the scholars of the post-1947 decades on the history of early India has so far been produced.

EXTRACTS FROM SOME VIEWS AND REVIEWS

'Your book shows a good deal of hard work and wide reading. I have high hopes that you will keep on making sustained progress with your good work.'

Professor R.S. Sharma, Patna.

'The author quotes the views of a large number of historians to demonstrates the change in historiographical interest from chronological reconstructions to socio-economic concerns and the inclusion of archaeological data in the study of early India.'

Professor Romila Thapar, New Delhi.

'It forms an important contribution to early period's historiography. You have done it so meticulously that I do not think that you have missed any writing on the subject. This shows your perspicacity in hunting out all the available literature.'

Professor M.K. Dhavalikar, Poona.

'It forms an excellent constructive critique on changing perceptions and approaches in the presentation of early Indian history. ...You have given a good idea of these approaches and in the process a good deal of dependable picture of the sources and historical reconstruction. You happen to be one of the very few scholars attending to historiographical issues objectively and have earned appreciation from serious students of early Indian history.'

Professor A.M. Shastri, Nagpur.

'Your work will help us understand better and evaluate the earlier researches and identify problems and pursue proper approaches.'

Professor Lallanji Gopal, Varanasi.

'Yours is indeed a well-informed and highly comprehensive treatment of the subject placing before the readers the different dimensions, discoveries and approaches regarding early history of India.'

Professor K.V. Raman, Chennai.

'The work gives a sober analysis of the data presented in a scholarly manner. It will serve as a basis for further research on the subject and shall be useful to students as well as scholars.'

Professor Ashvini Agrawal, Chandigarh.

4. The Image of Classical India : Its Changing Colours and Contours (Kusumanjali Prakashan, Jodhpur, 1997) : The history of India from the inception of the Gupta empire to the age of Harsha has attracted the attention of modern scholars from the beginning of Indological studies. It is generally regarded as the classical age or golden age of Indian history. But the attitudes of modern historians to this period have differed greatly. Specially in the recent past Marxist historians have painted the image of this period with quite a different brush—suggesting entirely different contours and using altogether different colours. This monograph by Shankar Goyal makes an indepth study of the changing image of classical or golden age of Indian history. No other work dealing so exhaustively with the changing attitudes and approaches of scholars on the history of this period has so far been produced.

EXTRACTS FROM SOME VIEWS AND REVIEWS

'All in all, this monograph provides a scholarly analysis of the changing pattern of historiography of the Gupta age and a couple of centuries after—from the golden or classical age to the iron age and back to the former. The book is written in a frank and straightforward manner. Shankar Goyal is analytical in his approach and is able to examine the views of various scholars on this subject dispassionately.'

***National Herald*, New Delhi.**

'In this highly thought-provoking monograph on the historiography of the classical age of India, Shankar Goyal has presented an indepth study of recently discovered material on the age of the Guptas and Harsha as well as the changing perceptions of modern historians. ... His work is very comprehensive, insightful and objective and deserves to be read by students and researchers in Indian history and culture.'

***The Hindu*, Chennai.**

'The work gives an excellent idea of the changing and growing patterns of the historiography of the imperial Guptas and a few after centuries, ... It will be found interesting and enlightening both by a scholar and a common reader and acquaint him/her with the views of all the scholars who have cared to write on any problem concerned with this phase dissected dispassionately. ... There are very few scholars working on historiography, and I wish you to continue your work with greater vigour and energy.'

Professor A.M. Shastri, Nagpur.

'I am happy to note that you have dealt with the Gupta age historiography at great length. This was necessary because a deliberate attempt is now being made to show that it was not the 'Golden Age' but an age of decline and decay. I congratulate you on this splendid achievement, and hope you will come out with volumes on the succeeding periods.'

Professor M.K. Dhavalikar, Poona.

'I enjoyed reading the book which have brought out clearly your thoroughness in going through the vast literature including the original and secondary sources and the absolutely scientific and critical assessment of them. You have taken up the important problems and issues that confront the historian and outline the different approaches.'

Professor K.V. Raman, Chennai.

'Goyal has taken account of the writings of almost every scholar who has had an occasion to write something on the subject under discussion and his analysis are quite cogent. ...Those familiar with his earlier writings on the historiography of ancient India shall find themselves at ease with his style of narrative and his suggestions on the subject. ... The monograph is a commendable effort and we look forward to the next enlarged and more exhaustive edition of the same.'

Professor Ashvini Agrawal, Chandigarh.

'It is very interesting, stimulating and refreshing.'

Professor J.K. Sharma, Chandigarh.

5. Recent Historiography of Ancient India (Kusumanjali Prakashan, Jodhpur, 1997) : Described by Bardwell L. Smith (Minnesota, U.S.A.) as 'a marvelous work' and 'a major contribution' and 'as an indispensable and dependable source-book' by R.N. Dandekar the present book entitled *Recent Historiography of Ancient India* is the doctoral dissertation of Shankar Goyal. It is a pioneer work which seeks to delineate the development of historiography of the political history of ancient India in the modern period, specially in the post-1947 decades. Divided into thirteen chapters it discusses the approaches of modern historians to the pre-Maurya and Maurya dynasties, the post-Maurya dynasties of the Śuṅgas and Kaṇvas, the ruling houses of the Indo-Greeks, Śakas, Pahlavas and Kushāṇas, the post-Maurya dynasties of the Sātavāhanas, Vākāṭakas and others, the imperial Guptas, Maukharis, Later Guptas and Pushyabhūtis, the post-Harsha political powers of north India up to Yaśovarman of Kanauj and the post-Vākāṭaka dynasties of the Deccan and the Far South including the Chālukyas of Vātāpi and the Pallavas of Kāñchi. Shankar Goyal has very successfully delineated the changing pattern of the approaches of modern scholars of various schools

— Imperialist, Nationalist, Marxist, etc.—varying from chronological reconstruction to socio-economic concerns, as well as their attitudes towards various types of sources—literary, epigraphical, numismatic and archaeological. Such a comprehensive treatment of the problems of the historiography of ancient Indian political history, with emphasis on the works of historians who wrote in the era of Independence, makes this volume a pioneer, comprehensive and uptodate work on the subject.

EXTRACTS FROM SOME VIEWS AND REVIEWS

'It is definitely a pioneering work on early Indian historiography. Shankar Goyal has discussed the major part of ancient Indian history with rare competence. He has also analysed the nature, content and development of the historiography of ancient India from the Vedic period to the fall of the kingdom of Thanesar in northern India (and also the age of the Rāshṭrakūṭas, the Choḷas and others of south India) in an unbaised manner, giving his own judgment on the views of earlier historians of India and abroad. His treatment is not on the pattern of traditional descriptive accounts. It is mainly an interpretative study, and, we, therefore, consider it to be a research work of great merit.'

***The Quarterly Review of Historical Studies*, Calcutta.**

'Shankar Goyal has certainly created a path for those who want to write history not based on more assumptions regarding social relations but on the rock-bottom of an adequate understanding of human nature. He has given birth to many questions and historians will have to answer them in order to create a new doctrine and methodology of writing history. This book will help those scholars who are attending to historiographical issues objectively and dispassionately. It will serve as a light house for the students of history of ancient India and its culture.'

***Vishveshvaranand Indological Journal*, Hoshiarpur.**

'...a marvelous book.'

Professor Bardwell L. Smith, Minnesota, U.S.A.

'Yours is a very important contribution. I congratulate you on this new achievement.'

Professor Maurizio Taddei, Napoli, Italy.

'...will serve as an indispensable and dependable source-book for every serious student of ancient Indian historiography.'

Professor R.N. Dandekar, Poona.

'It is the first detailed and critical study of the historiography of ancient India as practised today. It is at once critical and objective and may be described as a pioneering work.'

Professor G.C. Pande, Allahabad.

'It is one of the most original and welcome contributions to the study of ancient Indian history to appear in recent years.'

Professor V.S. Pathak, Gorakhpur.

'It would serve as a dependable source-book on ancient Indian historiography for a long time to come.'

Professor B.P. Sinha, Patna.

'Shankar Goyal's approach is critical and balanced. ... One cannot but admine the way he marshalls facts and analyses them.'

Professor K.K. Thaplyal, Lucknow.

'You have ransacked the literature on the subject thoroughly and have marshalled all the evidence judiciously. ...The book will be a great help to students and scholars alike.'

Professor M.K. Dhavalikar, Poona.

'The beauty of this work lies in that it acquaints the peruser not only with historiographical problems and developments but also gives him/her a dependable general idea of all the phases of early Indian historiography. ... It would hopefully be received well by all the serious students of Indian history.'

Professor A.M. Shastri, Nagpur.

'You have done admirably well. This is a very useful work.'

Professor N.N. Bhattacharyya, Calcutta.

6. Ancient Indian Numismatics : A Historiographical Study (Kusumanjali Book World, Jodhpur, 1998) : The study of ancient Indian coins is now a well-established discipline with a history of more than two centuries behind it. But strangely no monograph on its historiography has so far been published. The present full-length monograph on this subject is thus a pioneering study. It critically examines all the important works and a large number of research articles published during the last two hundred years. Divided into eleven chapters it begins with the progress of the study of the problems of the origin and antiquity of coinage in India (chapter one) and is followed by the historiography of Punch-marked coins, Local and Tribal coins, Indo-Greek coinage, coinages of the imperial Scythians and Pahlavas and the Western Kshatrapas and the coinage of the Kushāṇas (chapters second to sixth). Then in the next four chapters the numismatography of the Sātavāhanas, the Guptas, the Vākāṭakas and the post-Gupta dynasties has been discussed. In the last and concluding chapter some miscellaneous aspects of ancient Indian numismatics, not covered in the study of the coins of various periods and dynasties, have been examined.

EXTRACTS FROM SOME VIEWS AND REVIEWS

'I have enjoyed reading this book. It is a useful survey of the contents of writings on ancient Indian coins. ... I find that you present the views and arguments of both western and Indian numismatists clearly, ... I very much hope that you will continue your scholarly work and contribute more and more to ancient Indian studeis.'

Professor R.S. Sharma, Patna.

'This is indeed a unique work of its kind as though there are several illustrious works on Indian coinage in general and various series of early Indian coinage and scholars working on various aspects of early Indian coinage, no scholar has hitherto attempted stock-taking of different stages of the progress of study of the series of coins they are studying and enriching by their own contributions. And from this point of view your work will be of great utility to all students of early Indian coinage.'

Professor A.M. Shastri, Nagpur.

'Yours is a pioneering work on a neglected subject. It is a fitting tribute to several of our scholars, past and present, who have done valuable researches and discussions in this field. It is a painstaking work which covers a long period—from punch-marked and tribal to the post-Gupta dynasties. Important problems, issues and views have been covered with your own assessment.'

Professor K.V. Raman, Chennai.

7. Marxist Interpretation of Ancient Indian History (Bhandarkar Oriental Research Institute, Poona, 2000) : The Bhandarkar Oriental Research Institute has published this book of Shankar Goyal dealing with the Marxist interpretation of ancient Indian history. The Marxist approach to ancient Indian history is comparatively a recent phenomenon and with the passage of the time its popularity has gradually increased. Many a work has already come out reviewing many aspects of Indian history and culture from this point of view. There is yet no work which seeks to describe the theoretical suppositions of the Marxist approach and its practical application for the interpretation of ancient Indian history. The present monograph by Goyal seeks to fulfil this lacuna.

EXTRACTS FROM SOME VIEWS AND REVIEWS

'The book is a good introduction to the subject.'

Professor R.S. Sharma, Patna.

'It is a scholarly, analytical and useful book. I have not seen such a book in recent years.'

Professor S.N. Chaturvedi, Gorakhpur.

8. Problems of Ancient Indian History : New Perspectives and Perceptions (Book Enclave, Jaipur, 2001) : This monograph by Shankar Goyal seeks to study some problems of ancient Indian history and culture with a new approach. As Goyal's main area of interest is Indian historiography the present work includes several articles on the problems of historiography in which he has analysed the perceptions of earlier scholars thoroughly in the light of his own. Further, he has studied the new source materials which is coming to light every year. Goyal is extremely interested in Maurya, Gupta and Vardhana periods. He feels concerned with the theme of Gupta golden or classical age. That Bāna was a staunch follower of the Brāhmaṇical culture is basically true, but in his work Goyal has very cogently argued, and that too for the first time, that Bāṇa was also a great critic of such customs as *satī* and such concepts as the divinity of kings. He was also a critic of the then administrative structure. Such are some of the new dimensions which Goyal has boldly articulated in the present monograph.

EXTRACTS FROM SOME VIEWS AND REVIEWS

'Evidently the volume, well printed and neatly brought out, provides a rich fare and should find a place in the Indological libraries in India and abroad.'

***Nucleus*, Jaipur.**

9. Prāchīna Bhāratīya Itihāsa aura Saṁskṛti (Book Enclave, Jaipur, 2001) : This work of Shankar Goyal is divided into five parts. In the first part he has discussed the problems related with the cultural unity of the country. The second part discusses some problems connected with the political history of ancient India while the third part throws light on some aspects of the south Indian history. The fourth part deals with the changing perspectives of Indian historiography and, the fifth, tries to throw light on some miscellaneous problems.

EXTRACTS FROM SOME VIEWS AND REVIEWS

'It is specially useful for the students of postgraduate classes ... and sums of almost everything of value said about different aspects of India's ancient past.'

Professor S.N. Chaturvedi, Gorakhpur.

10. Contemporary Interpreters of Ancient India (Book Enclave, Jaipur, 2003) : In the era of Independence India has produced a large number of eminent historians. They are easily divisible into two categories—those who carried on the indigenous tradition of the pre-Independence period, and those who developed the theory and tools of Marxist approach to Indian historiography. In this work Shankar Goyal has studied eminent historians of both the schools. From amongst those who represent the flowering of the Indian tradition he has selected such great names as Professors R.C. Majumdar, V.S. Agrawala, G.C. Pande, V.S. Pathak, S.R. Goyal, Ajay Mitra Shastri and Lallanji Gopal while from the second category, he has emphasised on the contribution of Professors D.D. Kosambi, R.S. Sharma, Romila Thapar, D.N. Jha and V.K. Thakur. Shankar Goyal has not only given a short life-history, account of academic journey, contribution to learned bodies, etc., of each of them but has also provided an authoritative analysis of their approach to history along with a critical survey of their works. Thus, the present monograph seeks to give a complete picture of the life, personality, historical vision and contribution to Indology of each of the historians included in it.

EXTRACTS FROM SOME VIEWS AND REVIEWS

'In fine, the book of Shankar Goyal under review presents a fair and frank appraisal of some representative historians of recent times belonging to both the idealist as well as Marxist schools. ...Indeed, this book is a pioneer work on recent historiography of ancient India.'

***Nucleus*, Jaipur.**

11. Ancient India : A Multidisciplinary Approach (Kusumanjali Book World, Jodhpur, 2006) : In recent decades the popularity of the political history is declining very fast in India as well as in other countries. Therefore, in order to revitalise their discipline some political historians, both in India and the West, are pleading that now the concept of political history should be modified. They argue that now historians should cease to give emphasis only on the 'deeds' and 'dates' of the kings and should make a study of the political aspect of society their basic concern. In other words, they should give emphasis on 'how' and 'why' instead of only 'when' and 'what'. For this a study of the political events and institutions against various factors—religious, economic, social, etc.—is vital. This is what they call 'New Political History' or 'Integral Political History'. It needs not only a study of basic sources with a new angle but also a multidisciplinary approach to the political life of society and state. In India S.R. Goyal has been pleading for the adoption of this approach for several decades and now he is being supported by numerous others. Shankar Goyal seeks to show what S.R. Goyal has done to give a new definition and meaning to political history specially of ancient India and what more can be done in this field.

EXTRACTS FROM SOME VIEWS AND REVIEWS

'... the book *Ancient India : A Multidisciplinary Approach* forms a significant contribution to the study of early Indian history and historiography. It will be found immensely useful by all the scholars of early India.'

Professor S.N. Chaturvedi, Gorakhpur.

12. Harsha : A Multidisciplinary Political Study (Kusumanjali Book World, Jodhpur, 2006) : Described by R.S. Sharma as 'the best work on Harsha written so far' and as 'a compulsory reading for those working on ancient Indian history' by Romila Thapar, this research work on Harsha by Shankar Goyal, his D.Litt. thesis, looks upon the history of the age of Harsha not from the traditional 'what and when happened approach' but from multidisciplinary integral standpoint in which main political developments and events are put in their proper context by an analysis of their determining influences—social, economic, religious, geographical, etc., with the help of other branches of knowledge, of course without overlooking the need of reconsidering the 'what and when happened' problems afresh, wherever necessary. For example, on such problems as the motivations and reliability of Bāṇa and Yuan Chwang, social origins and early history of the Pushyabhūtis, reign of Rājyavardhana II, formative influences on the character and personality of Harsha, validity of his claim to the Maukhari throne, chronology of his campaigns, his political relations with the various regions of India and also with Iran, China, etc., the nature of the organisation of his empire, impact of his religious policies on his political activities, causes of his failure in establishing a permanent imperial structure, etc., Shankar Goyal has either thrown new light or has offered new cogent solutions for them. He has also given, probably for the first time, a psycho-sociological and religious analysis of the personality of Harsha. Further, he seeks to look upon the culture of the age of Harsha not only as an aggregate of the data found in the works of Bāṇa and other contemporary writers, but as the cultural situation which marked the end of the 'classicism' of the Gupta age and the beginning of the early 'medievalism'. When looked with the help of these two peepholes—the classical culture of the Gupta period and the medieval culture of the Rajput age—the works of Bāṇa and his contemporaries appear to yield a new meaning and light.

EXTRACTS FROM SOME VIEWS AND REVIEWS

'The book is written in a very fluid language and gives all that one can expect from a historian about the life and achievements of Harsha and also the socio-economic and religious conditions of that epoch. ...The book is recommended to all researchers in ancient Indian history.'

***History Today*, New Delhi.**

'Shankar Goyal's D.Litt. work on Harsha is the best book on the subject written so far.'

Professor R.S. Sharma, Patna.

'You have made a commendable coverage of sources and perspectives. ... It will be a compulsory reading for those working on ancient Indian history.'

Professor Romila Thapar, New Delhi.

'Shankar Goyal's work is lucid, readable and stimulating. I hope it will receive the attention and popularity it deserves.'

Professor G.C. Pande, Allahabad.

'This remarkable book is an amazing depository of information. The author has tapped all possible sources to substantiate his contentions. Unerring evidences and poignant arguments along with imaginative perceptions invariably uphold his conclusions. An uncommon objectivity has exalted the work to the height of almost, infallible, authenticity. 'Emperor' Harsha Śīlāditya has been thoroughly demistified, cut to size, and placed in the right niche of history. In short, the work is a remarkable achievement for Shankar Goyal in historical research and writing.'

Professor P.K. Mitra, Rajshahi, Bangladesh.

'This study is a genuine attempt to reorient the study of political history and this has widened the scope of such studies. Political history in Shankar Goyal's analysis is not a simple study of dynastic changes but a configuration of varying social and economic forces. He has projected Harsha in a new light and his conclusions are empirically so sound that it is difficult to ignore them.'

Professor V.K. Thakur, Patna.

'... Shankar Goyal is meticulous in presenting his evidence and acknowledging his debt to his precursors; but he has much new to say. I find his book refreshing in its critical method and unbiased conclusions. As one fed on Panikkar and Mookerji (read as an M.A. student in early fifties) it is disturbing to find Harsha's earlier carrier sullied possibly by fratricide; but facts are always stranger than fiction, it is said, and facts seem to be on Goyal's side quite decisively. However, there is much else of substance in Goyal's scholarly work, and all students of Harsha and his times should surely greatly welcome it.'

Professor Irfan Habib, Aligarh.

'I found the work as an extremely useful, careful attempt to broaden the scope of political history. ... The analysis is both interesting and perceptive.'

Professor Kumkum Roy, New Delhi.

'The present work, from start to finish, is objective as far as possible. The author is prepared to give what is due to Harsha; he will deny what is not due to him. Small wonder, this work, while it was in thesis form, brought D.Litt. degree to Shankar Goyal from the University of Jodhpur.'

Professor K.K. Kusuman, Trivandrum.

'Shankar Goyal's latest book *Harsha : A Multidisciplinary Political Study* is path-breaking in the sense that it looks at the age of Harsha from an integral time-point, discarding the old, traditional approach to the subject. A multidisciplinary approach adopted by Goyal adds a new dimension to the historiography of ancient India.'

Professor S. Gopalakrishnan, Tirupati.

'... On the whole, this work has cut a new ground in the historiography of the age of Harsha.'

Professor T.R. Ramachandran, Chennai.

'Shankar Goyal has successfully tried to explain how socio-economic and religious factors have contributed in the shaping of the political history of the age which justifies the 'multidisciplinary' subtitle of the work. To a great extent the author's claim that his book is different for many reasons from those of others is justified.'

Professor K.K. Thaplyal, Lucknow.

'... I heartily congratulate you on your obtaining D.Litt. degree for this book. I greatly admire your productivity. At a very young age you have already produced a dozen books and about 100 research papers. This is an enviable record for any scholar. ... I find that a lot of reading and thinking has gone into writing of this book. I am sure it will be very well received by all researchers and students of ancient and early medieval periods of Indian history.'

Professor V.N. Misra, Poona.

'...Shankar Goyal paints Harsha's age not with his hands but with his brain. A remarkable scholarly output of the author that cannot fail to attract attention.'

Professor L.S. Rathore, Jodhpur.

'... a very comprehensive, critical and uptodate account of the history of Harsha. ... Literary, epigraphic and numismatic evidence has been used with equal skill, meticulously and judiciously. It would prove a model for such studies in Indian history.'

Professor J.K. Sharma, Chandigarh.

'... It is a matter of happiness that the University of Jodhpur has conferred the degree of D.Litt. upon Shankar Goyal for his present work which he so richly deserves.'

Professor Ashvini Agrawal, Chandigarh.

13. 175 Years of Vākāṭaka History and Historiography (Kusumanjali Book World, Jodhpur, 2009): The following three works of Shankar Goyal published in the year 2009 are dedicated to the sacred and loving memory of his respected mother Mrs. Kusum Goyal who suddenly expired on September 27, 2008. In the present work Goyal seeks to deal with the history and historiography of the Vākāṭakas — one of the illustrious dynasties of the Deccan. Its first essay deals with the gradual changes in the historiography of the Vākāṭakas underlining the role of ideology in historical reconstruction. It also incorporates two appendices: in the first there is a critique of Hans T. Bakker's recent suggestions on art and culture of the Vākāṭakas and the second contains a criticism of K.M. Shrimali's article entitled 'Religions in Complex Societies : The Myth of the 'Dark Age'.' Then, there are two essays dealing with the new Vākāṭaka inscriptions discovered after the publication of V.V. Mirashi's *Corpus* in 1963, especially the Ramtek Prabhāvatīguptā Memorial Inscription which is of great value for the Vākāṭaka history. The fourth essay deals with some aspects of the economy of the Vākāṭakas and the question of the existence of their coins. Shankar Goyal finds it difficult to endorse the views of A. M. Shastri, Hans Bakker, Ellen M. Raven and some others who attribute some copper coins to the Vākāṭakas. His conclusion is also significantly different from Bakker's who finds economic prosperity in the Vākāṭaka kingdom which is not quite visible to Goyal. The rest of the essays focus on the varied problems of the history of the Vākāṭakas. As the influence of the imperial Guptas on the Vākāṭaka dynasty has been a major concern for most of the historians Shankar Goyal has also focused on this aspect of their history. But it is apparent from his studies that at the beginning of the twenty-first century the history of the Vākāṭakas has advanced from the stage of a chronological, dynastic study to an integral analysis of events and a detailed study of religion and art, agrarian expansion in central India and northern Deccan and state formation under the main branch.

EXTRACTS FROM SOME VIEWS AND REVIEWS

'*175 Years of Vākāṭaka History and Historiography* is yet another jewel in the academic crown of Shankar Goyal who has been tirelessly involved in maintaining the academic brilliance of the subject, ancient Indian history, with a number of monographs, edited works and books to his credit. This, of course, is a collection and edition of his presentations on the history of Vākāṭakas and Deccan as a whole at various seminars and conferences of repute which manifest his deep inroading into this otherwise less attended but historically highly important area and area of ancient Indian history.

'Besides a systematic historiography of the Vākāṭaka history and a critical updating of epigraphic and numismatic data around this period and region Shankar Goyal has made this work even worth by incorporating chapters on Vākāṭaka economy and culture with special reference to K.M. Shrimali and Hans Bakker. Though, it seems, he is a little more skeptical about the Marxist approach to the study of this period but at the same time he is good enough to put the Vākāṭaka history in perspective of economic and cultural development of the period. Vākāṭaka's relationship with the great Guptas, the Kadambas, the Vishṇukuṇḍins and the like reflecting the second wave of reemergence of the league of the Brāhmaṇas in the backdrop of Brāhmaṇical reaction to the foreign and non-Brāhmaṇical movements could well be derived from this serious documentation of the facts. So also, the connection of the paucity or absence of Vākāṭaka coins and the progress of land grants implying the growth of feudal structure may well lead to an important inference of interlinking Brāhmaṇical revival with feudal development in India. Thus Shankar Goyal has greatly contributed to the understanding of ancient Indian historical trends with successive dynasties. This is what the historians of present generation may rightly call the writing of integrated history, what his great father S.R. Goyal had been thoroughly arguing for.'

Professor M.V. Singh, Varanasi.

'This beautifully produced work on the Vākāṭaka history is a commendable contribution to Indological studies by Shankar Goyal. The Vākāṭakas have played a vital role in history and the development of economy and culture in the Deccan. Goyal has ably assessed the contributions of various scholars on the subject and has also offered his own views and suggestions which testify to his erudition and discerning mind. The book indeed is a ready reckoner for what has been said about the Vākāṭakas and provides clues to future possibilities in the field.'

Professor S.N. Chaturvedi, Gorakhpur.

14. Probings in Indian History (Kusumanjali Book World, Jodhpur, 2009) : This book by Shankar Goyal carries the reader from the post-Vedic age when coinage in India originated to the upheaval of 1857, making him enjoy the changing scenario throughout the journey. How did the coinage originate in India, what secrets the Avadānas reveal, what do the coinage of the imperial Guptas depose about the political ideology of their issuers, what Bāṇa and his *Harshacharita* seek not to reveal about Harsha, who was the real author of the plays ascribed to Harsha, the diplomatic manoeuvres of Harsha, the so far unknown aspects of the personality of Harsha, the making of early medieval India, the history writing of James Tod and the unknown facets of the great upheaval of 1857 in Rajasthan and many other aspects and secrets of Indian history are revealed to him.

EXTRACTS FROM SOME VIEWS AND REVIEWS

'Reading books is an excellent experience and reading history books is an exhilarating experience. Shankar Goyal's *Probings in Indian History* is a book of that genre. The articles included in this work furnishes very good information about India's glorious past. ... One will certainly get engrossed in this book the moment he starts reading it. Undoubtedly, it is an absorbing volume setting a trend to other scholars to follow on these lines. ... really a fascinating work which deserves high commendation.'

Professor A. Chandrasekaran, Chennai.

'*Probings in Indian History* is a collection of remarkable essays authored by Shankar Goyal. The essays included in this book cover a wide spectrum of issues in Indian hsitory. ... The essays on James Tod and the revolt of 1857 in Rajasthan highlight Goyal's deep understanding of British India. The essay on the comparison of the Gandhian and Ambedkarite approaches to untouchability brings to the fore Goyal's skill to analyse cogently a living issue in modern India.'

Professor G.J. Sudhakar, Chennai.

15. Studies in the History of the Deccan and South India (Kusumanjali Book World, Jodhpur, 2009) : This monograph of Shankar Goyal discusses some important aspects of the history of the Deccan and south India. Its first seven essays are concerned with the new source materials and recent suggestions on the history of the Vākāṭakas. In them Shankar Goyal has not only discussed some contributions of other great scholars, such as S.R. Goyal, A.M. Shastri, K.M. Shrimali, Hans T. Bakker and others, but has also thrown numerous suggestions of his own on this illustrious dynasty of the Deccan. Then follow a number of essays on varied problems of south Indian history, culture and historiography, including the historiography of K.A. Nilakanta Shastri, need of an integral view of the political history of south India, the Nāyanārs and Āḷvārs and their contribution to the bhakti movement in south India, Buddhism in early south Indian history and Harsha's relations with the Deccan and the Far South.

EXTRACTS FROM SOME VIEWS AND REVIEWS

'Shankar Goyal's *Studies in the History of the Deccan and South India* is a very readable collection of essays on an area of history that has suffered neglect at the hands of Indian historians in the past. ... In each of his essays, the primary focus is on new discoveries and new interpretation of events. This makes his book valuable to the students of history.'

Professor G.J. Sudhakar, Chennai.

'... The many significant aspects of the history of the Deccan and south India from ancient times are diligently discussed in this book. ... The author certainly deserves high praise and his work is a truly excellent addition to the existing historical literature.'

Professor A. Chandrasekaran, Chennai.

16. The 'Medieval' Factor and the Age of Harsha : A Cultural Study (Kusumanjali Book World, Jodhpur, 2016) : The reign of Harsha (606-647 A.D.) is a comparatively well-documented period of ancient Indian history. But it is indeed surprising that no full-length study of culture of the period has been attempted since the publication of V.S. Agrawala's classic work entitled *Harshacharita : Eka Sāṁskṛtika Adhyayana* from Patna in 1953. This work fills up this long felt need. It is divided into nine chapters— Introduction : The Making of Early Medieval Indian Society, Religion and the Medieval Trends in the Religious Activities of Harsha, Social Organisation in the Age of Harsha and the Impact of Feudalism, Society and Social Life in the Age of Transition, Economy and the Feudal Tendencies in the Economic Life of the Age of Harsha, Political Culture of the Age of Harsha and the Feudalization of Administrative Structure, The 'Medieval' Factor in Indian Art, Literary Activities under Harsha: (i) Bāṇa and the Writing of *Harshacharita*, Literary Activities under Harsha: (ii) The Problem of the Authorship of the Three Plays : *Ratnāvalī*, *Priyadarśikā* and *Nāgānanda*, and an appendix entitled Art and Architecture of the Age of Harsha as Known from the Literary Sources—and contains an exhaustive bibliography. This monograph is somewhat different from other existing works on the subject because it seeks to study the culture of the age of Harsha not only as an aggregate of the data found in the works of Bāṇa and other contemporary writers, but as the cultural situation which marked the end of the 'classicism' of the Gupta age and the beginning of the early 'Medievalism'. When looked with the help of these two peep-holes—the classical culture of the Gupta period and the medieval culture of the Rajput age—the works of Bāṇa, Yuan Chwang and their contemporaries appear to yield new meaning and light.

EXTRACATS FROM SOME VIEWS AND REVIEWS

'Shankar Goyal's book *The 'Medieval' Factor and the Age of Harsha : A Cultural Study* focuses on the age of Harsha as a watershed between the end of the ancient period and the coming of the medieval, subsequent to Harsha. Goyal uses the idea of a watershed in a very meaningful way to discuss elements of change that made the transition possible and recognisable. The span he covers is wide and the history is discussed with impressive detail. By examining changes in society, economy, religion and art, he shows the gradual evolution to medieval society. The many facets that he covers are well-integrated. 'Medieval' is a difficult term to define, but all credit to him that he defines it in the context of those times and does so with clarity.'

Professor Romila Thapar, New Delhi.

'Shankar Goyal provides an account of society, economy and cultural developments during the reign of Harsha, defining it as a crucial period in the transition to the medieval. He takes into consideration earlier scholarship on the theme and develops his arguments relying on a range of sources. Working broadly within the paradigm of Indian feudalism, Goyal provides a vivid and detailed description that will prove valuable for both the specialist and the more curious lay reader. His discussion based on Bāṇabhaṭṭa's work is particularly interesting as it provides scope for a critical evaluation of contemporary political and cultural practices, as well as of the narrative strategies adopted by one of the most renowned Sanskrit authors of the early medieval period.'

Professor Kumkum Roy, New Delhi.

'Shankar Goyal makes a serious attempt to give a new direction to study the culture of the age of Harsha against the feudal atmosphere of the period. He rightly argues that the age of Harsha is the focal point of change from ancient to medieval. His conclusions are sound and deserve very careful consideration. I am confident that this book will have the widest readership that it so thoroughly deserves.'

Professor R. Champakalakshmi, New Delhi.

'...the book definitely surpasses all earlier works on this theme.'

Professor A. K. Sinha, Bareilly.

'What distinguishes the present volume is Shankar Goyal's effort to survey the nature of state, society and culture (including court culture) in the age of Harsha. It is a work of both synthesis, taking into account the works of scholars such as R. S. Sharma, B. N. S. Yadava, Romila Thapar and others, and of exploration, based on his own extensive study of the sources of the period. To put it simply, Goyal argues that while the picture of India in the seventh century did correspond broadly to that of Europe after the decline of the Roman Empire, yet owing to important variations, such as the presence of caste system in India, Indian feudalism — for which he seems often to prefer the term 'medieval' — was different in important respects from its European counterpart. He sees similarities in the emergence of political decentralisation, sub-infeudation of land rights, and regionalisation of culture, while acknowledging a major point of differences in the absence of serfdom in India, balanced, so to speak, by an increasing rigour in the caste system. Goyal retains throughout an admirably objective spirit. Harsha, the biographers' delight, receives no benefit of doubt from him over shadowy events, like Rājyavardhana's murder or over his malexpenditure. His is a scholarly voice that needs to be heard, and I wish him a very wide readership.'

Professor Irfan Habib, Aligarh.

17. Origin and Growth of History Writing in Rajasthan, Volume I : Khyats and Allied Works of Historical Genre (D.K. Publishers Distributors Pvt. Ltd., New Delhi, 2017) : The Khyats are considered as significant sources for the proper understanding of Rajput history of the medieval Rajasthan. They were mostly written under the patronage of the rulers who were keen to perpetuate the memory of their exploits in various fields on the basis of past memories, speculations, traditions, personal records and experiences of the writers. They provide a detailed account of the histories of rulers, chiefs, nobles and other dignitaries of the period; their achievements, historical events, military strength and battles. They give wide information on various aspects of the life of rulers and their queens, the genealogies and successions, the palace intrigues and family feuds, and the fairs and festivals. They are more or less accurate and correct, despite imperfections of dates and chronology. They help in discovering vital information and reliable facts about the medieval Rajput history, despite slight exaggeration of local patriotism and exaltation of the rulers. They depict a broad framework of the history of medieval Rajasthan, though it may not be a complete one. Because they reflect the actual course of happenings in medieval Rajasthan, they are undoubtedly regarded as a valuable source of Rajput history. Shankar Goyal in this work has examined six prominent Khyats, namely, *Muhnot Nainsi ri Khyat*, *Bankidas ri Khyat*, *Dayaldas ri Khyat*, *Jodhpur Rajya ki Khyat*, *Marwar ri Khyat* of Tilok Chand Joshi, and *Jaisalmer ri Khyat* of Ajit Singh Mehta. In addition to the Khyats which constitute the primary source, he has also mentioned other auxiliary sources of the medieval Rajput history, namely, Vat (Bat), Vachanika, Davavait, Hal, Ahawal, Haqiqat, Vamshavali, Pattawali, Pidhiyawali, Vigat, Tahakikat, etc. Of these, he considers Vigats, Vamshavalis and Vats as important branches of historical literature. The factors which led to the decline of Khyat literature have also been carefully discussed. The main factors emphasized by him are : the lack of historical accuracy, not enough connected historical account of the period, rise of new forces of change, neglect of social upheavals and economic dissatisfaction, the end of the medieval traditions of chivalry and heroism and the like.

EXTRACTS FROM SOME VIEWS AND REVIEWS

'Shankar Goyal has done a great service for students, teachers and researchers of the history of Rajasthan in bringing to light such literature in English. His *Khyats and Allied Works of Historical Genre* is definitely the first and only account of its kind, at once critical, scholarly and uptodate. No scholar wishing to work on the subject can afford to ignore his book. ... It will create a new awareness and stimulate the interest of all those interested in the history and culture of Rajasthan. Goyal has laid the scholarly world under deep debt by writing this extremely useful book.'

Professor K.S. Gupta, Udaipur.

'Shankar Goyal's *Khyats and Allied Works of Historical Genre* is a neatly brought out, compact and comprehensive work on the Khyats, Vats, Vachanikas, etc. ... carried out with considerable patience and competence. ...The rich Bibliography adds to the value of the work.'

Professor V.S. Bhatnagar, Jaipur.

'The refreshing approach of Shankar Goyal have rightly put the works of Khyat writers in a novel perspective. All scholars seeking to work on the subject will have to reckon with his work which they would find most useful.'

Professor T.K.Mathur, Ajmer.

'... By writing this book in English, Shankar Goyal has done a great service of the academic world.'

Professor B.L. Bhadani, Aligarh.

'The saga of the valorous land of Rajasthan, known for its chivalry and sacrifices, was sung graphically in ballads and bardic tales since times immemorial. An outcrop of the traditional accounts was the emergence in medieval times of a genre of peculiar writings which, with the sifting of layers of romantic and panegyric coats, can be of great use for the fascinating history of the region. Shankar Goyal's present venture, I am sure, would provide a fresh impetus in that direction.'

Professor S.N. Dube, Jaipur.

'Shankar Goyal, known for his constructive researches in the historiography of ancient India, has now earned the gratitude of both students and scholars of the history of Rajasthan by writing an extremely invaluable work entitled *Khyats and Allied Works of Historical Genre*. Written in a very simple style the present work of Goyal investigates the contents of major Khyats and other historical works of Muhnot Nainsi, Bankidas, Dayaldas, Ai Dan Khidiya, Tilok Chand Joshi and Ajit Singh Mehta, their significance and relevance in the present-day historiography of Rajasthan, and also tries to analyse the factors in the decline of Khyat literature. As far as I know his work is the first study of Khyat literature of Rajasthan to be written in English language. He has brought together the results of earlier researches on the subject, and has added much that is his own, studying the original sources afresh in a truly critical and analytical spirit to produce a clear and concise account of the important Khyats which will be of great value and help to all students, researchers and teachers of the universities of Rajasthan who wish to make a specialized study of its literature, and to all others who are seriously interested in the past of this glorious land.

'All in all, a definite contribution to the history of Rajasthan.'

Dr. Hukam Singh Bhati, Jodhpur.

'Shankar Goyal is a well known authority on ancient Indian history and historiography, and by writing this work, I believe, he has successfully carved out a niche for himself in the field of Rajasthan studies. His present book is of utmost importance both for the scholars and researchers of the history of Rajasthan. It is a unique contribution in the said field, perhaps the only one of its kind. The presentation of the historical material is systematic, the narration is reliable and the analysis is objective. Based on facts, the work is logical, well organized and coherent; its contents are clear and easy to understand. The description of Khyats as basic sources of history has been given in such a delightful manner that the general readers can also derive pleasure and enjoyment by reading the book. All in all, it is a pioneering work, highlighting selective Khyats and other sources of the medieval Rajput history. Goyal deserves great appreciation for producing this useful work—a work that will be of benefit to every one concerned.'

Professor L.S. Rathore, Jodhpur.

'Shankar Goyal has done students of the history of Rajasthan a great service by bringing together in the present monograph detailed surveys of some major annals (*khyats*) of Rajasthan. His is a well-informed work which has given rise to many new thoughts. I am sure all those who are interested in the history of Rajasthan will greatly welcome this volume.'

Professor Shireen Moosvi, Aligarh.

18. Origin and Growth of History Writing in Rajasthan, Volume II : Historians and Historiography in Modern Rajasthan (D.K. Publishers Distributors Pvt. Ltd., Delhi, 2018) : This work demarcates the various stages or traditions that has dominated in the modern historiography of Rajasthan. The first tradition extended from James Tod to the dawn of Indian independence wherein the trend was of writing the chronological histories of the dynasties. The second tradition commenced from the mid-20th century showing a new trend of writing the history of Rajasthan against the perspective of national history. And lastly, a few more traditions that developed simultaneously in the later half of the 20th century were the writing of regional history, the study of the life of common people, the nature of freedom struggle or the liberation movements, poetic compositions about historical characters, and the study of culture of Rajasthan. While exercising his discretion in a fair manner Shankar Goyal has chosen eleven historians, namely, James Tod, Shyamaldas, G.H. Ojha,

V.N. Reu, Dasharatha Sharma, S.R. Goyal, G.N. Sharma, R.P. Vyas, L.S. Rathore, G.S.L. Devra and Sobhag Mathur, for being included in this work because they have been the pioneers in different traditions or areas of the history of Rajasthan.

EXTRACTS FROM SOME VIEWS AND REVIEWS

'Written in a lucid style, flawless language, and facts rigorously analysed, the book is extremely impressive and worth having. In fact, the book testifies Shankar Goyal's phenomenal ability to think and express his ideas clearly. That approach makes this work more reliable and more scholarly — indeed, well worth reading and enjoying.'

Professor L.S. Rathore, Jodhpur.

19. Harsha Revisited : A Re-interpretation of Existing Data (D.K. Publishers Distributors Pvt. Ltd., Delhi, 2018) : It is a first analytical study of the sources on Harsha. Divided into six chapters and three appendices, its first chapter is essentialy a new political biography of Harsha in the light of the decline of classical culture, rise of feudalism and transition to the medieval period in Indian history. The second chapter is a thorough investigative study of the *Harshacharita* of Bāṇa in the light of new methods in historical interpretation. It is highly critical in its approach and, perhaps, the most in-depth study of the *Harshacharita* as a work of history. The third chapter re-examines the problem of the authorship of the three plays — *Ratnāvalī, Priyadarśikā* and *Nāgānanda* — which are ascribed to Harsha, and their place in the history of the period. The fourth chapter re-analyses the contents of the copper plates of Harsha, including his recently discovered Kurukshetra-Varanasi grant of the year 23 of the reign of Harsha, which is, unfortunately, still unknown to the majority of Indian scholars. Its appendix provides the text and translation of this new inscription, and the seal attached to it. The fifth chapter takes up the numismatic evidence relating to Śrī Pratāpaśīla (Prabhākaravardhana) and Śrī Śīlāditya (Harsha). The last and the sixth chapter is an exhaustive study of the reliability of Yuan Chwang as a source of history. It is hoped that it will be a valuable addition to the existing literature on Yuan Chwang, and opens new areas for further research and analysis. The chapter is followed by two appendices—the first, on the *Life* of the Chinese pilgrim (a summary of chapters VI-X), and the second, on the approximate chronology of Yuan Chwang's travels (on the basis of A. Cunningham).

EXTRACTS FROM SOME VIEWS AND REVIEWS

'For decades, Shankar Goyal has been interested in researching on political history, and the early medieval king, Harshavardhana, has been amongst his favourite subjects. However, this concern is by no means an idiosyncratic fascination; on the contrary, Goyal recognizes and demonstrates the need to situate Harsha in terms of his times, so as to arrive at a more meaningful understanding. He casts his net wide, to locate the king within the context of contemporary polities within the subcontinent as well as beyond, creating space for exploring the complexities of political negotiations. ... Overall, Goyal provides us with a timely reminder of the value of intensive, painstaking scholarship, and shares with us the fruits of long years of research on a subject that has attracted scholarly attention for a variety of reasons, including the richness of sources. In enabling the reader to grapple with the specificities of these sources, their problems, perspectives, as well as the insights they yield, sometimes explicitly, but also inadvertently, Goyal successfully revisits the history of Harsha. This book marks a welcome addition to existing scholarship and will be of value to all those who recognize the importance of combining a broad perspective with an appreciation of finer details.'

Professor Kumkum Roy, New Delhi.

'It is gratifying to know that after D. Devahuti we again have a historian carrying out in-depth research on the times of Harsha. This book will be a valuable addition to the existing literature on the subject and the use of the then contemporary sources.'

Professor Bhairabi Prasad Sahu, Delhi.

'... A work of this kind needs to be highly appreciated for the thorough probe into the original sources of history and to be taken as an example for such other books to follow.'

Professor R. Champakalakshmi, New Delhi.

20. The Significance of Yuan Chwang in the Context of the Seventh Century : A Critical Assessment (D.K. Publishers Distributors Pvt. Ltd., Delhi, 2018) : This book *The Significance of Yuan Chwang in the Context of the Seventh Century : A Critical Assessment* is essentially a critique of the reliability of the Chinese pilgrim as a source of the history of Harshavardhana (606-647 A.D.). His travelogue *Hsi Yü Chi*, or *Buddhist Records of the Western World* assumes greater significance when it is studied against the background of the strengthening of feudal tendencies of the seventh century which for the first time became manifest in the Gupta age. Divided into six chapters and two appendices this painstakingly researched book of Shankar Goyal not only examines the credibility of Yuan Chwang as a source of history, it also discusses dispassionately his testimony on social organisation and social life, economic life and activities, Indian religions and religious condition, education and learning, and art and architecture, taking into consideration the distinctive feature— feudalism— of the age wheresoever possible. The book also contains two appendices—the first, on the *Life* of Yuan Chwang (a summary of chapters VI-X), and the second, on the approximate chronology of his travels in India (after A. Cunningham) in the light of which the testimony of the Chinese pilgrim sometimes assumes new significance. Perhaps there is no other book of this genre on the Chinese pilgrim by any scholar.

EXTRACTS FROM SOME VIEWS AND REVIEWS

'Shankar Goyal has a long standing interest in the history of north India in the seventh century. His present work, assessing the significance of Yuan Chwang, is part of this engagement. Scholars of ancient Indian history will benefit from his close, careful and critical assessment of Yuan Chwang. The book is likely to generate further debate and discussion.'

Professor Kumkum Roy, New Delhi.

'The book is a testimony of Professor Shankar Goyal's erudition and high standard of research. It will become indispensable for all students of the history of Harsha.'

Professor R. Champakalakshmi, New Delhi.

'Altogether we have here a valuable source book on that period of Indian history which is considered to be the most complicated. To the history of Indian civilization, the present book is certainly a welcome addition and a substantial contribution. Goyal has approached his question with an open mind with the result that his findings do not betray presuppositions and prejudices one often finds in such studies. I am sure the book will earn for Goyal much credit which he so eminently deserves.'

Professor Udai Prakash Arora, New Delhi.

'I am happy to read Shankar Goyal's new research work entitled *The Significance of Yuan Chwang in the Context of the Seventh Century: A Critical Assessment.* It is really the first book on the subject and Goyal deserves all praise. Shankar Goyal is a prolific writer and all his books are based on well-researched data. This book is yet another example of the same. Goyal has selected Chinese pilgrim's travelogue *Hsi Yü Chi* or *Buddhist Records of the Western World* which, according to him, assumes greater significance when studied against the background of the strengthening of the feudal tendencies in the seventh century. This, Goyal says, is best exemplified in the transformation of Nālandā Mahāvihāra and also other *vihāras* and the Brāhmaṇical temples in the age of Harsha. The description of Yuan Chwang and Hui-li is important in this context and appears to yield new meaning and light. ... On the whole, this work stands out for its serious research and use of Chinese sources. It will be a useful addition to the existing literature on Yuan Chwang, and opens new areas for further research and analysis.'

Professor D.N. Tripathi, Gorakhpur.

'...Shankar Goyal deserves all commendation for bringing out this monograph of a critical study on Yuan Chwang with a proper scientific zeal in history for the benefit of research and researchers in this era and area which no other Indian scholar has done so far.'

Professor M. V. Singh, Varanasi.

III. EDITED WORKS

21. King Chandra and the Meharauli Pillar (Kusumanjali Prakashan, Meerut, 1989) : The present work is a complete study of the Meharauli iron pillar and the inscription of King Chandra engraved on it. The Meharauli iron pillar is metallurgically unique and a fine specimen of Gupta art while the problem of the identity of King Chandra eulogised in its record is one of the most intriguing and baffling problems of ancient Indian history. This work seeks to present the views of the cream of Indologists on all the problems connected with history, epigraphy, art and metallurgy of the Meharauli pillar at one place. The book is divided into the following parts : Part I : contains papers on the art and metallurgy of the Meharauli pillar. Part II : reproduces text and translations of the inscription of King Chandra as given by eminent epigraphists from Fleet onwards with a short note on more modern inscriptions. Part III : contains the lead-paper of S.R. Goyal on the problem of the identification of King Chandra in which he proposes to identify this ruler with Samudragupta, contradicting the other established theories. Part IV : contains twenty-four reaction papers on the lead-paper of Goyal. Part V : reproduces extracts from the observations of some other scholars on the theory of Goyal. Part VI : contains the reappraisal of the problem of the identity of King Chandra by Goyal in the light of the papers given in parts IV and V. Part VII : is an appendix in which extracts from the views of earlier scholars from V.A. Smith onwards (1897) are reproduced.

What is most satisfying to us is that the contributors to the present volume are well known authorities on the subject representing nearly three generations of Indian scholarship and they have opined against as well as in favour of S.R. Goyal's hypothesis. A strong section of scholars has advanced arguments supporting the identification of Chandra with Chandragupta II but we have stalwarts like B.Ch. Chhabra, S.B. Deo, K. V. Raman, S.K. Gupta, Shankar Goyal and many others favouring S.R. Goyal's postulate. The controversy, however, continues to remain alive.

There is interesting and some altogether new material emerging out of the data presented or through the discussions which is, undoubtedly, informative in historical terms.

22. Political History in a Changing World (Kusumanjali Prakashan, Meerut, 1992) : In recent years the study of political history of ancient India has perceptibly declined. This problem has been critically analysed in the theme paper written for this monograph by S.R. Goyal. In it he has shown that it is the political history of 'traditional' type that has declined, that the decline of 'traditional' political history has taken place in the West also, and that scholars of this subject must invigorate their discipline with a multidisciplinary approach relegating the deeds and dates of the kings into the background and making the political life of ancient Indian society the focal point of their study. In the debate initiated by him more than fifty scholars of Indian and other countries participated, all of them arguing that political history of ancient India now needs a fresh approach and our attitude to the discipline must change. These include G.C. Pande, Allahabad; B.N. Mukherjee, Calcutta; B.N. Puri, Lucknow; B.P. Sinha, Patna; Sibesh Bhattacharya, Allahabad; S.V. Sohoni, Poona; V.S. Pathak, Gorakhpur; Lallanji Gopal, Varanasi; K.D. Bajpai, Sagar; A.V. Narasimhamurthy, Mysore; D. Balasubramanian, Annamalainagar; K.V. Raman, Madras; Upendra Thakur, Bodh-Gaya; Vivekanand Jha, New Delhi; Shankar Goyal (Jodhpur); and many others. Apart from them historians specialising in Epigraphy (Ajay Mitra Shastri, Nagpur; K.K. Thaplyal, Lucknow; and T.P. Verma, Varanasi), Archaeology (S.P. Gupta, New Delhi; K. Paddayya, Pune; and R. Nagaswamy, Madras), Numismatics (P.L. Gupta, Anjaneri), Literature (Jagannath Agrawal, Chandigarh) and Art (S.K.Gupta, Jaipur) have also commented on the suggestions of S.R. Goyal. Eminent scholars from other countries including Bongard-Levin (Russia), A.K. Warder (Canada), J.P. Sharma and A. K. Narain (U.S.A.), David N. Lorenzen (Mexico), Mubarak Ali (Pakistan), S.D. Singh (Australia), Alois Wurm (Austria), T.R. Vaidya (Nepal) and Priti Kumar Mitra (Bangladesh) have enriched the theme by their valuable observations. The real multidisciplinary nature of the book becomes evident by the fact that several scholars of other branches of knowledge including A.C.Angrish (Economics), S.K. Lal (Sociology), Kamini Dinesh (English), M.C. Joshi (Psychology), A.K. Tewari (Geography) and L.S. Rathore (Political Science) have participated in the discussion. In it are also included papers of Nurul Hasan, Romila Thapar and Buddha Prakash which cover some of the issues raised by S.R. Goyal.

23. Reappraising Gupta History for S.R. Goyal (Aditya Prakashan, New Delhi, 1992) : This collection of essays, all by reputed historians, both Indian and foreign, seek a reappraisal of the problems concerning historiography and political and cultural history of the Gupta age. Written in honour of S.R. Goyal by his friends and admirers, including A.M. Shastri, P.K. Mitra, David N. Lorenzen, Sibesh Bhattacharya, V.C. Pandey, Walter M. Spink, B.G. Gokhale, P.K. Agrawala, Lallanji Gopal, Shankar Goyal, etc., they endeavour to put his contribution to Gupta historiography in its proper perspective. They naturally do not provide a connected account of either political or cultural history of the Gupta age, but they do seek to analyse in depth some of the major problems of the history of this period from the angle of vision of their respective authors.

The first five essays collected in this volume throw light on the modern historiography of the Gupta age and the contribution of S.R. Goyal to Gupta studies while the rest are concerned with various aspects of the political and cultural history of the period. The articles collected here have not only evoked different reactions in different minds, but they have also generated huge interest in the problems touched in them.

24. S.R. Goyal : His Multidimensional Historiography (Aditya Prakashan, New Delhi, 1992) : This monograph is meant essentially to felicitate this great scholar and to acquaint those with his academic work who may not happen to be sufficiently familiar with it. His writings cover so very diverse branches as political history, religious history, social history, epigraphy, palaeography, numismatics, art, biographies, literature, and ancient world and have won him friends and admirers not only in India but in every country where Indian studies are popular. The learned authors have discussed in their respective papers his approach to history and contributions to historical studies in general and also to the specific areas on which he has worked. The variety of fields on which S.R. Goyal has worked and usually made original suggestions is the proof of his versatile scholarship. However, as an appreciation of his works involves a study of the changing pattern of Indian historiography during the last three decades or more, this work is useful not only for an evaluation of his multidimensional historiography, but also for a study of the entire spectrum of Indian historiography of the preceding three decades or so. The authors of this festschrift include A.M. Shastri, R. Nagaswamy, K.D. Sethna, P.K. Mitra, N.N. Bhattacharya, N.H. Samtani, G.N. Sharma, K.D. Bajpai, Shankar Goyal and many others.

25. Spectrum of Nehru's Thought (Mittal Publications, New Delhi, 1994) : Pt. Jawaharlal Nehru, the great nationalist leader and the first Prime Minister of India, is famous for his contribution to historical, political and socio-economic thought. The multifaceted dimensions of his thought include various other fields of national life. The present volume contains twelve papers in all which deal with the variegated colours of the spectrum of Nehru's thought. The first three papers deal with various aspects of Nehru's political thought. The first paper by L.S. Rathore is quite comprehensive in scope. It deals with the formative influences on Nehru's political ideas, the philosophical foundations of his political thought, his role in shaping the ideology of the Indian National Congress and the concept of socialism as propounded by him. The scope of the second and third papers is rather limited. The second paper by Sobhag Mathur analyses various radical aspects of Nehru's political thinking in the pre-Independence decades, while the third paper by S.R. Goyal deals with the impact of Marxist philosophy on his ideology. In his paper S.R. Goyal shows how Nehru's interest in Marxism was limited in his early political career, how and why did it increase in late 1920s and 1930s, and how and why did he become disillusioned with Marxist philosophy in the later years of his life. In the fourth paper L. L. Mehrotra studies Jawaharlal Nehru's place in the history of India and the world. Mehrotra evaluates Nehru on the basis of his perosnal contacts as well as study of Nehru's writings. The next two essays are by B.G. Gokhale. In his first essay he has discussed Nehru's view of and contribution to the discipline of history while in the second paper he has discussed Nehru's belief in new emergent Asia as an independent entity with its own 'spirit' poised to lead the world in the grand quest for world peace and his later disillusionment caused by the Chinese invasion of India and other developments. Nehru's Asianism rose as a dream in forties and died in the sixties, and in its birth and death it symbolised his hopes and disillusionments. Nehru took great interest in the making of the Indian Constitution. Later on a controversy arose whether or not there is something like the basic structure of the Constitution which the Parliament cannot touch. In the next article S.R. Bhansali has discussed Nehru's position *vis-a-vis* the concept of the basic structure of the Constitution. The following article by Anand Kishore D. Mathur brings into bold relief the theoretical bases of the foreign policy of free India which was given shape and direction by Nehru. In the next paper A.C. Angrish and Janardan Audichya deal with Nehru's vision of economic order, while the last three papers are devoted to various facets of Nehru's social thought. In her paper Anuradha Srivastava underlines Nehru's belief in rationalism or scientific temper, application of science for social progress, his criticism of the role of organised religion in society and the emphasis he gave on the need of ethical or moral approach to social problems while the paper of Alka Goyal examines critically Nehru's attitude to Indian women. The last paper, that of Shankar Goyal, outlines other main aspects of the social thought of Nehru, specially his integrated view of social welfare and his attitude to caste system, minorities, social justice, secularism, etc.

26-27. Rajasthan Bhāratī, in two volumes (Scientific Publishers, Jodhpur, 1995) : Shankar Goyal has also edited two volumes in Hindi titled *Rajasthan Bhāratī*, Volume I : *Bhāratīya Itihāsa ko Rajasthan kā Avadāna*, and Volume II : *Bhāratīya Saṁskṛti ko Rajasthan kā Avadāna.* These two volumes have been dedicated to S.R. Goyal. Volume I of *Rajasthan Bhāratī* deals with Rajasthan's contribution to Indian history. Apart from forty-five pages devoted to S.R. Goyal's works and his contribution to history, the book contains sixteen articles by scholars which depict important characteristics of the history of Rajasthan. Shankar Goyal has taken due care to show the glorious deeds of the history of Rajasthan which have added lusture to the history of India. Volume II of *Rajasthan Bhāratī* demonstrates that the cultural values of the history of Rajasthan form an illuminating part of Indian history. The book contains twenty-one interesting articles that show that despite its limited sources, Rajasthan's contribution to Indian culture has been highly magnificent. The cultural values for which Indian history is known, such as, patriotism, bravery, self-respect, secularism, patronage to arts, literature, music, architecture, etc., have all emanated from the land of Rajasthan. Rajasthan is the seedbed of Indian history and culture and this theme has been demonstrated in an attractive and scholarly manner by Shankar Goyal. The work is of great significance for the students of history who wish to know Rajasthan's contribution to the history and culture of India.

Shankar Goyal has also contributed substantially in *Rajasthan Bhāratī.* Apart from writing on S. R. Goyal's approach to history in Part I of both these works, in Part II of Volume I he writes an important paper on the historicity of Saṁyogitā, the heroine of *Pṛthvīrājarāso*, and refutes the arguments of Dasharatha Sharma who concedes that the tradition is unanimous in recognising her existence and there is nothing illogical and irrational about it. In Part II of Volume II he throws light on the works of Brahmagupta, a sixth century mathematician and astronomer, who is called *Bhillamālakāchārya.*

28. Prāchīna Bhārata kā Ādhunika Itihāsa-Lekhana (Kusumanjali Book World, Jodhpur, 2000) : It is the first and only work which deals with the subject in Hindi. Divided into 14 chapters it studies the modern history writing of the dynasties of the Vedic age, of the Janapada period and of the subsequent Maurya, Śuṅga, Kaṇva, Indo-Greek, Śaka-Pahlava, Sātavāhana, Gupta and post-Gupta periods up to the middle of the eighth century A.D. It analyses and throws light on all the tendencies found in the history writing of the works of the major historians of India of this period. The scholars who have contributed to the volume include T.P. Verma and M.V. Singh (Varanasi), S.R. Goyal (Jodhpur), J.K. Sharma and Ashvini Agrawal (Chandigarh), Man Mohan Kumar (Rohtak), V.B. Rao and Rajwant Rao (Gorakhpur), B.L. Sharma (Beawar) and Shankar Goyal himself. The book includes a critical study of the latest works on the subject.

29. Indian Art of the Gupta Age : From Pre-Classical Roots to the Emergence of Medieval Trends (Kusumanjali Book World, Jodhpur, 2000) : The Gupta period was admittedly the classical or golden period of Indian history when ancient Indian culture saw efflorescence in almost all aspects of life, including architecture, sculpture and painting. The art of this period has been a subject of study since the beginning of Indological studies in modern times. But the present monograph is different in approach and treatment. Firstly, it contains the fruits of the latest researches of some of the greatest authorities on the subject, including Frederick M. Asher, Walter M. Spink, B. G. Gokhale, P.K. Agrawala, S.R. Goyal, K. D. Bajpai, M.K. Dhavalikar, S.N. Chaturvedi and S.P. Gupta, apart from the contribution of Shankar Goyal. Secondly, despite being the result of the cooperation of numerous scholars of India and abroad, it has a unity in treatment of the subject. Its first three chapters form a sort of background. In the first chapter S.R. Goyal has outlined the historical and ideological background of the Gupta art while in the second chapter S.P. Gupta has discussed the process by which Kushāṇa art got transformed into the classical art of the Gupta age. Then follows the chapter of Frederick M. Asher in which he has given an overview of the art of the Gupta period, both of the imperial provinces and other regions. The next five chapters deal with various aspects of the Gupta art. The fourth chapter by P.K. Agrawala provides a detailed exposition of Gupta art and architecture while the fifth by S.N. Chaturvedi is concerned with various facets and factors of Gupta sculpture. The next three chapters, respectively by B.G. Gokhale, Shankar Goyal and S.R. Goyal, deal with the Buddhist art of the Gupta age, free-standing pillars of the Gupta age and the numismatic art of the period. The next three chapters of the volume are concerned with the study of some regional styles of the Gupta art. In chapter nine K.D. Bajpai discusses the art of central India and the Deccan, in chapter ten Walter M. Spink studies the art of the caves of Ajanta, Ellora, Elephanta, etc., with reference to their chronology, while chapter eleven by M.K. Dhavalikar is concerned with some cultural aspects of the paintings of the Ajanta caves. The twelfth or concluding chapter is by Shankar Goyal. In it he has shown how in the early post-Gupta centuries the classicism of the Gupta age gradually declined and medieval factor became more and more pronounced in Indian art. Thus, the story of the art of the Gupta age which begins with the emergence of classicism and the transformation of the Kushāṇa art into Gupta art comes to a close with the decline of classicism and the emergence of medieval factor in Indian art.

30-33. Reconstructing Indian History for S.R. Goyal (Book Enclave, Jaipur, 2003) : *Reconstructing Indian History for S.R. Goyal* is a stimulating survey of different periods and aspects of Indian history and culture in four volumes. This is a unique volume containing research articles dedicated to the multifaceted historiography of S.R.Goyal. With more than a hundred articles, a large number of photographs and a carefully chiselled intellectual and academic biography of S.R. Goyal this work successfully illumines many a shadowy corridor of India's past—from the earliest times to the present day. It provides an unparalleled source of insight into the changing pattern of Indian history and civilization incorporating the latest researches on the subject.

Through an evaluation of the life and works of S.R. Goyal the contributors of Volume I, *Professor S.R. Goyal : The Profile of a Historian*, all eminent historians, including A.K. Narain, (Varanasi), A.M. Shastri (Nagpur) V.B. Rao (Gorakhpur), B.N. Puri (Lucknow), Lallanji Gopal (Varanasi), Upendra Thakur (Bodh-Gaya), D.N. Tripathi (Gorakhpur), M. V. Singh (Varanasi), Shankar Goyal (Jodhpur), and many others have tried to delineate the changing pattern of Indian historiography at the turn of the century. *India's Ancient Past*, Volume II, is a study of some of the major problems of ancient Indian history and culture in the light of new discoveries and approaches which make it imperative for us to re-examine the contours of our ancient past afresh. It contains fifty-one articles which are divided subject-wise into five sections. They are contributed by eminent historians and archaeologists among whom are included the following : V.K.Thakur (Patna), S.P. Gupta (New Delhi), K.K. Thaplyal (Lucknow), A.M. Shastri (Nagpur), Om Prakash (Allahabad), S.V. Sohoni (Pune), I.K. Sarma (Hyderabad), Jagannath Agrawal (Chandigarh), Upendra Thakur (Patna), Lallanji Gopal (Varanasi), B.P. Sinha (Patna), V.B. Kolte (Nagpur), T.P. Verma (Varanasi), K.G. Krishnan (Mysore), David N. Lorenzen (Mexico), M.V. Singh (Varanasi), Vivekanand Jha (New Delhi), Priti K. Mitra (Bangladesh), Ashvini Agrawal (Chandigarh), P.K. Agrawala (Varanasi), Anupa Pande (New Delhi), S.K. Maity (Jadavpur), B.N. Mukherjee (Kolkata), K.D. Bajpai (Sagar), N.H. Samtani (Sarnath), J.P. Sharma (Hawaii, U.S.A.) Susmita Pande (Bhopal), Nisar Ahmad (Varanasi), Devendra Handa (Shimla), S.N. Chaturvedi, (Gorakhpur), Shashi Asthana (New Delhi), and Shankar Goyal (Jodhpur).

The history of medieval and modern India is the subject-matter of Volume III. In recent decades the texture of writing on these periods is changing fast due to the availability of new materials and changing attitudes of historians. Apparently, now more attention is being devoted to the study of socio-economic history, historiography, etc., instead of the age-old topics concerning the wars, intrigues and rivalries of royal potentates and dynasties. Thus, the Volume III, *India's Medieval and Modern Past*, gives emphasis on the new orientation which is being given to study of these periods. For example, it provides a detailed study of the Middle Class in Medieval India, Social Legislation and Public Reaction in Modern India, Status and Empowerment of Women in Modern India, and also Itihāsa-Darśana, Marxist View of History and Nehru's Universalistic View of History. Some old topics which have not lost their appeal such as Medieval Paintings, Akbar's Attitude towards Rana Pratap, British Relations with Mewar, Ideology of the Congress Socialist Party and the Muslims of the Indo-Pak Subcontinent have also been discussed and included in it. Among the contributors the following are included: K.S. Lal (New Delhi), R.P. Vyas and Shankar Goyal (Jodhpur), K.S. Gupta (Udaipur), Mubarak Ali (Sindh, Pakistan), A. Chandrasekaran (Chennai), and many others. The Volume IV, *Rajasthan : From Prehistory to the Independence Era*, seeks to re-study the history and culture of Rajasthan in the light of the new material which is being constantly discovered and in the light of new interpretations which have become imperative due to the changing historiographical attitudes. The contributors of this work include V.N. Misra and S.N. Rajaguru (Poona), B.D. Chattopadhyaya (New Delhi), K.C. Jain (Ujjain), V.K. Vashishtha (Ajmer), G.N. Sharma (Jaipur), Devendra Handa (Shimla), Dilbagh Singh (New Delhi), K.S. Gupta (Udaipur), R.P. Vyas and Shankar Goyal (Jodhpur).

34. Investigating Indian Society (Kusumanjali Book World, Jodhpur, 2013) : In this work some of the best minds of the Indological world discuss the formation and evolution of the ideals and patterns of Indian society. Dedicated to S. R. Goyal on the completion of his eightieth year, the volume throws welcome light on the various fundamental questions related with the social and ideological foundations of Indian culture, a subject so dear to him. It has been enriched, among others, by the scholarly contributions of such eminent historians as G.C. Pande (Allahabad), R. S. Sharma (Patna), Irfan Habib (Aligarh), Romila Thapar, Kesavan Veluthat and Kumkum Roy (New Delhi), R. Champakalakshmi (Chennai), S. N. Dube (Jaipur), K.K. Thaplyal (Lucknow), T. P. Verma and M. V. Singh (Varanasi). The volume also contains an Introduction by Shankar Goyal on S.R. Goyal's own contribution to the study of ancient Indian social institutions and ideas.

35. Indian Society : The Regional Contours (Kusumanjali Book World, Jodhpur, 2013) : Dedicated to S.R. Goyal on the completion of his eightieth year of life, this festschrift seeks mainly to study the regional contours of Indian society which have been conspicuous despite its overall fundamental unity. Containing the articles of eminent scholars such as R.P. Vyas, T.K. Mathur and Vinita Parihar (Rajasthan), A. Chandrasekaran, G.Venkataraman and G.J. Sudhakar (Tamilnadu), B.L. Bhadani (Uttar Pradesh), S.K. Panda (Odisha) and some others, it throws welcome light on the contribution of various regions of India to the formation of the pan-Indian personality of our society. The work also contains an Introduction by Shankar Goyal on S.R. Goyal's own contribution in this field.

36. Reinterpreting Indian History (Kusumanjali Book World, Jodhpur, 2014) : *Reinterpreting Indian History : Essays in Honour of Professor Sobhag Mathur* certainly owes a great deal to whom it seeks to honour. A perfect gentleman, Mathur's reputation lies in his scholarly contributions to the study of modern Indian history. As a mark of respect and affection for him on the occasion of his completion of 75 years of his life, seventeen historians, including L.S. Rathore, S.R. Goyal, P.R. Arya, T.K. Mathur, V.K. Vashishtha, B.K. Sharma, T.P. Verma, M.V. Singh, A. Chandrasekaran, Nalini Chandrasekaran, G.J. Sudhakar, A.K. Sinha, Vibha Upadhyaya, K. L. Mathur, Vinita Parihar and Meghna Goyal, have come together in this volume to produce a work worthy of both teachers and students. The intrinsic merit of these essays, the wide range of themes they encompass, the questions they raise and the facts they uncover make this a valuable collection in itself — of interest to any reader of history and historiography. The work also contains an Introduction by Shankar Goyal on Sobhag Mathur's own contribution to the study of modern Indian history and Rajasthan.

37. History and Politics (Kusumanjali Book World, Jodhur, 2015) : *History and Politics : Essays in Honour of Professor P. S. Bhati* definitely owes a great deal to whom it seeks to felicitate. Bhati's reputation lies in his remarkable contributions to the study of politics and history. As a mark of respect and affection for him, many scholars of both the disciplines, including L.S. Rathore, S.R. Goyal, Sobhag Mathur, A. Chandrasekaran, N. Rajendran, B.K. Sharma, M.V. Singh, A.K. Sinha, S.K. Panda, F. K. Kapil and Meghna Goyal, have come together in this volume to produce a work useful for teachers and students both. That history and politics are cognate disciplines is evident from their very nature and also from the contents of the problems these essays seek to elucidate. The work also contains an exhaustive and critical Introduction by Shankar Goyal on P. S. Bhati's own contributions to the study of politics and history, more particularly his studies on contemporary world.

Professor Shankar Goyal delivering the Presidential Address (Ancient India) to the 78th Session of the Indian History Congress at Jadavpur University, Kolkata, Dec. 2017. Professor R. Mahalakshmi on the right side.

Professor Shankar Goyal delivering the Presidential Address (Historiography) to the XXIII Annual Session of the Tamilnadu History Congress at Salem, Feb. 2016.

Professor Shankar Goyal delivering the Loyola College Endowment Lecture at Bangalore University, March 2006.

Professor Shankar Goyal delivering the Valedictory Address to the XXIII South Indian History Congress at Trivandrum, Feb. 2002.

Professor Shankar Goyal as a young scholar with Professor G.C. Pande.

Professor Shankar Goyal with Professor Romila Thapar during
the 69th Session of the Indian History Congress at Kannur, Kerala, Dec. 2008.

Professor Shankar Goyal with Professor Irfan Habib during
the 65th Session of the Indian History Congress held at Bareilly, Dec. 2004.

Professor Shankar Goyal with Dr. Mrs. Nalini Chandrasekaran and Professor A. Chandrasekaran.

38. Early India : Historical Probings : Essays in Honour of Professor S.R. Goyal on His 85th Birthday (Kusumanjali Book World, Jodhpur, 2015) : S.R. Goyal's reputation lies in the undoubted superiority of his works on early Indian history. As a mark of respect and affection for him some of his friends, which include not only some of the best minds of the Indological world such as Romila Thapar, Irfan Habib, R. Champakalakshmi, Kumkum Roy, Samaresh Bandyopadhyay, D.N. Tripathi, U.P. Arora and J.M. Rai, but also some young talent working on early India, such as Nanditha Krishna, Neekee Chaturvedi and Meghna Goyal, decided to put together a volume of essays in his honour. The intrinsic merit of these essays, the wide range of topics they cover within a broad framework of early India including political history, society, economy, religion, art and culture, the questions they raise and the facts they uncover make this a valuable collection in itself—of interest to any reader of history. The work also contains an Introduction by Shankar Goyal on S.R. Goyal's approach to history and his contribution to the study of ancient Indian history. This is no mean tribute and may as such be regarded as a evidence of the greatness of the man in whose honour it seeks to perpetuate through this work.

39. Origin and Growth of History Writing in Rajasthan, Volume III : Historions and Historiography in Contemporary Rajasthan (D.K. Publishers Pvt. Ltd., Delhi, 2019) : This edited book *Historians and Historiography in Contemporary Rajasthan* by Shankar Goyal is the third volume of his project entitled *Origin and Growth of History Writing in Rajasthan*, the two others being his own works on the subject, namely, *Khyats and Allied Works of Historical Genre* (New Delhi, 2017) and *Historians and Historiography in Modern Rajasthan* (Delhi, 2018). The Khyats are considered as the earliest sources of Rajput history of medieval Rajasthan. Therefore in Volume One Shankar Goyal examines some prominent Khyats, such as, *Muhnot Nainsi ri Khyat*, *Bankidas ri Khyat*, *Dayaldas ri Khyat*, *Jodhpur Rajya ki Khyat* of Ai Dan Khidia, *Marwar ri Khyat* of Tilok Chand Joshi, and *Jaisalmer ri Khyat* of Ajit Singh Mehta. In his Volume Two he appropriately demarcates the various traditions that has dominated in the modern historiography of Rajasthan. The first tradition extended from James Tod to the dawn of Indian independence wherein the trend was of writing the chronological histories of the dynasties. The second tradition commenced from the mid-20th century showing a new trend of writing the history of Rajasthan against the perspective of national history. And lastly, a few more traditions that developed simultaneously in the later half of the 20th century were the writing of regional history, the study of the life of common people, the nature of freedom struggle or the liberation movements, poetic compositions about historical characters, and the study of culture of Rajasthan. While exercising his discretion in a fair manner Shankar Goyal has chosen eleven historians, namely, James Tod, Shyamaldas, G.H. Ojha, V.N. Reu, Dasharatha Sharma, S.R. Goyal, G.N. Sharma, R.P. Vyas, L.S. Rathore, G.S.L. Devra and Sobhag Mathur, for being included in this work because they have been the pioneers in different traditions or areas of the history of Rajasthan. The story of history writing in modern and contemporary Rajasthan further continues in Volume Three of Shankar Goyal's *Origin and Growth of History Writing in Rajasthan* which includes some more historians who have contributed immensely to enrich the history and culture of Rajasthan and are pioneers in their respective fields of study. These include M. S. Jain, K.S. Gupta, V.S. Bhatnagar, S.P. Gupta, Dilbagh Singh, T.K. Mathur, Vinita Parihar and Shankar Goyal.

IV. ARTICLES

1. 1974. Pṛthvīrāja Chauhān ke Antim Din (in Hindi), *Shodha Patrika*, Udaipur, Year 25 (1). 11-15.
2. 1974. Saṁyogitā Kathā kī Aitihāsikatā (in Hindi), *Parishad Patrika*, Patna, Year 14 (2). 68-73.
3. 1976. Harsha aura Rajasthan (in Hindi), *Shodha Patrika*, Udaipur, Year 27 (1). 24-27.
4. 1977. Kumārajīva : The Yuan Chwang of India, *Journal of the Rajasthan Institute of Historical Research*, Jaipur, XIV (2). 36-40.
5. 1980. Maurya Sāmrājya ke Vighaṭan meṅ Aśoka kī Bhūmikā (in Hindi), *Parishad Patrika*, Patna, Year 20 (1). 37-45.
6. 1983. New Trends in Archaeology, *Vishveshvaranand Indological Journal*, Hoshiarpur, XXI (Pts. I-II). 73-77.
7. 1985. Gupta Samrāṭoṅ kī Sāmājika Pratishṭhā (in Hindi), *Parishad Patrika*, Patna, Year 25 (2). 74-80.
8. 1986. Social *Milieu* of the Pushyabhūtis : Significance of Some Hitherto Unnoticed Passages of the *Harshacharita*, in *Essays in Indian History and Culture* (Y. Krishan Ed.), pp. 167-170. New Delhi : The Indian History and Culture Society.
9. 1987. Kyā Akbar Sākshara Thā ? (in Hindi), in *Mughal Sāmrājya kā Prārambhika Itihāsa* (S. R. Goyal and S. K. Gupta Eds.), pp. 352-355. New Delhi : Munshiram Manoharlal Publishers Pvt. Ltd.
10. 1987. Pushyamitra Śuṅga and the Persecution of Buddhism, App. 2 in *A History of Indian Buddhism* (by S. R. Goyal), pp. 429-433. Meerut : Kusumanjali Prakashan.

11. 1987. Menander as a Buddhist King, App. 3 in *A History of Indian Buddhism* (by S. R. Goyal), pp. 434-437. Meerut: Kusumanjali Prakashan.
12. 1987. Buddhist Symbols and Buddha Image on Ancient Indian Coins, *Journal of the Numismatic Society of India*, Varanasi XLIX (Pts. I-II) : 109-114.
13. 1988. Śaśāṅka and Buddhism, in *Studies in Indian History and Culture* (T. P. Verma and O. P. Tandon Eds.), pp. 45-50. Varanasi : Bharat Kala Bhavan, Banaras Hindu University.
14. 1989. On the Identification of King Chandra of the Meharauli Pillar Inscription, in *King Chandra and the Meharauli Pillar* (Munish Chandra Joshi et al Eds.), pp. 150-156. Meerut : Kusumanjali Prakashan.
15. 1989. Some Observations on Magadha-Kosala Relations in the Age of the Buddha, in *History and Art* (Krishna Deva and Lallanji Gopal Eds.), pp. 240-244. Delhi: Ramanand Vidya Bhawan.
16. 1992. Political History : The Loss of Innocence, in *Political History in a Changing World* (G.C. Pande et al Eds.), pp.290-299. Jodhpur: Kusumanjali Prakashan.
17. 1992. Political Ideology of the Early Imperial Guptas, in *Reappraising Gupta History* (B.Ch. Chhabra et al Eds.), pp.215-223. New Delhi: Aditya Prakashan.
18. 1992. A Critique of Professor D. N. Jha's Evaluation of the Classicism of the Gupta Age, in *Reappraising Gupta History* (B. Ch. Chhabra et al Eds.), pp. 61-73. New Delhi : Aditya Prakashan.
19. 1992. S. R. Goyal's Approach to History, in *S. R. Goyal : His Multi-dimensional Historiography* (Jagannath Agrawal and Shankar Goyal Eds.), pp. 23-34. New Delhi : Aditya Prakashan.
20. 1992. S. R. Goyal and the Historiography of the Post-Gupta Period (c.550 - c.750 A.D.), in *S. R. Goyal : His Multidimensional Historiography* (Jagannath Agrawal and Shankar Goyal Eds.), pp. 123-146. New Delhi : Aditya Prakashan.
21. 1992. The Progress of Vākāṭaka Historiography, in *The Age of the Vākāṭakas* (A.M. Shastri Ed.), pp. 297-308. New Delhi: Harman Publishing House.
22. 1992. Rise of Medievalism in Indian History, *Vishveshvaranand Indological Journal*, Hoshiarpur XXX (Pts. i-ii) : 233-260.
23. 1992. Mahārāja Gupta se Samrāṭa Samudragupta tak Itihāsa-Lekhana kī Navīna Pravṛttiyāṅ (in Hindi), *Shodha Patrika*, Udaipur, Year 43 (1): 14-35.

24. 1992. Samrāṭa Chandragupta Vikramāditya se Samrāṭa Skandagupta tak Itihāsa-Lekhana kī Navīna Pravṛttiyāṅ (in Hindi), *Shodha Patrika*, Udaipur, Year 43 (2) : 36-53.
25. 1992. Coins of Prabhākaravardhana Pratāpaśīla and Harsha Śīlāditya, *Journal of the Numismatic Society of India*, Varanasi LIV (Pts. 1-2) : 65-69.
26. 1993. The Nature of the Early Buddhist Historiography, *The Indian Journal of Buddhist Studies*, Varanasi 5 (1) : 69-77.
27. 1993. Recent Historiography of the Age of Harsha, *Annals of the Bhandarkar Oriental Research Institute*, Poona LXXII-LXXIII (Amṛtamahotsava Volume) : 331-361.
28. 1993. Anusandhāna Paddhati kī Vivechanā (in Hindi), a Review Article, *Journal of the All India Philosophy Association*, Jabalpur, Year 38-39 : 98-106.
29. 1994. Social Thought of Jawaharlal Nehru, *The Quarterly Review of Historical Studies*, Calcutta XXXII (3-4) : 89-101.
30. 1994. Historiography of the Punch-Marked Coins, App. 1 in *Indigenous Coins of Early India* (by S. R. Goyal), pp. 205-218. Jodhpur : Kusumanjali Prakashan.
31. 1994. Historiography of the Tribal and Local Coins, App. 2 in *Indigenous Coins of Early India* (by S. R. Goyal), pp. 219-223. Jodhpur : Kusumanjali Prakashan.
32. 1994. The Rājyavardhana Murder Case, in *Heritage of India : Past and Present* (P. K. Mishra and S. K. Sullerey Eds.), Vol. II, pp.579-590. Delhi : Agam Kala Prakashan.
33. 1994. The Art of the Gupta Age, a script written for the film produced by the Educational Media Research Centre, Jodhpur, for the U.G.C. Programme.
34. 1995. Historiography of the Imperial Guptas : Old and New, *Annals of the Bhandarkar Oriental Research Institute*, Poona LXXVI : 1-33.
35. 1995. Dakshiṇa Bhāratīya Itihāsa ke Srota (in Hindi), Ch. 2 in *Dakshiṇa Bhārata kā Itihāsa* (by S. R. Goyal), pp. I. 5-13. Jodhpur : Kusumanjali Prakashan.
36. 1995. Saṅgama Sāhitya se Gyāta Rājanītika Itihāsa (in Hindi), Ch. 5 in *Dakshiṇa Bhārata kā Itihāsa* (by S. R. Goyal), pp. II. 67-72. Jodhpur : Kusumanjali Prakashan.
37. 1995. Vākāṭaka Itihāsa par Navīna Ābhilekhika aura Maudrika Prakāśa (in Hindi), App. in *Dakshiṇa Bhārata kā Itihāsa* (by S. R. Goyal), pp. III. 161-163. Jodhpur: Kusumanjali Prakashan.

38. 1995. Historiography of the Indo-Greek Coinage, in *The Dynastic Coins of Ancient India* (by S. R. Goyal), pp. 3-10. Jodhpur: Kusumanjali Prakashan.
39. 1995. A Note on the Date of Kanishka I, in *The Dynastic Coins of Ancient India* (by S. R. Goyal), pp. 45-47. Jodhpur : Kusumanjali Prakashan.
40. 1995. Historiography of the Kushāṇa Coinage, in *The Dynastic Coins of Ancient India* (by S. R. Goyal), pp. 47-49. Jodhpur: Kusumanjali Prakashan.
41. 1995. Historiography of the Sātavāhana Coinage, in *The Dynastic Coins of Ancient India* (by S. R. Goyal), pp. 86-89. Jodhpur: Kusumanjali Prakashan.
42. 1995. Historiography of Gupta Numismatics, in *The Dynastic Coins of Ancient India* (by S. R. Goyal), pp. 129-136. Jodhpur : Kusumanjali Prakashan.
43. 1995. Gupta Impact on the North Indian Coins of the Post-Gupta Century (550-650 A.D.) Ch. 4 in *An Introduction to Gupta Numismatics* (by S.R. Goyal), pp. 117-128. Jodhpur : Kusumanjali Prakashan.
44. 1995. Professor S. R. Goyal kī Itihāsa-Dṛshṭi (in Hindi), in *Rajasthan Bhāratī*, Vol. I (Sobhag Mathur and Shankar Goyal Eds.), pp. 19-28. Jodhpur : Scientific Publishers.
45. 1995. Bhinnamālakāchārya Brahmagupta (in Hindi), in *Rajasthan Bhāratī*, Vol. II (Sobhag Mathur and Shankar Goyal Eds.), pp. 11-15. Jodhpur : Scientific Publishers.
46. 1995. Recent Historiography of the Early Maurya Empire, in *Viśvambharā : Probings in Orientology* (A. M. Shastri Ed.), Vol. II, pp. 444-456. New Delhi : Harman Publishing House.
47. 1995. Dr. P. L. Gupta aura Guptakālīna Suvarṇa Mudrāyeṅ (in Hindi), in *Baḍhate Kadam-Badalte Āyāma* (Sarojini Kulshreshth Ed.), pp. 271-278. Varanasi : Vishwavidyalaya Prakashan.
48. 1996. Voices of Protest and Dissent in the Works of Bāṇa, in *Professor Shri Niwas Shastri Commemoration Volume*, pp. 650-660. Delhi : Parimal Publications.
49. 1997. Historiography of the Janapada Age and the Rise of Magadha, *Journal of Indian History*, Trivandrum LXVI : 13-28.
50. 1997. History as Biography in Sanskrit Literature, in *Professor D. N. Bhargava Felicitation Volume* (Narendra Awasthi Ed.), pp. 302-311. Jodhpur : Centre for Vedic Studies.
51. 1997. Guptakālīna Saṁskṛti aura Svarṇa Yuga kī Avadhāraṇā (in Hindi), in *Treasures in Indian Art and Culture* (K.K.

Chakravarty Ed.), Vol. II, pp. 613-617. Delhi: Sharada Publishing House.

52. 1998. Dr. R. P. Vyas : His Approach to History, in *Dr. R. P. Vyas Felicitation Volume* (Z. K. Mehar, S. K. Purohit and S. P. Vyas Eds.), pp. I. 69-72. Jodhpur : Rajasthani Granthagar.

53. 1998. Bhāratīya Itihāsa-Lekhana : Kuchha Vikṛtiyāṅ, in *Dr. R. P. Vyas Felicitation Volume* (Z. K. Mehar, S. K. Purohit and S.P. Vyas Eds.), pp. II. 78-84. Jodhpur: Rajasthani Granthagar.

54. 1999. Changing Historiography of the Pre-Buddha Period, *Annals of the Bhandarkar Oriental Research Institute,* Poona LXXIX (Pts. I-IV) : 29-59.

55. 1999. Professor G. C. Pande : A Philosopher-Historian Extraordinary, *Journal of the G. N. Jha Kendriya Sanskrit Vidyapeetha,* Allahabad L-LI : 5-17.

56. 2000. Free-standing Pillars of the Gupta Age, in *Indian Art of the Gupta Age* (S. R. Goyal and Shankar Goyal Eds.), pp. 139-149. Jodhpur : Kusumanjali Book World.

57. 2000. Prāchīna Bhārata kā Ādhunika Itihāsa-Lekhana : Pramukha Pravṛttiyāṅ (in Hindi), in *Prāchīna Bhārata kā Ādhunika Itihāsa-Lekhana* (Shankar Goyal Ed.), pp. 11-19. Jodhpur: Kusumanjali Book World.

58. 2000. Gupta Vaṁśa ke Itihāsa kā Lekhana : 1966 Tak (in Hindi), in *Prāchīna Bhārata kā Ādhunika Itihāsa-Lekhana* (Shankar Goyal Ed.), pp. 185-197. Jodhpur : Kusumanjali Book World.

59. 2000. 1966 ke Uparānta Gupta Itihāsa-Lekhana (in Hindi), in *Prāchīna Bhārata kā Ādhunika Itihāsa-Lekhana* (Shankar Goyal Ed.), pp. 198-225. Jodhpur : Kusumanjali Book World.

60. 2000. Prabhākaravardhana : A New Assessment, *Sri Venkateswara University Oriental Journal,* Tirupati 43 (Pts. 1-2) : 9-31.

61. 2000. Historiography of the Indo-Greek Coinage : A Revised Study, *Vishveshvaranand Indological Journal,* Hoshiarpur XXXIII-XXXIV (Pts. i-iv) : 295-314.

62. 2001. Chāṇakya in Graeco-Roman Tradition, Ch. 4 in *India as Known to Kauṭilya and Megasthenes* (by S. R. Goyal), pp. I. 61-68. Jodhpur : Kusumanjali Book World.

63. 2001. Kauṭilya and Machiavelli : A Comparison, Ch. 17 in *India as Known to Kauṭilya and Megasthenes* (by S. R.Goyal), pp. I. 166-174. Jodhpur : Kusumanjali Book World.

64. 2001. *Kauṭilīya Arthaśāstra* and Megasthenes' *Indica* : A Comparison, Ch. 18 in *India as Known to Kauṭilya and Megasthenes* (by S. R. Goyal), pp. I. 175-180. Jodhpur : Kusumanjali Book World.

65. 2001. Megasthenes on the Geography of India, Ch. 2 in *India as Known to Kauṭilya and Megasthenes* (by S. R. Goyal), pp. II. 15-22. Jodhpur : Kusumanjali Book World.

66. 2001. Megasthenes on Indian History, Royal Life and Allied Matters, Ch. 3 in *India as Known to Kauṭilya and Megasthenes* (by S. R. Goyal), pp. II. 23-32. Jodhpur: Kusumanjali Book World.

67. 2001. Buddhism and the Indo-Greeks, *Sri Venkateswara University Oriental Journal*, Tirupati XLIV (Pts.1-2) : 19-26.

68. 2002. Protest against Untouchability : A Comparative Study of Gandhian and Ambedkarite Approaches, *The Quarterly Review of Historical Studies*, Kolkata XLI (4) : 23-27.

69. 2002. Historiography of the Punch-Marked Coins : A Revised Study, *Journal of the Numismatic Society of India*, Varanasi LX-LXI : 73-84.

70. 2002. Bāṇa ke 'Harshacharita' meṅ Abhivyakta Itihāsa-Dṛshṭi (in Hindi), *Shodha Samaveta*, Ujjain XI (1-2) : 140-147.

71. 2002. Comparative Reliability of the Avadānas and Aśokan Edicts, *Annals of the Bhandarkar Oriental Research Institute*, Poona LXXXII : 251-257.

72. 2002. Bhāratīya Saṁskṛti kā Artha aura Svarūpa (in Hindi), *Pratisruti*, Jodhpur 7: 23-34.

73. 2002. Wajid Ali Shah : An Assessment, in the *Seventh Annual Conference of the Association of the Third World Studies, South Asia Chapter* (Prema Kasturi Ed.), pp. 28-30. Chennai : Sir C. P. Ramaswamy Aiyar Foundation.

74. 2002. Prajātīya Vaividhya se Sampanna Bhāratīya Rāshṭrīyatā (in Hindi), *Vaichariki*, Bikaner 17 (4) : 56-62.

75. 2002. Historiography of James Tod, in *Some Aspects of Rajasthan History and Culture* (Pema Ram Ed.), pp. 245-253. Banasthali : Department of History, Banasthali Vidyapith.

76. 2002. Harsha's Relations with the Deccan and the Far South : Some Problems and Suggestions, in the *Proceedings of the Twenty-second Annual Session of the South Indian History Congress*, Thiruvananthapuram, 2002, pp. 135-137.

77. 2002. Need of an Integral View of the Political History of South India, Valedictory Address, published in the *Proceedings of the Twenty-second Annual Session of the South Indian History Congress*, Thiruvananthapuram, 2002, pp.515-517.

78. 2002. Political History as an Integral Study of Political Life and Institutions, *Khyat*, Bikaner 7: 61-74.

79. 2002. Bhārata kī Bhāshātmaka aura Sāhityika Ektā (in Hindi), *Vaichariki*, Bikaner 18 (2):36-45.

80. 2003. Vartamāna Samaya aura Rāshṭrīya Ektā kā Praśna (in Hindi), *Pratisruti*, Jodhpur 9:18-26.

81. 2003. Acquisition of the Maukhari Empire by Harsha, *Journal of the Asiatic Society*, Kolkata XLV (2) : 53-62. Abstract also published in the *Proceedings of the Indian History Congress*, 62nd Session, Kolkata, 2002, pp. 1090-1091.

82. 2003. V. S. Agrawala : Historian *Par Excellence* of Art and Culture, *Vishveshvaranand Indological Journal*, Hoshiarpur XXXVII-XXXVIII (Pts. i-ii) : 193-209.

83. 2003. Buddhism in Early South Indian History, in the *Proceedings of the Twenty-third Annual Session of the South Indian History Congress*, Tiruchirappalli, 2003, pp. 539-542.

84. 2003. S. R. Goyal's Integral Approach to History, in *Professor S.R. Goyal : The Profile of a Historian* (Shankar Goyal Ed.), pp. 199-221. Jaipur : Book Enclave.

85. 2003. S. R. Goyal's Probings into the History and Sources of the Pre-Gupta Period, in *Professor S. R. Goyal : The Profile of a Historian* (Shankar Goyal Ed.), pp. 261-316. Jaipur : Book Enclave.

86. 2003. S. R. Goyal's Appraisal of the History and Sources of the Gupta and Post-Gupta Periods, in *Professor S. R. Goyal : The Profile of a Historian* (Shankar Goyal Ed.), pp. 353-421. Jaipur : Book Enclave.

87. 2003. Wajid Ali Shah : His Life and Character as Described by His Contemporary Abdul Halim Sharar, in *India's Medieval and Modern Past* (Shankar Goyal Ed.), pp. 81-94. Jaipur : Book Enclave.

88. 2003. L. S. Rathore : A Poet-Historian of Rajasthan, in *Rajasthan: From Prehistory to the Independence Era* (Shankar Goyal Ed.), pp. 343-368. Jaipur : Book Enclave.

89. 2003. The Historiography of Gaurishanker Hirachand Ojha, in *Jijñāsā* (A Journal of the History of Ideas and Culture), Jaipur IX: 67-76.

90. 2003. A Brief Historiography of Professor Lallanji Gopal, *Journal of the Numismatic Society of India*, Varanasi LXII-III: xxix-xxxii.

91. 2003. On Dr. P. L. Gupta's Contribution to Gupta History and Coinage, *Journal of the Numismatic Society of India*, Varanasi LXIV-V : xxx-xxxiii.

92. 2003. Political Ideology of the Early Guptas as Reflected on their Coins, *Journal of the Numismatic Society of India*, Varanasi LXIV-V: 24-28.

93. 2004. Main Stages in the Study of Maurya Epigraphy, in *Methodology of Epigraphical Studies and History Writing* (Sita Ram Dube Ed.), pp. 36-46. Delhi : Pratibha Prakashan.
94. 2004. Vikramāditya Kathā kā Janma aura Vikāsa (in Hindi), in *Ujjain and Its Glorious Past* (R. K. Ahirwar Ed.), pp. 63-70. Jaipur : RBSA Publishers.
95. 2004. Meharauli Abhilekha kā 'Chandra' : Dvitīya Chandragupta yā Samudragupta? (in Hindi), in *Ābhilekhika Adhyayana kī Pravidhi evaṁ Itihāsa-Lekhana* (Sita Ram Dube Ed.), pp. 140-151. Delhi : Pratibha Prakashan.
96. 2004. Harsha ke Abhilekha : Kuchha Samasyāyeṅ aura Sujhāva (in Hindi), in *Ābhilekhika Adhyayana kī Pravidhi evaṁ Itihāsa-Lekhana* (Sita Ram Dube Ed.), pp. 183-189. Delhi: Pratibha Prakashan.
97. 2004. Psycho-Sociological Analysis of Harsha's Personality, *Journal of Indian History*, Thiruvananthapuram LXXVI-LXXVIII : 7-14.
98. 2004. Professor Dasharatha Sharma : His Contribution to the Historiography of Rajasthan, in the *Proceedings of the Rajasthan History Congress*, Vol. XIX, Proceedings of the Sheoganj Session, 2001, Jodhpur, 2004, pp. 71-84.
99. 2004. Chandragupta II's Relations with the Vākāṭakas during the Regency of Prabhāvatīguptā, *Journal of the Asiatic Society*, Kolkata XLV (4) : 53-58.
100. 2004. Factors in the Making of Early Medieval Society in India, *Journal of Indian History and Culture*, Chennai XI : 25-52.
101. 2004. Professor Ajay Mitra Shastri's Contribution to Ancient Indian Numismatics, *Journal of the Numismatic Society of India*, Varanasi LXVI : xl-xliv.
102. 2005. Political History as the Study of Power against the Background of Factors and Forces Operating in Society, *Vishveshvaranand Indological Journal*, Hoshiarpur XLI-XLII (Pts. i-ii) : 195-207. Abstract also published in the *Proceedings of the Summaries of Papers*, 42nd Session, All India Oriental Conference, Varanasi, 2004, p. 398.
103. 2005. Main Stages in the Study of Gupta Epigraphy, Ch. 13 in *Ancient Indian Inscriptions: Recent Finds and New Interpretations* (by S.R. Goyal), pp. 110-114. Jodhpur : Kusumanjali Book World.
104. 2005. The Recently Discovered Kurukshetra-Varanasi Grant of Harsha : Year 23, in the *Proceedings of the Indian History Congress*, 65th Session, Bareilly, 2004 (Kolkata, 2005),

pp. 178-189. Also published in the *East and West*, Rome, Italy, Vol. 57 (1-4), December 2007, pp. 193-203 and *Epigraphia Indica*, New Delhi, Vol. XLIII, Part I, 2011-12, pp. 40-51.

105. 2005. Meaning and Significance of New Integral Political History, in *Brahma Śrī : Researches in Archaeology, History and Culture in the New Millennium* (P. Chenna Reddy, Ed.), Vol. II, pp. 375-392. Delhi : Sharada Publishing House.

106. 2005. A.S. Altekar and the Bayana Hoard, *Journal of the Numismatic Society of India*, Varanasi LXVII : 80-84.

107. 2005. Historiography of Professor K.A. Nilakanta Sastri, *Journal of Indian History and Culture*, Chennai XII : 36-50.

108. 2005. Historiography of Professor R.C. Majumdar, *Journal of Indian History*, Thiruvananthapuram LXXXIV (Pts. 1-3) : 283-296.

109. 2005. Professor G.N. Sharma as a Historian, in the *Proceedings of the Rajasthan History Congress*, Vol. XX, Proceedings of the Udaipur Session, 2004, Jodhpur, 2005, pp. 84-94.

110. 2005. Professor K.A. Nilakanta Sastri's Approach to History, in the *Proceedings of the Twenty-fifth Annual Session of the South Indian History Congress*, Madurai, 2005, pp. 694-699.

111. 2005. Nandoṅ kā Itihāsa meṅ Mahattva : Eka Naī Dṛshṭi kī Jaroorata (in Hindi), *Pratisruti*, Jodhpur 17 : 33-39.

112. 2006. Archaeological Sources for the Reconstruction of the Maurya Dynasty (With Special Reference to the Aśokan Edicts), in *Pañcatantra : Recent Researches in Indian Archaeology* (K.M. Suresh et al Eds.), Vol. II, pp. 201-216. Delhi : Bharatiya Kala Prakashan.

113. 2006. Role of the Doctrines of Āpaddharmas and Kalivarjyas in the Transition from the Vedic to the Paurāṇika Age, in *Vedic Culture and Its Continuity* (Sita Ram Dube Ed.), pp. 86-90. Delhi : Pratibha Prakashan.

114. 2006. A Plea for Writing a New Political History of Ancient India, *Purābhāratī* (*Commemoration Volume in Respect of Professor B.P. Sinha*), Vol. I (B.R. Mani and S.C. Saran Eds.), pp. 139-146. Delhi : Sharada Publishing House.

115. 2006. Historiography of Professor V.S. Pathak, *Jñāna-Pravāha*, Varanasi IX : 215-237.

116. 2006. Historiography of the Vākāṭaka-Gupta Relations, Appendix in *A History of the Vākāṭaka-Gupta Relations* (by S.R. Goyal), pp. 125-142. Jodhpur : Kusumanjali Book World.

117. 2006. The Vākāṭakas in the History of the Deccan : A Fresh Appraisal in the Light of Recent Discoveries and New Interpretations, The Loyola College Endowment Lecture, published in the *Proceedings of the Twenty-sixth Annual Session of the South Indian History Congress*, Bangalore, 2006, pp. 689-702.

118. 2006. The Myth of the Vākāṭaka Coins, *Journal of Indian History*, Thiruvananthapuram LXXXV (Pts. 1-3) : 9-25. A revised version of this article has also appeared in the *Indian Historical Review*, New Delhi, Vol. 34, No. 2, July, 2007, pp. 1-15.

119. 2006. Professor V.S. Pathak's Contribution to Numismatic Studies, *Journal of the Numismatic Society of India*, Varanasi LXVIII : 121-125.

120. 2006. Historiography of Dr. R.P. Vyas, *Khyat*, Bikaner 10 : 108-116.

121. 2007. Professor V.S. Pathak's Contribution to Epigraphical Studies, *Journal of the Epigraphical Society of India*, Mysore XXXIII : 23-33.

122. 2007. A Note on the Paurāṇika Portrayal of the Emergence of the Middle Ages in the Form of the Kali Age Crisis, in *Purāṇoṅ meṅ Bhāratīya Saṁskṛti* (S.K. Purohit Ed.), pp. 280-283. Jodhpur : Rajasthani Granthagar.

123. 2007. Historiography of Pt. V. N. Reu, in the *Proceedings of the Rajasthan History Congress*, Vol. XXI, Proceedings of the Jodhpur Session, 2005, Jodhpur, 2007, pp. 156-163.

124. 2007. Kavirāja Shyamaldas and His *Vir Vinod*, in *Professor K.S. Gupta Felicitation Volume* (D. P. Sharma et al Eds.), pp. 191-197. Udaipur : Professor K. S. Gupta Felicitation Organizing Committee.

125. 2007. Buddhism in Bengal in the Early Medieval Period, *Journal of the Institute of Bangladesh Studies*, Rajshahi, Bangladesh XXX : 43-50.

126. 2008. Bearing of the Recent Epigraphical Data on the History of the Vākāṭakas, in the *Proceedings of the Twenty-eighth Annual Session of the South Indian History Congress*, Anantapur, 2008, pp. 37-43.

127. 2008. Religious Analysis of Harsha's Personality, in the *Proceedings of the Indian History Congress*, 68th Session, Delhi, 2007 (Delhi, 2008), pp. 136-148.

128. 2008. Harshacharita as a Source of History, in the *Papers from the Aligarh Historians Society* (Irfan Habib Ed.), 69th Session of the Indian History Congress, Kannur University, Kannur, pp. 122-152.

129. 2009. The Nāyanārs and Āḷvārs and their Contribution to the Bhakti Movement in South India, Presidential Address to the Cultural History Section of the South Indian History Congress, published in the *Proceedings of the Twenty-ninth Annual Session of the South Indian History Congress*, Tirunelveli, 2009, pp. 370-379.

130. 2009. Notes on Professor Lallanji Gopal's Contribution to Numismatic Studies, *Journal of the Numismatic Society of India*, Varanasi LXXI : 118-124.

131. 2009. The Authenticity of the Plays Ascribed to Harsha, in the *Proceedings of the Indian History Congress*, 69th Session, Kannur, 2008 (Kolkata, 2009), pp. 86-93.

132. 2009. A History of the Emergence of the Indian Coinage, in *Studies in Indian Numismatics* (J.P. Singh and P.N. Singh Eds.), pp. 53-88. Varanasi : The Numismatic Society of India.

133. 2010. Vākāṭaka Historiography : The Old and the New, in the *Proceedings of the Indian History Congress*, Delhi, 2009-10 (Kolkata, 2010), pp. 101-117.

134. 2011. Caste System as Reflected in the Works of Bāṇa and Yuan Chwang, in the *Papers from the Aligarh Historians Society* (Irfan Habib Ed.), 71st Session of the Indian History Congress, Gaur Banga University, Malda, pp. 124-147.

135. 2012. A Comment on Hans Bakker's Suggestion on the Vākāṭakas, published in the *Proceedings of the Thirty-second Annual Session of the South Indian History Congress*, Chennai, 2012, pp.839-842.

136. 2012. An Investigation into the Feudal Nature of the Vākāṭaka Economy : A Study of the Epigraphic Evidence, General President's Address delivered to the XXXVII Annual Congress of the Epigraphical Society of India, Baroda, published in the *Journal of the Epigraphical Society of India*, Vol. XXXVIII, 2012, pp. 1-38.

137. 2013. Professor S.R. Goyal's Contribution to the Study of Ancient Indian Social Ideas and Institutions, in *Investigating Indian Society* (Shankar Goyal Ed.), pp. xv-xxix. Jodhpur : Kusumanjali Book World.

138. 2014. Professor Sobhag Mathur's Contribution to the Study of Modern Indian History and the History of Rajasthan, in *Reinterpreting Indian History* (Shankar Goyal Ed.), pp. xiii-xxiii. Jodhpur : Kusumanjali Book World.

139. 2014. Some Notes on T.V. Mahalingam as a Historian, published in the *Proceedings of the Thirty-fourth Annual Session of the South*

Indian History Congress, Poondi, 2014, pp. 734-738.

140. 2014. Ideas and Movements in the Age of the Mauryas, a Review Article, *Aitihya*, Journal of Ancient History, Culture and Archaeology, Bareilly V : 146-155.

141. 2015. Professor P. S. Bhati's Contribution to the Study of Politics and History, in *History and Politics* (Shankar Goyal Ed.), pp. xxiii-xlviii. Jodhpur : Kusumanjali Book World.

142. 2015. Feudalization of Polity in the Age of Harsha : An Analysis, in *History and Politics* (Shankar Goyal Ed.), pp. 143-167. Jodhpur : Kusumanjali Book World.

143. 2015. Professor S. R. Goyal's Approach to History and His Contribution to Ancient India, in *Early India : Historical Probings* (Shankar Goyal Ed.), pp.xvii-xxxii. Jodhpur : Kusumanjali Book World.

144. 2015. The 'Medieval' Factor in Indian Art, in *Early India : Historical Probings* (Shankar Goyal Ed.), pp. 248-261. Jodhpur : Kusumanjali Book World.

145. 2015. Reflections on the Upheaval of 1857 in Rajasthan, in the *Proceedings of the Rajasthan History Congress*, Vol. XXX, Proceedings of the Udaipur Session, 2015, Jodhpur, 2015, pp. 297-317.

146. 2016. Professor S.R. Goyal's Contribution to the History of Rajasthan, in the *Proceedings of the Rajasthan History Congress*, Vol. XXXI, Proceedings of the Jodhpur Session, 2016, Jodhpur, 2016, pp. 238-254.

147. 2016. Yuan Chwang's India and the Problem of the Extent of Harsha's Empire and Sphere of His Influence, in the *Papers from the Aligarh Historians Society* (Irfan Habib Ed.), 77th Session of the Indian History Congress, Kerala University, Thiruvananthapuram, pp. 104-116.

148. 2016. The Madras School of Ancient Indian Historians, Presidential Address to the Historiography Section of the Tamilnadu History Congress, published in the *Proceedings of the Twenty-third Session of the Tamilnadu History Congress*, Salem, 2016, pp. 445-465.

149. 2017. The Historiography of Professor K.S. Lal, in the *Proceedings of the Rajasthan History Congress*, Vol. XXXII, Proceedings of the Jaipur Session, 2017, Jodhpur, 2017, pp. 291-301.

150. 2017. Some Observations on India's Intercourse with Iran in the Seventh Century A.D., in the *Papers from the Aligarh Historians Society* (Irfan Habib Ed.), 78th Session of the Indian History Congress, Jadavpur University, Kolkata, pp. 11-16.

151. 2018. Harsha : A Retrospective, Presidential Address to the Ancient India Section of the Indian History Congress, published in the *Proceedings of the Indian History Congress*, 78th Session, Jadavpur University, Kolkata, 2017 (Delhi, 2018), pp. 27-41.

152. 2018. Inscriptions of Harsha : Some Problems and Suggestions, Professor Ku. Si. Haridas Bhat Shashtipoorti Endowment Lecture, published in the *Studies in Indian Place Names*, Proceedings of the Place Names Society of India, Vol. XXXVII, Mysore, 2018, pp. 18-32.

153. 2018. Dr. H.S. Bhati and His Edited Work *Marwar ri Khyat*, in *Dr. H.S. Bhati Felicitation Volume* (S.K. Purohit and Saddiq Mohammed Eds.), pp. 263-265. Jodhpur : Itihas Anusandhan Sansthan.

154. 2018. The Problem of Chandragupta II's Political Influence on the Vākāṭakas : A Revised Study of the Epigraphic Sources, in *Epigraphic Studies*, Select Papers from the Panel on Epigraphy at the 16th World Sanskrit Conference, 2015, Sanskrit Studies Centre, Silpakorn University, Bangkok, Thailand (D.P. Dubey Ed.), pp. 129-137. New Delhi : D.K. Publishers Distributors Pvt. Ltd.

V. CONCLUSION

To sum up, Shankar Goyal belongs to that genre of historians whose contributions are not restricted to a single specialized field of study. He has worked on a very wide canvas and published about forty works and more than 150 articles on a broad range of varied subjects pertaining to different branches of Indological studies. Most of his works have been acclaimed as important contributions of enduring value combining all the qualities of scientific scholarship and reflecting his command over original sources. His work on the Vākāṭakas has been described as an excellent piece of research and testifies to his mastery over epigraphic materials. The history of Harsha, which is his first love, and for which he earned his D.Litt. degree, has been minutely studied by him in almost all its aspects. Described by R.S. Sharma as 'the best book on the subject written so far' and as 'a compulsory reading for those working on ancient Indian history' by Romila Thapar, here he looks at the events of the history of Harsha in the context of their situation which is responsible for his critical approach to political history. Besides this, he keeps himself abreast with the latest researches and discoveries and modifies his views without hesitation. His work on the recent historiography of ancient India is the first detailed and critical study of the subject and described by R.N. Dandekar as 'indispensable' and 'dependable' source-book for every serious student of ancient Indian history. His works and numerous papers in the fields of epigraphy, numismatics, art and culture are also worth appreciation. His three-volume study on the origin and growth of history writing in Rajasthan is acclaimed as 'a definite contribution to the history and historiography of medieval/modern Rajasthan' and will be difficult to be replaced. Goyal, therefore, deserves the compliments of all for his illuminating contribution to historical studies.

Chapter Two

Shankar Goyal on the Modern Historiography of Ancient India

MAHESH VIKRAM SINGH
Professor of History
Kashi Vidyapith, Varanasi

THE PROBLEM OF WRITING HISTORY

Howsoever old may be the civilization and culture of the Indian sub-continent, its ancient history is as much like a discovery of modern age! Because there we find just some stories about our past as history mainly knit into our enormous religious literature, whether in the shape of Purāṇas or great epics or in the form of legends or folklores, in the absence of any scientific tradition of writing history in ancient period of Indian history. We do have to come down to the twelveth century A.D. to find out *Rājataraṅgiṇī* of Kalhaṇa telling us about the history of Kashmir from the time of Aśoka, the great Mauryan emperor, which has applied some scientific and relatively modern methodology of writing history. While discovering and defining sources of any event or period of history and their reliability in itself is a tedious exercise, saying/explaining anything against the popular notions further, becomes an issue of delicate handling of information. Things about ancient history have become even more complicated with the ideological assertions or biases/prejudices of Colonial historians, Imperialists, Orientalists, Nationalists, Marxist and Sectarian writers. Thus, it is a challenge to any scholar to review the modern historiography of ancient India with complete honesty and comprehension.

MAJOR WRITINGS ON THE HISTORIOGRAPHY OF ANCIENT INDIA

Shankar Goyal took up this challenge, which most of the scholars would like to skip, by bringing out his masterpiece on the subject with the title *Recent Historiography of Ancient India* in 1997. There were quite a few studies on the historiography before this updated and serious work of Shankar Goyal. And these too were in the form of some analysis of works of one or other great historian, or as some felicitation or co-memorial volume on some historian, or else as review of literature on some particular topic or subject of research. It was firstly in 1961 *Historians of India, Pakistan and Ceylon* edited by C.H. Philips was published from London to be followed by *Historians and Historiography in Modern India* edited by S.P. Sen from Calcutta (now Kolkata). Both these volumes have listed selected works on all the periods and aspects of Indian history. But, as it can be presumed, they are confined to the description of works done until the mid of the last century and that too in a very brief manner. Then, *The Evolution of Historiography in Modern India–1900-1960* by S.K. Mukhopadhyay published in 1981 from Kolkata refers only to a few select modern historians in its view.

A brilliant review of the works on social and economic history, however, came out in *Perspectives in Social and Economic History of Early India* presented by Ram Sharan Sharma in 1983 from New Delhi. And a similar approach he had made in the presentation of his study on the political institutions of early India way back in 1959 with the title *Aspects of Political Ideas and Institutions in Ancient India* published from Delhi itself. Then, it was Vijay Kumar Thakur who brought out his book *Historiography of Indian Feudalism* in 1989 from Patna presenting in detail his studies on the genesis and form of feudalism in ancient India. Whereas, Shankar Goyal sticks to the writings on political history of ancient India and the works related to social, religious, art and economic aspects, etc., are referred to as and when required to be mentioned in the context of political history. An introduction to the new approach to the analysis of political history had also been found in *S.R. Goyal: His Multidimensional Historiography* edited by Jagannath Agrawal and Shankar Goyal published from New Delhi in 1992. This has incorporated views and articles of other historians on the writings of S.R. Goyal on different periods and aspects of ancient Indian history. But the first and only work of presenting a complete and comprehensive work in the field of modern historiography on ancient India was finally brought out by Shankar Goyal updating the contributions and new ideas from the time of independence also along with its backdrop.

WRITINGS OF SHANKAR GOYAL ON THE MODERN HISTORIOGRAPHY OF ANCIENT INDIA

This independent work on the modern historiography of complete political history of ancient India was in a way expansion and conclusion of Shankar Goyal's own project on the subject beginning with *History and Historiography of the Age of Harsha* in 1992 published from Jodhpur and followed by his another title *Aspects of Ancient Indian History and Historiography* discussing the main historiographical issues published in 1993 from New Delhi. Adding to these were his next title *History Writing of Early India: New Discoveries and Approaches* published in 1996 from Jodhpur and yet another presenting the modern historiography on the Gupta period with the title *The Image of Classical India : Its Changing Colours and Contours* published in 1997 again from Jodhpur. All these efforts of Shankar Goyal in fact are mainly the outcome of his serious Ph.D. work with the title *Main Trends in Indian Historiography Since Independence* and further extension of his studies in this field incorporating all the other left-over periods of ancient Indian history.

The book *Recent Historiography of Ancient India* by Shankar Goyal presents the modern historiography on different periods of ancient Indian history in thirteen chapters in all. Chapter thirteen contains the views of various modern historians and their historical methodology as a conclusion, wherein the author has advocated a neutral approach to the study of history referring to the limitations and shortcomings of different ideological historical methodologies. Division of all the other chapters as per the periods of ancient Indian history appears to be quite logical, according to which it begins with the pre-Buddha period followed by the Janapada age and the rise of Magadha, the Maurya period in two chapters, the period of Śuṅgas, Indo-Greeks, Śakas, Pahlavas, Kushāṇas and Sātavāhanas in two chapters, the period of Gupta dynasty in three chapters, the period of early Kanauj empire in two chapters, and the history of the Deccan and Far South dynasties in the twelveth chapter. Thus, this book may be rightly considered as a comprehensive source-book for the modern historiography of the ancient history of India. Enlisting all the notable works and updating all the new analysis from 1947 to 1997 on the political history of ancient India Shankar Goyal's claim of using the term 'recent' in the title is quite justified too.

The political history happened to be long seen as independent and unrelated sequence of political events and remained focusing upon the chronology of origin and fall of different dynasties and importance of certain activities of some notable kings or emperors. Seldom there was an attempt of explaining political history in the chronological contexts of socio-economic developments or changes *per se* as well as the religious and cultural tendencies therein of different communities and regions. But now if revisited with new ideological methodologies, it requires study of the impact of all the social, religious and material conditions as well as the expectations of the time and space. Hence, there arise a number of views of explaining the political history depending upon the emphasis upon one or other or all the factors related to it. For example, considering the sequence of political events a by-product of the time and situations, or holding one or many factors responsible for a certain political event, or again, considering the political events itself as cause of new developments which, of course, refer to the personality and actions of a political person, all this comes into the purview of writing political history nowadays. Further, it is important also to keep away from indulging in one sided interpretations or explanations which certainly demands scrutiny of any historical writing. Keeping all this in mind Shankar Goyal has tried to undertake this tedious work of chronological study of the ideas and writings of various historians explaining at the same time their contributions as well as their limitations. Besides, he has tried to underline the debates related to some important points and contexts of history in order to discover all the relevant dimensions with a view to reach to a neutral understanding of historical developments in our remote past. Historian's prejudice remains a big hurdle in impartial writing of history. It is almost obligatory for anyone writing or re-writing history to know about the pre-established as well as new ideas and explanations beforehand. Shankar Goyal's book is undoubtedly a big leap in this direction. A good many discussions about important literary, numismatic, epigraphic and archaeological sources have also been incorporated in his book in order to scrutinize the merits or demerits of any work on history.

HISTORIOGRAPHY OF THE PRE-BUDDHA PERIOD

Shankar Goyal has touched upon various dimensions of political developments of the pre-Buddha period which in the absence of any inscriptional and commonly accepted material fall into proto-history. Historians have largely depended upon the traditional literature, viz., Vedic texts, epics, Purāṇas, Buddhist and Jaina religious and other narrations which in itself demand scrutiny as to reliability of the stories contained therein. He has specially discussed the problem of the historicity of the central tales of the two epics and the date of 'Bhārata War' and has also tried to reconstruct the traditional history and chronology. Besides making a discussion on the literary sources Shankar Goyal has given sufficient attention to the debates over the original home of Aryans and their racial identity. He has tried to analyze proposed co-relation between the information available from traditional sources and archaeological finds said to be of this period under a separate heading. And so he has done with the discussion on ideas about the origin of society and the state as a new dimension of the pre-Buddha historiography. Another dimension of the study of modern historiography of this period, as pointed out by him, is the writing of regional traditional history of the period.

RELIABILITY OF SOURCES

Referring to the reliability of the literary sources of traditional history Shankar Goyal has enlisted the suggestions and logics of various scholars. He does agree to the views of H.C. Raychaudhuri and Hopkins that both the great epics *Rāmāyaṇa* and *Mahābhārata* are the extended versions of some original happenings which went on to be composed quite late after the Vedic period. Hence, it is difficult to accept all of it as the history of Vedic period. Shankar Goyal also goes on to review the opinion of Smith, according to which there are so many narrations in the Purāṇas and epics which could hardly be acceptable. Yet Shankar Goyal is of the view that all that is there could not be set aside altogether and one has to glean relevant historical material from these sources as well. Epigraphic and numismatic evidences of the Sātavāhanas, Ābhīras, Vākāṭakas, Nāgas, Guptas and many other dynasties sufficiently support their existence who found mention in this traditional literature too. As far as the history of pre-Buddha or pre-Bimbisāra age is concerned, Shankar Goyal, however, acquiesces to the opinion of Raychaudhuri that the epics and Purāṇas are definitely later compositions in their present shape and the information about earlier periods contained therein could be relied upon only to the extent *Mahāvaṁsa* and *Aśokāvadāna* are reliable for the activities of great Mauryas. It would not be wise to negate everything preserved in them and there is certainly enough of historical value to us. Thus, whatever caution Smith has suggested in dealing with the Pali literature does apply to the Sanskrit epics and Purāṇas also.

Further, Shankar Goyal has given serious attention to the various views about the relative reliability of Vedic and Purāṇic literature. R.C. Majumdar, H.C. Raychaudhuri and D.C. Sircar are not in favour of Purāṇic literature for the reconstruction of history of the pre-Buddha period and depend much upon the information suppressed in the Vedic texts in this matter. Whereas scholars like F.E. Pargiter reject the validity of Vedic literature for history writing considering it merely a 'Brāhmaṇical tradition' and uphold Purāṇic literature as a 'Kshatriya tradition' coming down from the Vedic times as a major source of history of that period. Shankar Goyal comes forward with a third view in this regard by saying that there could be nothing like 'Brāhmaṇa tradition' and 'Kshatriya tradition', as suggested by Pargiter, and referring to the views of S.R. Goyal, he considers that even if the earliest Purāṇas available in their present form are not older than the Gupta period, they could not be entirely divorced from the unwritten Purāṇic tradition of the Vedic age. Hence, it would not be altogether unjustified using its material for the reconstruction of pre-Buddha history although it demands careful corroboration and comparison with the information available in the contemporary Vedic texts and other sources of history. Thus, a rational use of both the Vedic texts and Purāṇas would be welcome. At the same time, Shankar Goyal also emphasizes upon the use of Buddhist *Tripiṭakas* and Jaina *Āgamas* in this context.

The Pali Buddhist literature stands just below the Vedic age chronologically. Referring to *Pre-Buddhist India* of Rati Lal Mehta, Shankar Goyal is of the view that they could be used alike the Purāṇas in the reconstruction of Vedic history. Nevertheless, he leaves this question to the wisdom of scholars of history because they may have their selection of giving less or more importance to one or other information as per their own ideas for the lack of unanimity or coherence in the information available in literature of different literary traditions or texts. There we find always a tendency among historians in the selection of information as per their own biases or prejudices when it comes to the matter of traditional sources. This makes the reconstruction of history even more difficult. We earnestly hope that the new technology of computation of information may help us to reach to some precise neutral conclusions.

PROBLEMS RELATED TO THE VEDIC HISTORY

The problems of identity and original home of the Vedic Aryans have been a big puzzle for the historians. A good many ideas have been propounded about it in the last few decades. Shankar Goyal has specially mentioned the views of S.R. Rao and S.P. Gupta in this regard, as both of them have contended that the Vedic Aryans were quite related to the Harappan civilization and that the Harappan civilization be renamed as 'Sārasvata Civilization' for having arisen in the vicinity of the river Sarasvatī. There has come up another view in this context that the culture of Vedic Aryans was an outcome of the combination of different local cultures and that Aryans should not be treated as some particular ethnic or linguistic entity but as containing several ethnic and lingual elements. In *Recent Perspectives of Early Indian History* edited by Romila Thapar this view has been clearly upheld suggesting that seeing from archaeological, lingual and cultural angles there appears to be all the possibilities of coexistence of different communities among the Aryans of the Vedic age. Thus, a single racial or ethnic identity of the Aryans has been put to question in this view as well. Ram Sharan Sharma and D.N. Jha have also consented to this view of denying any racial identity to the Aryans. But it is also important to note here that majority of scholars have yet to find sufficient ground to equate Vedic culture with that of the Harappans. And so, it has not been possible to reframe the long and generally accepted sequence of ancient Indian history. Despite a little addition of knowledge and new explanations this period of Indian history is presented the same way it happened to be presented earlier. In fact, Shankar Goyal appears to skip the arguments against the thesis of equating Vedic culture with Harappan culture. Just a reference to the views of K.C. Chattopadhyaya questioning any similarity between Aryan and Harappan cultures has been made in a footnote to the whole discussion on the subject. Similarly, he did not care to mention a very important book *Ārya Saṁskṛti kī Khoja* of Ram Sharan Sharma which has fresh discussion on the origin and sources of Aryan culture and which tries to distinguish the latter from the Indus-Harappan civilization. Nevertheless, Shankar Goyal's presentation on the problems of identity and original home of the Aryans is quite useful.

Taking up the issue of the historicity of the original narrations of the epics and the date of 'Bhārata War' Shankar Goyal refers to questions raised by H.C. Raychaudhuri and indication of many contexts of the *Mahābhārata* in the Vedic literature. He accedes to the opinion of Raychaudhuri referring as well to later studies in this regard, such as, the *Mahābhārata : Myth and Reality* edited by S.P. Gupta and K.S. Ramachandran published from Delhi in 1976. He has also indicated about the politicization of the issues of historicity of the *Rāmāyaṇa* and the birth place of Rāma without, however, going into the details of it. He merely mentions H.D. Sankalia's work *The Rāmāyaṇa in Historical Perspective* (Delhi, 1982) and D.C. Sircar's *Problems of the Rāmāyaṇa* (Hyderabad, 1979) in footnotes.

Shankar Goyal's discussion on the date of 'Bhārata War' is quite compact which entails the views of Pargiter dating it around 950 B.C. and that of H.C. Raychaudhuri's pulling it down to 850 B.C. Shankar Goyal himself agreeing to the solution put forward by S.R.Goyal in this matter speculating about the existence of two Parīkshits and two Janamejayas, earlier of both of them having been born after the 'Dāśarājña Yuddha', i.e., the battle with ten kings mentioned in the *Ṛgveda*, and latter two of them having been the successors of the 'Bhārata War', suggests the dates of the two wars as 1400 B.C. and 950 B.C. respectively. A similar view was put forward by P.L. Bhargava in his *India of the Vedic Age* sometime earlier. But Shankar Goyal seems to skip the views of S.R. Rao and some others in this regard.

As far as the studies done on the traditional Indian history in the pre-independence period are concerned, Shankar Goyal has given a detail account of the suggestions made by Radha Kumud Mookerji and H.C. Raychaudhuri. Then, he refers to a big contribution of A.D. Pusalker to this era of study in the *The Vedic Age* in independent India. However, *Dates and Dynasties in Earliest India* of Morton R. Smith published in 1975 from Delhi may be considered as the latest effort in this direction which has quite rationally tried to reconcile the contradictions arising in the lists of traditional dynasties preserved in Purāṇas with a comparative study, even though failing in taking into account the scientific editions of the same. Shankar Goyal, of course, has rightfully used this work in his discussion on the subject.

WRITINGS ON VEDIC REGIONAL HISTORY

A new trend of looking at the early history of certain northern and eastern regions separately from the beginning of Vedic civilization and culture early in Punjab and later in the Gangetic plains has also been noticed by Shankar Goyal. This has been referred to as studies of Bihar, Mithilā, Videha, Vaiśālī and ancient Kosala by D.S. Triveda, Upendra Thakur, R.R. Diwakar, Yogendra Mishra and Vishuddhanand Pathak respectively. Besides this Shankar Goyal has also mentioned the works of K.A.N. Sastri and G. Yazdani on the history of south India and Deccan and that of H.K. Mehtab on Orissa. But he does not seem to be in favour of considering the work of Buddha Prakash on ancient Punjab as regional history all away from the beginning of the Vedic culture in that area.

RECONCILIATION OF TRADITIONAL HISTORY WITH RECENT ARCHAEOLOGICAL DISCOVERIES

Shankar Goyal has tried to review the efforts in the direction of reconciliation of traditional history with recent archaeological discoveries in quite a detail. This problem remains quite pertinent in view of making any idea about the political situations of the Vedic age without comparing the history of dynasties mentioned in the later literary sources with the archaeological finds of the time. He has rightly discussed B.B. Lal's suggestions about relating the Painted Grey Ware culture found in Kurukshetra and Hastinapur to the *Mahābhārata* age and also the views of Romila Thapar about the archaeological chronology of ancient India. But here again he skips from mentioning some very recent findings of the pre-iron phase of PGW in Punjab and Haryana by J.P. Joshi and Madhubala Joshi as well as the processes involved in moving from the copper age cultures to the iron age in the reconstruction of ancient Indian history.

RESEARCHES ON THE FORMATION OF SOCIETY AND STATE

The writings on the formation of society and state in the pre-Buddha period have been taken up as a new dimension of historiography by Shankar Goyal. Here, he has given sufficient attention to the notable works of Romila Thapar with the titles *From Lineage to State* and *Ancient Indian Social History* and also to Ram Sharan Sharma's *Material Culture and Social Formations in Ancient India* describing the growth of political institutions and politics in the backdrop of contemporary socio-economic situations.

MODERN HISTORIOGRAPHY ON THE AGE OF JANAPADAS

The age of the Janapadas and the rise of Magadha form a very interesting part of the discussions on modern historiography by Shankar Goyal. In order to have a clear picture of the recent historiography on the period he has gone back to the pre-independence period in quite detail which includes the works of D.R. Bhandarkar, H.C. Raychaudhuri as well as of Kashi Prasad Jayaswal. Besides, a good many works on social, economic, cultural and religious aspects, especially those related to Buddhism and Jainism, of the history of this period have been taken into account so as to make a comprehensive understanding of the political situation of the age. *The Age of Imperial Unity*, edited by R.C. Majumdar and A.D. Pusalker, is certainly a milestone in this direction of historical study. Shankar Goyal goes on to discuss the works like *Ancient India* by R.C. Majumdar, *Groundwork of Ancient Indian History* by J.S. Negi, *Bimbisāra to Aśoka* by Sudhakar Chattopadhyaya and *Māgadha-Sātavāhana-Kushāṇa Sāmrājyoṅ kā Yuga* by S.R. Goyal. He does also refer to Vimal Chandra Pandey's work *Prāchīna Bhārata kā Rājanītika evaṁ Sāṁskṛtika Itihāsa*, Part I, in this regard and specially commends the work of S.R. Goyal for its comprehension of complete political, social, economic, religious and cultural background in order to look into the political developments of this period. Shankar Goyal has all praise for J.S. Negi for his work free of any biases and also for Sudhakar Chattopadhyaya for a detailed chronological study of kings and events of this period.

A separate section of Shankar Goyal's study of modern historiography of this period is devoted to the *gaṇas* or republics. He considers all the studies in this direction after 1947 as some extension of the works of pre-independence period, particularly that of B.C. Law. He refers to Mamata Choudhury's work *Tribes in Ancient India* (1977) as of special importance in this regard. It attracts attention for her efforts going into some anthropological explanations as well as her study of transformation of tribes into castes. *Republics in Ancient India* (1968) by J.P. Sharma has deserved commendation for its authoritative use of Buddhist and Jaina sources. Then, it is in *Ancient Indian Republics* (1976) by S.N. Mishra we get a detail description of the history and constitutional system of the republics of this period. Shankar Goyal is, however, a little skeptical about this work for the study of different subjects confined to just one or other source only which fails to create a total perspective of the thing. The same error is visible in Mishra's work in the presentation of chapters of the history of republics for having based upon some particular sources only. Another shortcoming of this work, as pointed out by Shankar Goyal, is its lack of perspective about change in the form and functions of the republics in all their existence for almost 1500 years. Reviewing the book *A Complex Study of Ancient India: A Multidisciplinary Approach* by G.M. Bongard-Levin published in 1986 Shankar Goyal finds it of much importance from the point of view of a new approach in the history writing for its discussions on the sources, class structure, socio-economic layers of the society, major features of political organization, etc.

As far as the regional history of this period is concerned Shankar Goyal has dealt with it separately, referring to the researches of Sudhakar Chattopadhyaya, K.C. Ojha, D.C. Shah, A.K. Narain and Buddha Prakash about the Greek invasions and settlements of the Greek kings in the north-western part of India. However, no other information about the regional history writing of this period is available in his work.

One of the most noteworthy features of the study of recent historiography by Shankar Goyal is his discussion on the Marxist historians and their writings. It has been an entirely new approach to the writing of Indian history after 1947. Quite a detailed discussion on *A History of India*, Part I, by Romila Thapar, *Ancient India : An Introductory Outline* by D.N. Jha and *Material Culture and Social Formations in Ancient India* by Ram Sharan Sharma has been done by Shankar Goyal in his reference to the Marxist writings pointing out the limitations and biases appearing therein. Considering each and every change or happenings in social, religious and political domain a by-product of the economic causes has been underlined as standing shortcoming of this type of writing. However, it is also surprising to note that Shankar Goyal has entirely left out D.D. Kosambi in his discussion who is otherwise supposed to be the father figure of Marxist approach to Indian history. Similarly, while Shankar Goyal has definitely mentioned the works of N.R. Banerjee and Dilip K. Chakravarty on the origin and use of iron in ancient India in a footnote, he has left out any discussion on the impact of their researches on Indian historiography.

PRE-INDEPENDENCE MODERN WRITINGS ON THE MAURYAN AGE

The writings on the Mauryan age in the pre-independence era have been divided into four parts by Shankar Goyal. The first part is confined to the discovery of new material about the Mauryas, the second is devoted to the ascertainment of the time of composition of the ancient literature, the third deals with the comparative importance of literary, epigraphic and archaeological sources, and the fourth gives the details of writings on the Mauryan dynasty. Independent monographs on Chandragupta and Aśoka have also been listed among the studies on the Mauryan age. Shankar Goyal has underlined different viewpoints held in the writing of history of the age of Mauryas which include imperialist, nationalist and scientific or mixed views. A discussion on the sources of Mauryan age is very useful in this regard. The literary sources include Jaina, Buddhist and Brāhmaṇical literature besides narratives of foreign writers. A chronological presentation of the discoveries and studies and translations of Aśokan inscriptions by both Western and indigenous scholars, such as, by James Prinsep, A. Cunningham, G. Bühler, F.W. Thomas, E. Hultzsch, D.R. Bhandarkar, B.M. Barua, D.C. Sircar and others has been made. Adding to that is the important information about the studies on numismatic and archaeological sources. Much emphasis is there on dating and comparative reliability of the same. References of different views related to the utility of literature like the *Arthaśāstra* of Kauṭilya, *Indica* of Megasthenes, *Mudrārākshasa* and *Aśokāvadāna* are worthwhile. It has also been pointed out that who and who among the scholars has given less or more importance to which one of the sources, such as, D.R. Bhandarkar and B.M. Barua giving more importance to the Aśokan inscriptions, Radha Kumud Mookerji basing his discussion upon the Western narratives and V.R.R. Dikshitar on Kauṭilyan *Arthaśāstra*. Studies on Mauryan art have also been indicated as a source of Mauryan history. A critical evaluation of the researches of Vincent Smith, D.R. Bhandarkar, R.K. Mookerji and H.C. Raychaudhuri has also been made to cover the pre-independence modern historiography of the Mauryan age.

MAURYA HISTORY WRITING IN INDEPENDENT INDIA

Shankar Goyal has given quite a long space to the discussions over the history writing of Mauryan period after 1947. This includes the description of newly found Aśokan inscriptions. He has taken sufficient pain in explaining the synonyms of the term *dhamma* and some other words used in his reference to major and minor bilingual rock-edicts in Aramaic and Greek languages found in the north-western India and Afghanistan coming out with some of his own explanations in this regard. Further, he has indicated the importance of other information available in other inscriptions. A worthwhile debate is obviously there with regard to S.R. Goyal's suggestion about the Brāhmī script as the product of Mauryan period with

Aśoka himself being its inventor. Similarly, sufficient attention has been given to the question of re-dating the *Arthaśāstra* as well as about its real author which contains a re-analysis of different sections or portions of the *Arthaśāstra* with their separation by scholars like Thomas R. Trautmann and some others. The views of S.R. Goyal have been rightly referred to in connection with the limitations of the use of materials of the *Arthaśāstra* and *Indica* in the reconstruction of Mauryan history.

Works of R.C. Majumdar, R.K. Mookerji, H.C. Raychaudhuri, K.A.N. Sastri and the like scholars have been firstly referred to in the discussion regarding their ideas and methodology about the Mauryan rule putting all of them in the category of nationalist writings of scientific nature. Further, a separate discussion has been made about the works of Sudhakar Chattopadhyaya and Buddha Prakash before explaining in detail the approach of Marxist writings as that of D.D. Kosambi, Romila Thapar, Ram Sharan Sharma, Dwijendra Nath Jha and G.M. Bongard-Levin. *The Mauryas Revisited* by Romila Thapar captures special attention in this regard which explains the economic basis of the empire of the Mauryas along with presenting a hypothesis of the tensions arising out of the nature of interaction between metropolitan state and peripheral regions. This is of course a product of fresh and genuine scientific acumen of the scholar like Romila Thapar. Thus, Shankar Goyal has made a big contribution to the recent historiography of ancient India by explaining the Marxist approach of writing in quite a detail. Besides, he has also tried to put S.R. Goyal's criticism of such approach in the right perspective. The views of S.R. Goyal are worth quoting in this context, according to which the developments around each and every dynasty of the Magadhan empire, beginning with Bimbisāra and ending with the Kaṇvas, including that of the Mauryas, may be compared with changes occurring with the Roman empire. S.R. Goyal has upheld the views of Har Prasad Shastri and also H.C. Raychaudhuri for considering the decline and fall of the Mauryas as a result of Aśoka's over-indulgence in Buddhism and annoyance and reaction of the Brāhmaṇical forces thereby instead of its economic and administrative structure, as suggested by Romila Thapar.

Shankar Goyal has made a brief mention of some cartographic works also on the Maurya period. The efforts of Irfan Habib and Faiz Habib have been rightly discussed in this regard which helps us in understanding actual and practical situation of the empire of the Mauryas. Some notable works about the Later Mauryas and on the decline of the Mauryan empire have also been taken into account which include that of Romila Thapar, Buddha Prakash, Sudhakar Chattopadhyaya and Hector Alahakoon.

HISTORIOGRAPHY OF THE POST-MAURYAN PERIOD TO THE RISE OF KUSHĀṆAS

It has been a challenge to the historians to organize all the works done about the period between the Mauryas and Guptas because of the existence of a number of minor and major indigenous and foreign political powers belonging to this interregnum. It has remained difficult for the scholars to ascertain the origin and nature of these powers as well as the actual boundaries of their states and areas of their impact. Numerous scholars have published independent studies on one or other political power of this period. But a comprehensive picture about the trends of the time has failed to emerge out of all that had been done earlier. While it remained a dark period of Indian history for quite a long time, the recent Marxist writings have tried to light it up as the period of utmost activity and life in the whole of Indian history. This refers to the industrial and commercial progress of this period which includes expansion of industrial guilds, both inland and foreign trade, established practice of coins and currency and the rise of urban centres specially.

Introducing the works on the Śuṅgas and Kaṇvas, Shankar Goyal has pointed out to the approaches of historians regarding different questions related to their period. The studies on the Bactrian and Indo-Greeks have been largely based on the numismatic finds of their reigns and Shankar Goyal has discussed the pre-1947 and post-1947 studies separately. The works of A.K. Narain, Buddha Prakash, A.N. Lahiri, Vasishtha Mohan Dev Mehta and G.R. Sharma have been described in detail as the post -1947 studies. In addition to a discussion on the works published on the Scytho-Parthians, Shankar Goyal has tried to treat all the perceptible aspects of this era, such as, the problems about the Śakas, question about the historicity of Vikramāditya and also studies about the urban centres under separate headings which enhances the utility of this work even more. He has specially discussed the work of Bela Lahiri, to say *Indigenous States of Northern India* (*circa 200 B.C.-320 A.D.*), which gives an account of contemporary autonomous and self-governed cities and also that of many a major and minor political powers with suffix 'Mitra'. Next to this, he underlines the importance of B.C. Sinha's work on the Śuṅgas following soon the work of Bela Lahiri.

Shankar Goyal has quite successfully organized the researches related to the sources of this period. This include studies pertaining to numismatics, epigraphy, philology and art which are quite helpful in explaining the nature and importance of the political powers of this age, like, the Indo-Greeks, Śakas, Kushāṇas, Sātavāhanas and others. Discussions about economic and other aspects, like, art and crafts, trade and commerce, guilds and urban culture, etc. are much noteworthy. Shankar Goyal has rightly mentioned the works of Kameshwar Prasad, Buddha Rashmi Mani, Vijay Kumar Thakur, Himanshu Prabha Ray, Ram Sharan Sharma and others in this context. Further, he has also tried to put in order the political history of this period by reviewing the debates over the issues of origin and authorship of Kṛta (Mālava, Vikram) and Śaka Saṁvat.

HISTORIOGRAPHY OF THE KUSHĀṆA-SĀTAVĀHANA ERA

Discussion on the historiography of Kushāṇa and Sātavāhana dynasties specially brings to notice new dimensions and aspects touched upon in the recent studies about it besides the description of international conferences held to resolve the issues related to the Kushāṇas. The views and contributions of European, Soviet, Chinese and Indian scholars have been underlined separately in this regard. Special mention has been made of the works of Buddha Prakash, B.N. Puri, Baldev Kumar, B.N. Mukherjee, Bhaskar Chattopadhyaya and some others among the Indian scholars. Some light has been thrown upon the Marxist approach to the problems separately in this context. A note on the historiography of different indigenous states and tribal powers of the age of the Śakas and Kushāṇas is another contribution of Shankar Goyal. Enlisting the epigraphic and numismatic studies on the Sātavāhanas he goes on to discuss the works of Sudhakar Chattopadhyaya, Ajay Mitra Shastri and some Marxist historians. A separate study of the history of Kaliṅgarāja Khāravela has been incorporated.

HISTORIOGRAPHY OF THE GUPTA AGE

Historiography of the Gupta age has been taken up in quite a detail by Shankar Goyal under three separate headings. The first part of it deals with the beginning of writings on the Gupta age and its various dimensions taking into account the studies related to the sources of Gupta history, viz., epigraphic, numismatic, literary, both Indian and foreign, and archaeological sources. This part also includes a separate discussion on the early Western writings as that of Vincent A. Smith, E.B. Havell and Louis de la Vallée Poussin and thence goes on to review the works of early Indian scholars like R.G. Bhandarkar, H.C. Raychaudhuri, S.K. Aiyangar, R.D. Banerji, Kashi Prasad Jayaswal, R.G. Basak, Vasudeva Upadhyaya, R.N. Dandekar and R.N. Saletore on the Gupta period. An exclusive discussion is also there on *A New History of Indian People*. As about the writings of post-1947 era, Shankar Goyal has described the works of scholars like Radha Kumud Mookerji, R.C. Majumdar, A.S. Altekar, B.P. Sinha, A.L. Basham, B.G. Gokhale, Lallanji Gopal and Buddha Prakash. A separate description is there on the essays presented in the *Vikram Volume*. Referring to all these traditionally known studies, Shankar Goyal has also pointed out that they all go by the concept of a golden age during Gupta rule.

Discussing the pattern of writings on Gupta period after 1966, Shankar Goyal specially names R.C. Majumdar, D.C. Sircar, S.K.Maity, B.P. Sinha, Jai Prakash Singh, Radhesharan, D.K. Ganguly, T.R. Sharma, Ashvini Agrawal, Lallanji Gopal, T.P. Verma and David N. Lorenzen besides mentioning the works like *A Comprehensive History of India*, Vol. 3, Pt. 1, *Essays on the Gupta Culture* and *King Chandra and the Meharauli Pillar*. He seems to be quite justified in making a separate note on all the works of S.R. Goyal on Gupta history claiming it to be a fresh contribution to the researches in this direction. It brings us to a happy situation when various dimensions and aspects related to the history of Gupta period are well comprehended. Shankar Goyal rightly approves of the emphasis of S.R. Goyal upon treating political history of the Guptas in its complete political, social, economic, cultural and religious backdrop. Shankar Goyal has also incorporated the writings on regional history, arts, etc., in his attempt to cover almost all the dimensions and aspects of the Gupta age.

Shankar Goyal has very rightly pointed out that though there have been sufficient studies on cultural, scientific and literary progress of the Gupta period considering all that as big achievements of the great Guptas but hardly there had been an effort in explaining how far the Gupta emperors were themselves remained under the influence of their age and also that what role they had to play in giving any direction to future course of history. S.R. Goyal has been acknowledged as giving a new direction to the writings on Gupta history raising freshly a number of issues regarding it in this very context. This includes quite interestingly the questions about the origin along with the place of origin of the Guptas, chronology of early and later Gupta emperors, area covered under the military campaigns of Samudragupta, and the religious policies of early and later Gupta emperors.

S.R. Goyal's arguments about the Brāhmaṇa origin of Guptas and considering Prayāga as their place of origin do not just make it interesting but also matches with conditions of space and time. The Brāhmaṇa origin of Guptas also fits in the early history of India in view of the Brāhmaṇa caste identity of the post-Mauryan indigenous dynasties who claimed for themselves to be the preserver and protector of the *varṇāśrama* system. And it can be well presumed that the Guptas while taking over reigns thereafter seemed to have avoided disclosing their own identity as Brāhmaṇas as for this period of transition of restoring back the power to rule to the Kshatriyas ultimately as per the dictates of the caste system which can also be gathered from the trend of later political powers identifying themselves as Kshatriyas/Rājputs (please also refer to the opinion of the author of this article in *India Rediscovered: A New Vision of History and Call of the Age*, New Delhi, 2006, pp. 134-35). Further, it is worth noting here that the importance of Prayāga for Brāhmaṇa-Vaishṇava tradition came to be established from this period itself. However, S.R. Goyal in his analysis of the religious policy of the Gupta kings do accept the continuing importance of non-Brāhmaṇical traditions during the period of the Guptas. And it is quite plausible that it was finally the feudal system supporting the Brāhmaṇical system in the main which tended to de-establish the latter. An altogether new history of the imperial Guptas has been proposed by S. R. Goyal with his discussions on the problem of Rāmagupta, identification of 'Chandra' of Meharauli inscription with Samudragupta, a new evaluation of Chandragupta II, the question of Bālādityas in Gupta history, etc. Although many of the aspects brought to light by S.R. Goyal in re-defining the political history of the Guptas are, more or less, now being taken note of by some scholars but, Shankar Goyal appears to be disappointed with not much takers of the views of S.R. Goyal on the concept of 'new political history'.

Reviewing the Marxist approach to the Gupta history Shankar Goyal goes on to describe recent studies on various political, administrative, social and economic aspects and arguments pertaining to the origin and nature of Indian feudalism. Among these are the works of D.D. Kosambi, Ram Sharan Sharma, Romila Thapar, Dwijendra Nath Jha, B.N.S. Yadava and Vijay Kumar Thakur. The mainstay of Marxist writing, according to Shankar Goyal, has been the study of the nature of feudalism, weakening of economic activities and criticism of the traditional concept about Gupta era as the golden age of ancient Indian history. Shankar Goyal, agreeing with the opinion of some scholars, like, M.G.S. Narayanan, has pointed out that many an explanations of the Marxists in this context are contradictory to their own Marxist dictum. Damodar Dharmanand Kosambi, considered to be the initiator of Marxist explanation of Indian history, has been referred to by Shankar Goyal as describing the rise of feudalism in India at two levels. Firstly, it is at the level of politics and administration with the transfer of powers by central authority to its chiefs which has been explained as 'feudalism from above'. And secondly, it has been assumed as the rise of feudal lords containing/carrying economic, administrative and military powers with the establishment of the class of new landlords at local level which has been termed as 'feudalism from below'. Quite visibly, D.D. Kosambi's concept about 'feudalism from above' does not fit into the Marxist frame of the rise of feudalism. Ram Sharan Sharma, another Marxist historian, has found the roots of Indian feudalism in the nature and practice of land and village grants which having begun from the Sātavāhana and

Kushāṇa period became a common culture during the time of Guptas and thereafter. Sharma has also proposed to relate this process/phenomenon with the contraction of economic mobility and decline of urban centres and urbanism from the Gupta period. Nevertheless, he refrains from going further to question the concept of Gupta age as the golden age of Indian history, as has been done by other Marxist historians, like, D.N. Jha. Similarly, Romila Thapar does not seem to approve of the view about decline of urban centres in the Gupta period itself. Thus, Shankar Goyal has found a number of differences in the opinions of different Marxist scholars themselves.

Shankar Goyal has taken up the issue, 'concept of iron age' (iron as model), raised by D.N. Jha about the Gupta age in quite a detail and has presented the views of Lallanji Gopal, Ajay Mitra Shastri, T.P. Verma and S.R. Goyal challenging the same. In his book, *Ancient India: An Introductory Outline*, D.N. Jha puts the concept of iron age with the title, 'The Myth of the Golden Age'. He quite skeptically asks why there are no other court-writings or poetry carrying any laurels about the Gupta kings but just their own epigraphs. Jha has argued that that the condition of peasants was akin to the bonded peasant-slaves and bonded labourers due to feudalization of economic structure. The urban centres and trade were on the decline because of heavy taxation. The condition of women had worsened and the practice of *devadāsī* and prostitution was on the rise. There was also a growth of untouchables along with the multiplication of castes. Religion was being made the scapegoat for infusing social disparities and even Vaishṇavism became instrumental in promoting superstitions/blind faith instead of logical discourse. There were luxuries available, of course, for the affluent class of the society but social inequality and tension were the order of day. Further, whatever achievements were there of the Gupta age were the contribution of the Buddhists, Jainas, Greeks and Romans, and not of the Hindu revivalism. Shankar Goyal has also added to this the views of S.K. Maity presented in latter's work *Economic Life in Northern India in the Gupta Period* wherein questions have been raised about the concept of golden age citing pitiful condition of the common masses during the period of Guptas. But Shankar Goyal is not in favour of measuring the merits and demerits of any era of ancient history with the yardstick of modern age ideologies. He is of the view that there were sufficient elements in the culture of Gupta age which provide some glitter to it. He goes on to quote further the arguments of Lallanji Gopal, T.P. Verma and others who come out with open challenge to the Marxist approach and suggest that there are enough literary, numismatic and archaeological evidences to prove the economic mobility and affluence prevailing in the Gupta age. Overall, this discussion about the

Gupta historiography has been much contributory in bringing the issue to the forefront and it is much needed to understand the tendencies of the Gupta period which also set trend for later history of India. Any lopsided explanation in this context could blur the overall understanding of ancient past of India.

HISTORIOGRAPHY OF THE POST-GUPTA PERIOD

Shankar Goyal has dealt with the historiography of post-Gupta period in two parts. Focusing upon the history of early empires of Kanauj the first belongs to Maukharis, Pushyabhūtis and Yaśovarman. Beginning with the break-up of the Gupta empire, Shankar Goyal has attempted to discuss the studies evaluating major sources of the period, viz., Chinese and Bāṇa's texts and other Indian sources. Then, he refers to four stages of modern day writings on the post-Gupta period which often encroach upon one another. With regard to the first stage he discusses the works of scholars like M.L. Ettinghausen, Sampurnanand, C.V. Vaidya, K.M.Panikkar, R.K. Mookerji, R.S. Tripathi and G.S. Chatterji. Among other scholars writings on this period he refers to Vincent A. Smith, R.G. Basak, D.C. Ganguly and K.C. Chattopadhyaya. He has made special mention of the views of R.C. Majumdar and R.S. Tripathi, according to which Harsha was not the last of the great emperors of Hindu India and there came about even greater emperors after him. Describing the researches done by V.S. Agrawala on Harsha and the *Harshacharita*, Shankar Goyal then considers the minute historical analysis undertaken on the *Harshacharita* and other *charita kāvyas* by V.S. Pathak, a milestone of study in this direction. He has all praise for D. Devahuti's independent work on Harsha also.

Further, Shankar Goyal gives quite a detail of the contribution of S.R. Goyal to the study of history of the empire of Kanauj. Commenting upon the earlier traditional approach of studies of this period he says that it remained confined to the questions of 'what and when', whereas, S.R. Goyal has been able to deal with 'how and why' dimension of its history bringing many a new aspects to light. Shankar Goyal has rightly pointed out that that the traditional writings have largely accepted the versions of the *Harshacharita* and Yuan Chawng on their face value and little has gone into a discussion about comparative importance of these sources. Some light does appear about it in the works of V.S. Pathak and D. Devahuti. S.R. Goyal has, however, made a critical analysis of the administration of Harsha and its religious motives and has presented the history of Harsha in a new way.

Finally, Shankar Goyal has also incorporated the works on the Deccan and south India in his study of recent historiography of ancient India. These include pre-1947 and post-1947 studies on the Vākāṭakas, Chālukyas and other major dynasties of the south. Thus, he has tried to cover the whole of ancient India for the purpose of his study of historiography and presented a critical account of almost all the recent works referring back at the same time traditional writings earlier to this.

It is worth mentioning that Shankar Goyal has no where hesitated in assessing critically all these writings wherever he has found it wanting. He has been quite straight in treating the subject and has underlined the new trends and practices to end his discussion. He deserves all the praise for this valuable contribution to the study of ancient India adhering to the rational view of the study of history asserting as well the scientific temper required for it, particularly at a time when history writing is being influenced by communal and cultural assertions on the one hand and the Marxists biases on the other. Here, I would like to put the concerns of Shankar Goyal in his own words, "Modern historians of ancient India, therefore, have to be on their guard against becoming slaves of a doctrine and a methodology instead of their masters." The study of history like any other subject needs to be done with utmost neutrality and no conclusions be drawn with any bias or prejudice which may harm the whole of humanity, lest it amount to a massacre!

REFERENCES

Agrawala, V.S., *Harsha Charita—Ek Sāṁskṛtika Adhyayana* (in Hindi), Patna, 1953.

Agrawal, Jagannath and Goyal, Shankar, eds., *S.R. Goyal : His Multidimensional Historiography*, New Delhi, 1992.

Basham, A.L., *The Wonder that was India*, London, 1954.

—, *Studies in Indian History and Culture*, Calcutta, 1964.

—, ed., *Papers on the Date of Kanishka*, Leiden, 1968.

Beal, S., *The Life of Hiuen-Tsiang*, New Delhi, 1973.

—, *Si-Yü-Ki* or *Buddhist Records of the Western World*, Delhi, 1969.

Bhattacharya, Sibesh, 'Political History of Ancient India and Its Social Context', in *Political History in a Changing World*, ed. G.C. Pande et al, Jodhpur, 1992, pp. 116-34.

Carr, E.H., *What is History?*, London, 1964.

Chattopadhyaya, D.P., ed., *Marxism and Indology* (for Walter Ruben's 80th Birthday), Calcutta, 1981.

Chhabra, B. Ch., Agrawala, P.K., Agrawal, Ashvini and Goyal, Shankar, eds., *Reappraising Gupta History for S.R. Goyal*, New Delhi, 1992.

Collingwood, R.G., *The Idea of History*, OUP, 1961.

Craig, Gordon, 'Political History', in *Daedalus*, Cambridge, Mass., Winter 1971, pp. 323-38.

Devahuti, D., *Harsha : A Political Study*, 2nd edn., Oxford University Press, New Delhi, 1983; 1st edn., Oxford, 1970.

—, ed., *The Unknown Hsüan-tsang*, New Delhi, 2001.

—, ed., *Problems of Indian Historiography*, Delhi, 1979.
—, ed., *Bias in Indian Historiography*, Delhi, 1980.
—, ed., *Historical and Political Perspectives*, New Delhi, 1982.
Dhavalikar, M.K., 'The Golden Age and After : Perspectives in Historical Archaeology', his Presidential Address delivered to the Diamond Jubilee Session of the Indian History Congress, Calicut, 1999.
Finberg, H.P.R., ed., *Approaches to History*, London, 1962.
Fleischer, H., *Marxism and History*, London, 1973.
Ganshof, F.L., *Feudalism*, London, 1952.
Gardiner, Patrick, ed., *The Philosophy of History*, OUP, London, 1974.
Ghoshal, U.N., *The Beginnings of Indian Historiography and Other Essays*, Calcutta, 1944.
Goff, E.G., 'Is Politics Still the Backbone of History?', *Daedalus*, Cambridge, Mass., Winter 1971, pp. 1-19.
Gopal, S. and Thapar, R., ed., *Problems of Historical Writing in India*, New Delhi, 1963.
Goyal, Meghna, *Welding the Plural Society of India : The Nanda-Maurya Experiment*, Jodhpur, 2013.
Goyal, Shankar, *History and Historiography of the Age of Harsha*, Jodhpur, 1992.
—, *Recent Historiography of Ancient India*, Jodhpur, 1997.
—, *Harsha : A Multidisciplinary Political Study*, Jodhpur, 2006.
—, *Ancient India : A Multidisciplinary Approach*, Jodhpur, 2006.
—, *Studies in the History of the Deccan and South India*, Jodhpur, 2009.
—, *175 Years of Vākāṭaka History and Historiography*, Jodhpur, 2009.
—, *The 'Medieval' Factor and the Age of Harsha : A Cultural Study*, Jodhpur, 2016.
—, *Harsha Revisited : A Re-interpretation of Existing Data*, Delhi, 2018.
—, *The Significance of Yuan Chwang in the Context of the Seventh Century : A Critical Assessment*, Delhi, 2018.
—, ed., *Reconstructing Indian History for S.R. Goyal*, in 4 volumes, Jaipur,2003.
—, ed., *Early India : Historical Probings*, Jodhpur, 2015.
—, '*Harshacharita* as a Source of History', in the *Papers from the Aligarh Historians Society*, ed. Irfan Habib, 69th Session, Indian History Congress, Kannur University, Kannur, 2008, pp. 122-52.
—, 'Harsha : A Retrospective', his Presidential Address, Section I : Ancient India, 78th Session, Jadavpur University, Kolkata, 28-30 December, 2017.
Goyal, S.R., *A History of the Imperial Guptas*, Allahabad, 1967.
—, *A Religious History of Ancient India*, Vol. I, Meerut, 1984.
—, *A Religious History of Ancient India*, Vol. II, Meerut, 1984.
—, *Harsha and Buddhism*, Meerut, 1986.
—, *Harsha Śīlāditya*, Meerut, 1986.
—, *A History of Indian Buddhism*, Meerut, 1987.
—, *Nanda-Maurya Sāmrājya kā Itihāsa*, Meerut, 1988.
—, *India as Known to Kauṭilya and Megasthenes*, Jodhpur, 2001.

—, *The Imperial Guptas : A Multidisciplinary Political Study*, Jodhpur, 2005.

—, *Brāhmī Script : An Invention of the Early Maurya Period*, Jodhpur, 2006.

—, ed., *Māgadha Sāmrājya kā Udaya*, New Delhi, 1981.

Habib, Irfan, *Interpreting Indian History*, Shillong, 1985.

—, 'Problems of Marxist Historiography', *Social Scientist*, Vol. XVI, No. 12, December 1988.

Harshacharita of Bāṇa, tr. E.B. Cowell and F.W. Thomas, 2nd ed., Delhi, 1968.

Jha, D.N., *Ancient India : An Introductory Outline*, New Delhi, 1977; revised edn., 1998.

—, his Presidential Address to the Ancient India Section of the 40th Session of the Indian History Congress, Waltair, *Proceedings of the Indian History Congress*, 1979, pp. 15-45.

—, ed., *Feudal Social Formation in Early India*, Delhi, 1987.

Jha, Vivekanand, 'Rewriting Ancient Indian Political History : Possibilities and Pitfalls', in *Political History in a Changing World*, ed. G.C. Pande et al, Jodhpur, 1992, pp. 60-80.

Kādambarī of Bāṇa, tr. C.M. Ridding, Bombay, 1956.

Kosambi, D.D., *An Introduction to the Study of Indian History*, Bombay, 1956.

—, *Myth and Reality : Studies in the Formation of Indian Culture*, Baltimore, 1962.

—, *The Culture and Civilization of Ancient India in Historical Outline*, New Delhi, 1982.

Lorenzen, David N., 'Imperialism and the Historiography of Ancient India', in S.N. Mukherjee, ed., *India : History and Thought*, Calcutta, 1982, pp. 84-102.

Majumdar, R.C., *Historiography in Modern India*, Bombay, 1970.

—, *Readings in Political History of India*, ed. by S.P. Gupta, Delhi, 1976.

Majumdar, R.C. and Pusalker, A.D., eds., *The Age of Imperial Unity*, Bombay, 1953.

—, *The Classical Age*, Bombay, 1954.

Marc Bloch, *Feudal Society*, London, 1961.

—, *The Historian's Craft*, tr. from the French by Peter Putnam, reprint, Manchester University Press, 1984.

—, 'Feudalism', *Encyclopaedia of Social Sciences*, Vol. VI.

Mitra, P.K., 'Rewriting Political History of Ancient India', in *Political History in a Changing World*, ed. G.C. Pande et al, Jodhpur, 1992, pp. 100-15.

Mukherjee, B.N., *The Rise and Fall of the Kushāṇa Empire*, Calcutta, 1988.

Mukhopadhyay, S.K., *Evolution of Historiography in Modern India : 1900-1960, A Study of the Writing of Indian History by Her Own Historians*, Calcutta, 1981.

Narain, A.K., *The Indo-Greeks*, Oxford, 1962.

—, 'Writing a New History of Ancient India : A Study of Problems, Sources and Methods', in *Problems of Historical Writing in India*, New Delhi, 1963, pp. 1-10.

—, his Presidential Address, Ancient India Section, 30th Indian History Congress, Bhagalpur, 1968.

Pande, G.C., Gupta, S.K. and Goyal, Shankar, eds., *Political History in a Changing World*, Jodhpur, 1992.
Pathak, V.S., *Ancient Historians of India*, Bombay, 1966.
Philips, C.H., ed., *Historians of India, Pakistan and Ceylon*, London, 1961.
Problems of Historical Writing in India, Proceedings of the Seminar held at the India International Centre, New Delhi, 1963.
Ray, Niharranjan, 'Indian Historiography and Marxist Thought', in *Marxism and Indology*, ed. Debiprasad Chattopadhyaya, Calcutta, 1981.
Raychaudhuri, H.C., *Political History of Ancient India*, Calcutta, 1953; with 'Commentary' of B.N. Mukherjee, Oxford, 1996.
Sastri, K.A.N., *A History of South India*, 4th edn., Madras, 1974.
—, ed., *The Age of Nandas and Mauryas*, Varanasi, 1952.
Sen, S.P., ed., *Historians and Historiography in Modern India*, Calcutta, 1973.
Sharma, R.S., *Perspectives in Social and Economic History of Early India*, New Delhi, 1983.
—, *Material Culture and Social Formations in Ancient India*, Delhi, 1983.
—, *Urban Decay in India* (c. 300-1000 A.D.), New Delhi, 1987.
—, *Early Medieval Indian Society : A Study in Feudalisation*, Kolkata, 2001.
Shastri, A.M., *Early History of the Deccan*, New Delhi, 1987.
—, *The Sātavāhanas and the Western Kshatrapas : A Historical Framework*, Nagpur, 1998.
—, ed., *The Age of the Vākāṭakas*, New Delhi, 1992.
—, ed., *The Age of the Sātavāhanas*, in two volumes, New Delhi, 1999.
Singhal, D.P., 'Battle for the Past', in D. Devahuti, ed., *Problems of Indian Historiography*, New Delhi, 1979.
Singh, M.V., *India Rediscovered*, New Delhi, 2005.
Thakur, V.K., *Urbanisation in Ancient India*, New Delhi, 1981.
—, *Historiography of Indian Feudalism*, Patna, 1989.
—, 'The Marxist View of Ancient Indian History', *Journal of the Bihar Research Society*, Patna, Vol. LXII, Pts. 1-4, 1976.
—, 'Decline or Diffusion : Constructing the Urban Tradition of North India during the Gupta Period', in *The Indian Historical Review*, New Delhi, Vol. XXIV, Nos. 1-2, 1997-98, pp. 20-69.
Thapar, Romila, *Aśoka and the Decline of the Mauryas*, Oxford, 1961; 2nd edn., Delhi, 1997.
—, *A History of India*, Vol. I, Harmondsworth, 1966.
—, *Ancient Indian Social History*, Hyderabad, 1978.
—, *The Mauryas Revisited*, Calcutta, 1988.
—, *Interpreting Early India*, Delhi, 1992.
—, *From Lineage to State*, 2nd edn., Delhi, 1996.
—, *The Penguin History of Early India*, New Delhi, 2003.
Thapar, Romila et al, *Communalism and the Writing of Indian History*, New Delhi, 1969.
Warder, A.K., *An Introduction to Indian Historiography*, Bombay, 1972.
Watters, T., *On Yuan Chwang's Travels in India*, Delhi, 1961.

Chapter Three

Shankar Goyal's Studies on the Marxist Interpretation of Ancient India

VIBHA UPADHYAYA
Professor, Department of History and Indian Culture
University of Rajasthan, Jaipur

One doesn't have to be a Marxist to acknowledge that Karl Marx was one of the greatest thinkers in the history of the world. Most of the political scientists, economists, sociologists, philosophers and historians refer to Marx's works irrespective of whether they agree with him or not. No thinker of the nineteenth century has such a direct, deliberate and powerful influence on mankind as Marx. He has worldwide organized following in each discipline. Normally, whenever there is some reference to Marxism or Marxist doctrines these days, the general reaction of the people is that it is dead or irrelevant today, with disintegration of the Soviet Union. This is not true. The world over, particularly in poor and developing countries, including India, impact of Marxist ideology has been increasing. This impact can also be seen in the history writing in India in the post-independence period. Marxism has influenced the Indian historiography in many ways. It has been used in the study of feudalism, socio-economic history and even in the Indian nationalism and Indian renaissance also. This influence is known as 'paradigm shift' in Indian historiography and Romila Thapar credits D.D. Kosambi (1907-1966) for this effort. Kosambi defines history "as the presentation, in chronological order, of successive developments in the means and relations of production." But he also considered Marxism as a method which could be usefully applied for the study of Indian society and history.

The Marxist historiography was first used vaguely in the works of

James Tod, but clearly used by B.N. Dutta, S.A. Dange, D.D. Kosambi, Romila Thapar, R.S. Sharma and many others.[1] They use Marxist interpretation of history to analyse Indian history from 700- 1200 CE. It is also noteworthy to understand their approaches to study Indian history, as R.S. Sharma says, "I am always willing to use the non-Indian phenomenon including the African for understanding social, economic and political process in India."[2] Similar approaches have been used by Marxist historians to understand Indian society with profound differences of their approaches within the Marxist interpretation of Indian history. Though the scholars like D.C. Sircar and Lallanji Gopal did try to argue against this interpretation their efforts were devalidated under the strong influence of Marxist historiography in India. It is remarkable that now Professor Shankar Goyal has provided an insight into the true nature of the writings of Marxist historians. He has set a new trend into the field of critical evaluation of the Marxist historians with analytical research. Shankar Goyal is a brilliant scholar with main interests in major historiographical trends of ancient Indian history. He has authored a number of works on ancient Indian history, historiography, feudalism and culture. He has documented various periods of ancient Indian history with an in-depth study of the available sources. He has dealt with gradual changes in the historiographical studies of ancient India and also underlined the role of ideology in the historical reconstruction.

A monograph written by Shankar Goyal entitled *Marxist Interpretation of Ancient Indian History* has been published by the well known, prestigious academic institute, Bhandarkar Oriental Research Institute, Pune, in 2002. It is divided into the following subheadings: 'Beginning of Marxist Approach to Indian History', 'Process of Social and State Formations in the Vedic Age', 'Marxist Approach to the Problem of the Correlation of 'Traditional' History with Archaeological Cultures', 'Marxist Interpretation of the History of Janapada Age', 'Marxist Historians' Interpretation of the Maurya Period', 'Criticism of the Marxist Approach to Maurya History', 'Marxist Approach to Kushāṇa- Sātavāhana Period', 'Marxist Perception of the Gupta Age', 'Criticism of the Marxist Approach to Gupta History', and 'Marxist Interpretation of Ancient Indian History: Some Pitfalls and Dangers'. This monograph does not cover the post-Gupta period of Harsha. Shankar Goyal studies this period extensively within the paradigm of Indian feudalism in some other works and has given a new direction to the subject. From the subsequent discussion it is apparent that he is not against utilizing the models provided by the Marxists; he only wants to be certain that the model concerned is in consonance with the data provided by our sources. According to Shankar Goyal, "The Marxist view of history, which is both dialectical and materialist, draws the historian away from the traditional path of history writing and involves him in an objective reconstruction of the historical past in terms of social contradiction overlying the material conditions of life and perpetuating the dialectical process of history."[3] S.A. Dange was known as the earliest Marxist writer, but his work *India from Primitive Communism to Slavery* was not accepted as an authoritative interpretation of ancient India, even by the Marxist historians. Basically, according to Shankar Goyal, the true Marxist interpretation of ancient India took significant place with the emergence of writings of D.D. Kosambi. Dealing with the Vedic age Kosambi describes the changes in the Vedic and Early Buddhist periods as 'From Tribe to Society'. According to D.N. Jha, the Aryans came to India as a semi-nomadic people and Romila Thapar dealt with the theme of the gradual movement from a lineage based society to the emergence of state system. In continuation of these types of understanding, R.S. Sharma also discusses in-depth the problem of state formation in the Vedic age. Utilizing both literary and archaeological sources, he comes to the conclusion that the cattle pastoralism of the *Ṛgveda* supplemented by farming was a far cry from Harappan urbanism and that in contrast to the Ṛgvedic society, the Later Vedic society was marked by the dominance of the priestly class which appears to be as important as the nobles and warriors. According to R.S. Sharma, the class and the state were not well-established in the Later Vedic age. But with reference to the problem of the correlation of 'traditional' history, known by the literary sources, with archaeological cultures, their views seem to be contradictory. Dealing with the history of Janapada age, they emphasized that the developments of the Janapadas depends on the use of iron, emergence of trading system, trade with Western Asia, introduction of monetary system, tribal small geographical republics, etc. All of them (R.S. Sharma, D.N. Jha and others) clearly demonstrated the importance of economic factor in the political and social formations in the Early Buddhist period. With the emergence of Marxist approaches in Indian history writing, the history of the Maurya period also received a new orientation. Shankar Goyal evaluated their approaches and methods to visit the Maurya age in a new light. According to him, the main contribution of D.D. Kosambi is the application of statistical analysis of the Punch-marked coins in order to determine their chronology and identification.[4] He evaluated the works of Romila Thapar entitled *Aśoka and the Decline of the Mauryas* and *The Mauryas Revisted.* According to Shankar Goyal, all the Marxist historians assign the *Arthaśāstra* to the Maurya period and explains the Maurya administration and socio-economic developments on the line of *Arthaśāstra.*[5] According to the Marxist historians, the whole of India under the Mauryas was conquered with the help of a huge army and vast bureaucracy. Shankar Goyal also discussed the contribution of G.M. Bongard-Levin to the Maurya history. His *Mauryan India, A Complex Study of Ancient India : A Multidisciplinary Approach* and *Kuṇālāvadāna* makes an important contribution to Maurya history. But Shankar Goyal says that on certain points Bongard- Levin's observations are difficult to be accepted. For example, the prevailing theme of slavery and tribal system in Maurya times. Bongard-Levin also emphasized on the interrelationship between the Graeco-Roman and Indian civilizations in this perspective. Levin also suggested the use of Graeco-Roman sources to analyse the Maurya history. But S.R.Goyal[6] has adopted the holistic approach with the help of epigraphy, palaeography, numismatics, etc. According to Shankar Goyal, he raises the discussion on the problems of Maurya history to a high level.[7] According to Shankar Goyal, the most important aspect of the history writing of S.R. Goyal is that he goes much beyond the deeds and dates of Maurya kings and studies the political events of the period in their situational context.[8] He explains the growth of Magadhan empire, from Saptasindhu to Brahmāvarta, Āryāvarta and the whole subcontinent.[9] S.R. Goyal argues that the objective of Aśoka was not to encourage the tendencies of political and cultural unity; he merely wanted to become *Dhamma-chakkavattī* and was keen to spread Buddhism. The political and cultural unity was a by-product of his aim of becoming *Dhamma-chakkavattī* just as the awareness of the unity of India in the modern age was a by-product of the administrative measures adopted by the Britishers in India, who were themselves not at all interested in promoting the awareness. This perception of S.R. Goyal runs counter to Romila Thapar's view according to which the *dhamma* of Aśoka was devised to promote integration of his large empire.[10]

Dealing with the Marxist approach to Kushāṇa-Sātavāhana period, Shankar Goyal analysed the works of Romila Thapar, G.M. Bongard- Levin (Russian historian), Xinru Liu (Chinese historian and alumnus of Pennsylvania University) and Himanshu Prabha Ray (Indian archaeologist) in detail. All the Marxist historians opined that in the period of Kushāṇas and Sātavāhanas, Central Asia came in the orbit of Indian merchant and this in turn led to trade with China.[11] Shankar Goyal also described the initiative of Indian and Soviet scholars to launch a joint project of comparative study of archaeology, ethnolinguistics and ancient history of India and Central Asia. Shankar Goyal has also given the details of the contribution of Chinese sources to Kushāṇa historiography.[12] For the Marxist approach to study the period of the Sātavāhanas, Shankar Goyal evaluated the work of K. Satyanarayana entitled *A Study of the History and Culture of the Andhras*, Volume I, *From Stone Age to Feudalism.* Shankar Goyal critically examined the contradictory statements of Satyanarayana entitled who described the post-Sātavāhana period (third century A.D. to seventh century A.D.) as 'the Early Phase of Asiatic Society'.[13]

Himanshu Prabha Ray's approach has been found informative and well-argued by Shankar Goyal.[14] He admires the arguments of H.P. Ray as the constant royal support and encouragement contributed to the remarkable growth of trade, commerce and crafts in the Sātavāhana period and brought many a scattered tribal unit under one umbrella.[15]

There are many historical debates regarding the rise of feudalism, urban decay and economic decline in the Gupta age which gave strong platform for the Marxist interpretation. Specially, D.D. Kosambi,[16] R.S. Sharma,[17] Romila Thapar,[18] D.N. Jha[19] and V.K. Thakur[20] have examined the Gupta age form various points of view. Kosambi made the statement that "far from the Guptas reviving nationalism, it was nationalism that revived the Guptas."[21] Definition of feudalism, significant features of feudalism and feudalism as a system of government have been explained by Marxist historians with relation to the Gupta history. According to D.D. Kosambi, there are two processes of feudalism, he terms them as, 'feudalism from above', when the kings began to transfer their fiscal and administrative rights over land to subordinate chiefs and 'feudalism from below', when a class of land-owners developed within the village between the state and peasantry, gradually to wield armed power on the local population.[22] R.S. Sharma has expanded this view of feudal character of the Gupta administration. Inspired by Kosambi and R. S. Sharma, many other scholars[23] started to study the parallels proposed by R.S. Sharma but the Marxist formulation of Indian history was challenged by D.C. Sircar[24], Lallanji Gopal[25] and so many others on the basis of empirical data dealing with trade and commerce, availability of coins and currency, arts and crafts, trading centres and cities and also with the empirical base of *bhūmidāna* as pointed out by Sima Yadav.[26] But, finally, Shankar Goyal presented the view of S.R. Goyal regarding the decline of Gupta empire, and for the decline of Gupta empire he spoke about the rise of a class of the Brāhmaṇa feudatories which came into existence as a result of the practice of *bhūmidāna.*[27] Marxist criticism of the Hindu Gupta age, the golden age of history and the period of Hindu renaissance, has been described in detail by Shankar Goyal. V. K. Thakur came forward with Marxist interpretation of the social roots of the *Bhagavadgītā*. Shankar Goyal analysed the view of Thakur in a way that "The *bhakti* and *śraddhā* doctrines of the *Gītā* involving complete devotion and surrender to the Lord also suited the feudal ideology."[28] Shankar Goyal has also given a detailed criticism of the Marxist approach to Gupta history by S. R Goyal, Lallanji Gopal, A. M. Shastri and others. But, following Romila Thapar, Shankar Goyal admits that the classicisim of the Gupta period is not an innovation emanating from Gupta rule but the culmination of a process that began earlier.[29]

With reference to the Marxist interpretation of the history of

Vākāṭakas, Shankar Goyal has written many papers and a very invaluable work titled *175 Years of Vākāṭaka History and Historiography* (Jodhpur, 2009) with this approach. He critically examines Hans T. Bakker's suggestions on the art and culture of the Vākāṭakas[30] and rejects his thesis that the kingdom of the Vākāṭakas is to be seen "on a par with the Gupta world". To Shankar Goyal it appears to be somewhat exaggerated proposition. According to him, most historians have accepted the importance of the Vākāṭaka age in central India and the Deccan within the Gupta empire. "Even Hans Bakker in his 'Preface' to *The Vākāṭaka Heritage*", Shankar Goyal points out, "has categorically stated that at the crossroads of the Indo-Aryan north and Dravidian south, the northern culture of the Gupta kingdom reached the Deccan and developed a character of its own." In a highly illuminating and offbeat Presidential Address delivered to the XXXVIIth Annual Congress of the Epigraphical Society of India on 24-26 February, 2012, Shankar Goyal explains his ideas on the feudal nature of Vākāṭaka economy and the question of the existence of their coins in detail.[31] He finds it difficult to endorse the views of A.M. Shastri, Hans Bakker, Ellen M. Raven and some others who attribute some copper coins to the Vākāṭakas. Shankar Goyal's conclusion is notably different from Bakker's who finds economic prosperity in the Vākāṭaka kingdom which is surely "not quite visible" to him. On the whole, Shankar Goyal is of the view that "a study of the known inscriptions of the Vākāṭakas indicates the comparative paucity of coins resulting in the large-scale mechanism of land grants, growth of small village settlements and relatively declining urban economy."

With regard to the Marxist interpretation of the age of Harsha, there is no full-length study on Harsha and his times by any Marxist scholar. But Shankar Goyal has done a lot to give a new dimension to study this period. He studies the age of Harsha against the background of the strengthening of feudal tendencies of the seventh century, which, according to him, for the first time became manifest in the Vākāṭaka-Gupta age. His *Harsha : A Multidisciplinary Political Study* (Jodhpur, 2006) is essentially a new political biography of Harsha in the light of the decline of classical culture, rise of feudalism and transition to the medieval period.[32] Working broadly within the paradigm of Indian feudalism, Shankar Goyal, in his *The 'Medieval' Factor and the Age of Harsha: A Cultural Study* (Jodhpur, 2016), provides an account of society, economy and cultural developments during the reign of Harsha, defining it as a crucial period in the transition to the medieval.[33] He argues that while the picture of India in the seventh century did correspond broadly to that of Europe after the decline of the Roman Empire, yet owing to important variations, such as, the presence of caste system in India, Indian feudalism was different in important respects from its European counterpart. He sees similarities in the emergence of politcial decentralisation, sub-infeudation of land rights, and regionalisation of culture, while acknowledging a major point of differences in the absence of serfdom in India by an increasing rigour in the caste system.[34] Shankar Goyal's *Harsha Revisited : A Re-interpretation of Existing Data* (Delhi, 2018) brings together all the existing data, freshly interpreted. He recognizes and demonstrates the need to situate Harsha in terms of his times, so as to arrive at a more meaningful understanding. He casts his net wide, to locate the king within the context of contemporary polities within the subcontinent as well as beyond creating space for exploring the complexities of political negotiations.[35] In his *The Significance of Yuan Chwang in the Context of the Seventh Century : A Critical Assessment* (Delhi, 2018), Shankar Goyal not only examines the credibility of the Chinese pilgrim as a source of history, but also discusses dispassionately his testimony on social organisation and social life, economic life and activities, Indian religions and religious condition, education and learning, and art and literature, taking into consideration the distinctive feature – feudalism – of the age wheresoever possible.[36]

From the above discussion it is obvious that Shankar Goyal does not follow blindly the theories of Marxist scholars, howsoever eminent, and tries to establish what the evidence at his disposal suggests. While recognising the all-important role played by economic factors in shaping the course of history, he is happily able to keep himself free from dogmatism characterising the writings of some modern Marxist historians. As a historical thinker and writer, his approach is characterised by logical treatment of the subject and intellectual honesty. As he approaches his subject with an open mind, and without any prejudice, despite some deep disagreements, he has stood on similar lines on certain issues with them in course of his own academic journey of about three decades or so in the university. According to Shankar Goyal," the Marxist approach has served as a corrective for the over-sentimentalised and over-spiritualised account of ancient India."[37] He further states that "Marxist interpretation has made it imperative for the traditional historion to justify the literary accounts against the background of the archaeological sources and has given encouragement to the study of economic and material aspects of ancient Indian culture." But, as pointed out by him, the Marxist approach has given over-emphasis on the economic factor and made the theory of unchangeableness of Asiatic societies. This theory was based on the knowledge of European situation, it may not be applied in India. Shankar Goyal opines that Marxist approach to Indian history often implies the application of modern European criteria to ancient India. For example, Marxist historians identified the *varṇas* in ancient India with the economic classes of Marxism. Shankar Goyal strongly warned the historians in such a way that "One would also do well to remind oneself that research in the economic field in India is still in a nebulous condition and that adequate evidence is still not available to justify the assumption of any conscious class struggle. Finding socialist trends in the reign of Aśoka and the theory of proletarian reaction as the basis of Buddhism may appear 'saucy' but they do not add much to our knowledge. All human institutions do not follow the same line of development everywhere. The laws of social change are by no means as predictable as the laws of physical change."[38] According to Shankar Goyal, the Marxist interpretation has no doubt served as a corrective approach, but, it is feared, it is tending to err in the opposite direction. Their application of dialectical materialism to the interpretation of the history of India is grossly mechanical rather than critically discerning. This cannot claim to provide the only scientific approach to historical research relating to India; but at the same time, it cannot be ignored altogether. We only want to be certain that the models provided by the Marxists are in consonance with the data provided by our sources. We should not try to bring our data in conformity with the model. With particular reference to ancient Indian history, all different aspects of human life – political, social, economic, religious and cultural – should be studied as parts of one organic reality, each of them studied in its relation with others and not in isolation from each other.[39] With a rigorous assessment of Marxist interpretation of ancient Indian history, one feels, Shankar Goyal adopts a more balanced approach to understand our ancient past. On the whole, Shankar Goyal cautioned the modern historians of ancient India that "they have to be on their guard against becoming slaves of a doctrine and a methodology instead of their masters."[40] It is remarkable that Shankar Goyal has provided an insight into the true interpretation of ancient Indian history with reference to the correct understanding of Marxist approaches. By his interpretation we can say that "the supersitition that history has to be similar in all countries must be abandoned. ... All fields do not yield the same crop. One who knows this and thus looks for proper crop in the proper field, is truly a wise person."[41]

REFERENCES

1. James Tod, *Annals and Antiquities of Rajasthan*, London, 1957, 1960; B.N. Dutta, *Studies in Indian Social Polity*, Calcutta, 1944; S.A. Dange, *India from Primitive Communism to Slavery*, Delhi, 1949; D.D. Kosambi, *An Introduction to the Study of Indian History*, 2nd revised edn., Bombay, 1975; Romila Thapar, *Ancient Indian Social History*, New Delhi, 1984; idem, *From Lineage to State*, Delhi, 1984; R.S. Sharma, *Material Culture and Social Formations in Ancient India*, New Delhi, 1983; idem, *Indian Feudalism*, Calcutta, 1965.

2. R.S. Sharma, 'The Segmentary State and the Indian Experience', in *The Feudal Order*, ed. D.N. Jha, New Delhi, 2002, p.137.

3. Shankar Goyal, *Marxist Interpretation of Ancient Indian History*, Poona, 2002, p. 1; for further details, also see his *Contemporary Interpreters of Ancient India*, Jaipur, 2003, pp. 185-273.

4. *Ibid.*, p. 23.

5. *Ibid.*, pp. 22 ff.

6. *Ibid.*, p. 43.

7. *Ibid.*, pp. 43-48.

8. *Ibid.*, p. 45.

9. S.R. Goyal, *Māgadha-Sātavāhana-Kushāṇa Sāmrājyoṅ kā Yuga*, Meerut, 1988, pp. 28-34.

10. Cf. Shankar Goyal, *op.cit.*, pp. 47-48.

11. *Ibid.*, p. 49.

12. *Ibid.*, pp. 53 ff.

13. *Ibid.*, p. 55.

14. *Ibid.*, pp. 57-58.

15. *Ibid.*, p. 58.

16. D.D. Kosambi, *An Introduction to the Study of Indian History*, *op.cit.*; idem, *The Culture and Civilisation of Ancient India in Historical Outline*, 7th edn., New Delhi, 1982, pp. 166 ff.

17. R.S. Sharma, *Indian Feudalism*, pp. 76, 265-67; idem, *Perspectives in Social and Economic History of Early India*, New Delhi, 1983, Chs. 9 and 10.

18. Romila Thapar, *A History of India*, Vol. I, Harmondsworth, 1966, pp. 133-66; idem, *Early India*, New Delhi, 2002, pp. 280-325.

19. D.N. Jha, ed., *Feudal Social Formation* in *Early India*, New Delhi, 1987. In his 'Introduction' he gives a brief outline of Marxist literature on Indian feudalism.

20. V.K. Thakur, *Historiography of Indian Feudalism*, Patna, 1989, pp. 87 ff.

21. Shankar Goyal, *op.cit.*, p. 59.

22. *Ibid.*, p. 61.

23. *Ibid.*, pp. 61-63.

24. E.g., D.C. Sircar, *Land System and Feudalism in Ancient India*, Calcutta, 1966.

25. Lallanji Gopal, 'On Feudal Polity in Ancient India', *Journal of Indian History*, Vol. 41, 1963, pp. 405-13.

26. See, Sima Yadav, *The Myth of Indian Feudalism*, Delhi, 2005, Chs. I, II and V.

27. Shankar Goyal, *op.cit.*, pp. 72 ff.

28. *Ibid.*, p. 71.

29. Romila Thapar, *Early India*, p. 281; Shankar Goyal, *op.cit.*, pp. 72-82.

30. Shankar Goyal, *175 Years of Vākāṭaka History and Historiography*, Jodhpur, 2009, pp. 28-30.

31. Shankar Goyal, 'An Investigation into the Feudal Nature of the Vākāṭaka Economy : A Study of the Epigraphical Evidence', his Presidential Address delivered to the XXXVII Annual Congress of the Epigraphical Society of India,

Journal of the Epigraphical Society of India, Vol. XXXVIII, 2012, pp. 1-38; also see his 'The Myth of Vākāṭaka Coins', in *Indian Historical Review*, Vol. 34, No. 2, July, 2007, pp. 1-15.

32. The refreshing approach of Shankar Goyal in his *Harsha : A Multidisciplinary Political Study* (Jodhpur, 2006) brought him encomium from a large number of Marxist historians. For example, it has been acclaimed as 'the best work on the subject written so far' by R.S. Sharma and as 'a compulsory reading for those working on ancient Indian history' by Romila Thapar.

33. Kumkum Roy on Shankar Goyal's *The 'Medieval' Factor and the Age of Harsha : A Cultural Study*, Jodhpur, 2016, p. ii.

34. Irfan Habib, in his 'Foreword' to Shankar Goyal's *The 'Medieval' Factor and the Age of Harsha : A Cultural Study*, p. viii.

35. Kumkum Roy, in her 'Foreword' to Shankar Goyal's *Harsha Revisited: A Re-interpretation of Existing Data*, Delhi, 2018, p. vii.

36. R. Champakalakshmi on *The Significance of Yuan Chwang in the Context of the Seventh Century : A Critical Assessment*, Delhi, 2018, by Shankar Goyal.

37. Shankar Goyal, *Marxist Interpretation of Ancient Indian History*, p. 83.

38. *Ibid.*, p. 85.

39. *Ibid.*, p. 86.

40. *Ibid.*

41. Rabindra Nath Tagore, 'The History of Bhāratavarsha', the little known seminal text of Tagore, written in August, 1903, and translated from Bengali by Sumita Bhattacharya and Sibesh Bhattacharya.

Chapter Four

Shankar Goyal's Probings in Epigraphical and Numismatic Studies

T.S. RAVISHANKAR
Former Director (Epigraphy)
Archaeological Survey of India
Mysore

My acquaintance and friendship with Professor Shankar Goyal has been more than two and a half decades. In the fraternity of epigraphists I consider him as one of the foremost members. More than a great scholar and academician, his down to earth nature endeared me most. He was elected General President of the XXXVII Annual Congress of the Epigraphical Society of India in 2012 for his continuous association with and contribution to epigraphical studies. I am extremely happy to share my views on some of his writings and offer this article as a bouquet for his festschrift.

There are very few scholars whose critical acumen is amply reflected in their writings. One such committed scholar is Shankar Goyal, whose deep erudition in understanding and interpreting the historical facts, whether in the realm of epigraphy or numismatic studies, is of a very high order. Inheriting rich academic traditions from his great father, the late Professor S.R. Goyal, a renowned historian and a prolific writer, whose contribution to historical writings was unfathomable, Shankar Goyal continued his legacy and contributed immensely to the scholarly world. I have the privilege and pleasure of going through his writings which has come to us in the form of his Presidential Addresses, forewords, articles and books which are multidimensional in nature, belonging particularly to ancient and early medieval periods of Indian history. Some of his writings are analysed here to understand his rich contribution in the realm of epigraphy and numismatics. Though Shankar Goyal has dealt with many aspects connected with Indian epigraphy, his *forte* is his masterly treatment of Gupta and Vākāṭaka inscriptions.

I. EPIGRAPHY

PRESIDENTIAL ADDRESS OF SHANKAR GOYAL TO THE EPIGRAPHICAL SOCIETY OF INDIA (2012)

In the XXXVII Annual Congress of the Epigraphical Society of India, held at Baroda (*Journal of the Epigraphical Society of India*, Vol. XXXVIII, 2012, pp. 1-38), Shankar Goyal chose to tread a less trodden path and gave an exceptionally brilliant address entitled 'An Investigation into the Feudal Nature of the Vākāṭaka Economy : A Study of the Epigraphic Evidence'. To address this issue, he examined the entire gamut of writings by various scholars both in the area of numismatics and epigraphy. He has beautifully narrated how the structure of the empire which Samudragupta established was feudal-federal. In the beginning of his highly researched address, he raises certain basic issues connected with Vākāṭaka economy, an aspect which would be incomplete without referring to their coinage. He analyses various views expressed by different scholars regarding one or two copper coins of the Vākāṭaka period and goes into a detailed discussion on the problem of the absence of coins in a society which is usually regarded as a feature of feudal economy. He has critically examined all the available sources at that point of time and makes a serious attempt to give a new direction to the subject. He differs with A.M. Shastri, Hans T. Bakker, Ellen M. Raven and some others and observes that "the question of the existence of the currency of an extensive kingdom, as that of the Vākāṭakas, cannot be decided by one or two copper coins." On the whole, according to Shankar Goyal, "no credence should be given to such coins unless they are obtained from regular archaeological excavations and their authenticity is proved by detailed investigations."

Further, coming to the epigraphical sources, Shankar Goyal has investigated several land grants of the Vākāṭakas and has made a complete analysis of them to drive home the fact of the existence of feudal structure in the Vākāṭaka territories. Under the subheadings, 'Mechanism of Land Grants in the Vākāṭaka Economy', 'Privileges and Obligations of the Donees in the in Vākāṭaka Inscriptions', 'Impact of Land Grants on the Economic Condition of the Vākāṭakas : Burgeoning of the Rural Settlements' and 'Decline of Urban Settlements in the Vākāṭaka Territories', he extensively refers to all the available epigraphs — old and new — to substantiate his views on this issue on the federal nature of economy. He concludes by stating that "...The two and a half centuries of the Vākāṭaka ascendency in parts of central India and the northern Deccan, with its non-monetary small-scale village settlements and relatively declining urban economy, presents a *milieu* in which we find some elements of feudalism."

LOYOLA COLLEGE ENDOWMENT LECTURE OF SHANKAR GOYAL (2006)

Another well-researched lecture which Shankar Goyal delivered in the 26th Annual Session of the South Indian History Congress, Bangalore (published in the *Proceedings of the Twenty-sixth Annual Session of the South Indian History Congress*, Bangalore, 2006, pp. 689-702), is entitled 'The Vākāṭakas in the History of the Deccan: A Fresh Appraisal in the Light of Recent Discoveries and New Interpretations'. Here he has made a complete and an in-depth study of the Vākāṭaka history, of course, based on inscriptions. This study underlines the role of ideology in historical reconstruction. Focusing on the varied problems of the history of the Vākāṭakas, Shankar Goyal has either thrown new light or has offered new cogent solutions for them. As the influence of the imperial Guptas on the Vākāṭaka dynasty has been a major concern for most of the historians he has also concentrated on this aspect of their history. He also shows how in the beginning of the twenty-first century the history of the Vākāṭakas has advanced from the stage of a chronological, dynastic study to an integral analysis of events and a detailed study of religion and art, agrarian expansion in central India and northern Deccan and state formation under the main branch (for further details, see his *175 Years of Vākāṭaka History and Historiography*, Jodhpur, 2009).

SELECT PAPERS OF SHANKAR GOYAL ON EPIGRAPHICAL STUDIES

In the book entitled *Methodology of Epigraphical Studies and History Writing* edited by Sita Ram Dubey (2004) Shankar Goyal has penned an article named 'Main Stages in the Study of Maurya Epigraphy' (pp. 36-46). He has made an exhaustive and critical study of the sources and appropriately demarcates the important stages in the study of Mauryan epigraphy. He has categorised them in two types. Firstly, he mentions both the literary and archaeological sources. Since the epigraphs form one of the major sources, he has dealt with in detail all the earlier edicts of Aśoka and their critical editions by various scholars. Secondly, he has given a list of new Aśokan epigraphs with their detailed references. Further, he has included in this discussion the debate on the origin of Brāhmī script and succinctly mentions S.R. Goyal's theory that "the questions of the antiquity of Brāhmī and antiquity of the knowledge of the art of writing in India are quite separate and different," and that "the Brāhmī script was invented in the reign of Aśoka and that the Indians of the post-Indus and pre-Aśokan period, barring the people of the north-west, were illiterate." Finally, he concludes the article by mentioning cartographic studies on Aśokan inscriptions.

Shankar Goyal has vigorously involved himself in studying the early history of India, especially the Gupta-Vākāṭaka phase. He has a thorough understanding of not only epigraphs of this phase, but also the historiography of Gupta and Vākāṭaka inscriptions. In the work *Ancient Indian Inscriptions: Recent Finds and New Interpretations*, written by S.R. Goyal (2005), Shankar Goyal has contributed a chapter entitled 'Main Stages in the Study of Gupta Epigraphy' (pp. 110-14). He has beautifully narrated the attempts made by various scholars in deciphering Gupta inscriptions at different point of time. It's not a mere narration of the historiography of Gupta inscriptions but he has also tried to show the advancement in the knowledge of Gupta history through the medium of inscriptions. Shankar Goyal has also mentioned the immense contribution made by various scholars, both indigenous, as well as foreign scholars, including Captain Troyer, who successfully read a part of the Allahabad pillar inscription in the year 1834, to S.R. Goyal, whose *Guptakālīna Abhilekha* was published from Meerut in 1984.

Another brilliant piece of writing of Shankar Goyal appears in the work *King Chandra and the Meharauli Pillar*, ed. by Munish Chandra Joshi, S.K. Gupta and Shankar Goyal (Meerut, 1989, pp. 150-56). To quote his own words, "To prove the identity of King Chandra of the Meharauli pillar inscription with Chandragupta II Vikramāditya much has been theorised about Chandragupta II's influence on the Vākāṭakas and the Kadambas, for the Meharauli *praśasti* explicitly refers to the military achievements of Chandra up to the southern Ocean." Shankar Goyal delineates various aspects of Vākāṭaka-Gupta relations. Citing many copper plate inscriptions to prove his point, he argues that the achievements of King Chandra in the south are applicable to Samudragupta, and not to Chandragupta II.

More critical approach and thorough understanding of the subject could be seen in Shankar Goyal's another article entitled 'The Problem of Chandragupta II's Political Influence on the Vākāṭakas : A Revised Study of the Epigraphic Sources', presented at the 16th World Sanskrit Conference, Silpakorn University, Bangkok, Thailand, in 2015, and published in the *Epigraphic Studies : Select Papers*, edited by D.P. Dubey (pp. 129-37). The article refutes various arguments put forth by different scholars to prove Chandragupta II's influence on the Vākāṭakas. Here Shankar Goyal stresses the need for greater critical scrutiny than has been accorded to them so far. On the whole, according to Shankar Goyal, "The evidence of Pune and Rithpur copper plates and the recently discovered Ramtek stone inscription cited to prove Chandragupta II's influence on the Vākāṭaka court during the regency of Prabhāvatīguptā do not prove the case. We do not mean to suggest that such an influence was impossible. Indeed, in the circumstances are known to us some sort of Gupta influence on the Vākāṭakas during the minority of the sons of Rudrasena II may easily be presumed but there is nothing to prove any Gupta interference in the Vākāṭaka kingdom. Our submission is simple: the evidence cited in favour of this presumption does not prove the point; even the Ramtek inscription only concedes the overlordship of Chandragupta II in the southern peninsula only in theory."

'Some Observations on the Ramtek Prabhāvatīguptā Memorial Fragmentary Stone Inscription', published in the *Proceedings of the Twenty-sixth Annual Session of the South Indian History Congress*, Bangalore (2006), contains entire details of the inscription (pp. 25-27). Verse by verse Shankar Goyal has given the translation of the inscription and highlighted its importance, of course, giving his own observations, which enable us to appreciate the relevance of the inscription in full measure.

Another very interesting article, which is published in the *Proceedings of the Twenty-eighth Annual Session of the South Indian History Congress*, Anantapur (2008) is on the bearing of the recent epigraphical data on the history of the Vākāṭakas (pp. 37-43). In this article Shankar Goyal has brought to light new copper plate and stone inscriptions which were discovered after the publication of *Corpus* of the Vākāṭaka inscriptions in the year 1963 and has given a brief account of all the fourteen inscriptions, of which, eleven belong to the main branch and other three belong to Vatsagulma branch.

Shankar Goyal's contribution of an article entitled 'The Recently Discovered Kurukshetra-Varanasi Grant of Harsha : Year 23' (published in the *East and West*, December, 2007, pp. 193-203), speaks of his popularity as an academician in international circle. He has critically edited this inscription, which is quite exhaustive, and provided his own translation of the text of the inscription as well as the seal. The facsimile of both the copper plate and the seal enhances the value of the article.

The article published in *Studies in Indian Epigraphy* in Vol. XXXIII, 2007, Mysore, on V.S. Pathak's contribution to epigraphical studies, running into five small sections, brings in full measure, the personality of V.S. Pathak, the doyen among historians and epigraphists. Shankar Goyal has made a deep study of his works and brought before us the impressive span of research of Pathak.

Shankar Goyal has also authored many articles in Hindi : One of them 'Harsha ke Abhilekha : Kuchha Samasyāyeṅ aura Sujhāva', edited by Sita Ram Dubey in *Ābhilekhika Adhyayana kī Pravidhi evaṁ Itihāsa-*

Lekhana (2004), offers interesting glimpses on the copper plate charters of Harsha in manifold ways.

II. NUMISMATICS

SHANKAR GOYAL'S MAGNUM OPUS : *ANCIENT INDIAN NUMISMATICS*

Shankar Goyal's contribution in the realm of numismatic studies, especially of early India, has been extraordinarily rich and immense. His deep erudition and scholarship could be discerned in his writings which have come down to us in the form of a book *Ancient Indian Numismatics : A Historiographical Study* (Jodhpur, 1998) and numerous articles. There are very few numismatists who have worked on the historiography of numismatics studies, but Shankar Goyal's writings in an abundant measure focus on the historiographical studies of ancient Indian numismatics. Apart from the highly appreciated work, mentioned above, which covers the entire gamut of ancient Indian numismatic studies, he has written extensively on the great contributions made by stalwarts in the area of numismatics, such as, P.L. Gupta. A.S. Altekar, Ajay Mitra Shastri, V.S. Pathak, S.R. Goyal and Lallanji Gopal. His own papers on the origin and antiquity of coinage in India, Buddhist symbols and Buddha image on ancient Indian coins, political ideology of the early Guptas as reflected on their coins, the myth of the Vākāṭaka coins, coins of Prabhākaravardhana Pratāpaśīla and Harsha Śīlāditya, etc., amply reflect his deep understanding of the subject.

It won't be an exaggeration if I say that the book *Ancient Indian Numismatics : A Historiographical Study* is a great addition to our numismatic literature. Admired by R.S. Sharma, one of the best minds of the Indological world, it is definitely the first and only account of its kind, at once critical, scholarly and uptodate. Especially for the students and serious research scholars, who want to gain knowledge and to understand the vast literature and immense contributions made by foreign and indigenous scholars to ancient Indian numismatics, this book is of enormous value. It also offers as a source-work to understand the growth of numismatic studies beginning from the origin and antiquity of coinage in India up to the coins of the north Indian dynasties of the post-Gupta period (550 -750 A.D.). The monograph spread over in eleven chapters has given a detailed account of the history of ancient Indian numismatic studies from the late eighteenth century to 1998. Much effort has gone in gathering information from the vast numismatic material found in different research works and publications and arranging them in chronological sequence in the land mark time zones, such as, the punch marked coins, the tribal and local coins, the Indo-Greek coinage, the imperial Scytho -Parthian and Western Kshatrapa coinage, the Kushāṇa coinage, the Sātavāhana coinage, the coinage of the Gupta empire, etc., and also bringing together a host of scholars mentioning their contributions under different categories. At the end of the book a vast Bibliographical Index is given. Surely, this is the only historiographical study attempted by any scholar as far as ancient Indian numismatics is concerned.

SELECT PAPERS OF SHANKAR GOYAL ON NUMISMATIC STUDIES

'The Origin and Antiquity of Coinage in India', published in *Studies in Indian Numismatics*, eds. Jai Prakash Singh and Paras Nath Singh, Varanasi, 2009, pp. 53-88, embodies an exhaustive treatment at the hands of Shankar Goyal. Apart from mentioning all the earlier works done in this direction, he has provided a full and comprehensive picture of the origin and antiquity of coinage in India. This painstakingly researched piece is one of Shankar Goyal's major contributions to the subject and adds a new dimension to the study of the subject. Here he has analysed the contribution of various scholars in the field, such as, D.D. Kosambi, A.S. Altekar, P.L. Gupta, A.M. Shastri, S.C. Ray, Michael Mitchiner, M.K. Dhavalikar, V.S. Pathak, Joe Cribb, B.N. Mukherjee and S.R. Goyal. Finally, he sums up his article by stating that "Though metallic pieces of fixed weight might have been in circulation in the Later Vedic age, coinage proper originated in India in the sixth-fifth centuries B.C."

Another very scholarly and fascinating writing of Shankar Goyal is on the Buddhist symbols and Buddha image on ancient Indian coins (*Journal of the Numismatic Society of India*, Vol. XLIX, Parts I and II, 1987, pp. 109 -14). We are all aware how in the understanding of early Indian history, Buddhism occupies a place of vital significance. Its value and abundance can least be exaggerated in the areas of art, architecture, inscriptions and coins; especially in the study of early coins there are innumerable symbols appearing on them. It is quite interesting to note that Shankar Goyal has systematically drawn our attention to various symbols appearing on early coins which has strong Buddhist affiliations, beginning from D.B. Spooner to various other scholars who have embarked on the subject. The detailed narration from the appearance of symbols to the images of Buddha and different aspects of iconography of the Buddha makes the article very fascinating.

Numismatic studies offer a fair ground to understand the socio-economic, religious and many other aspects of the contemporary world. Shankar Goyal in his article 'Political Ideology of the Early Guptas as Reflected on their Coins', *Journal of the Numismatic Society of India*, Vol. LXIV -V, 2002-03, pp. 24-28, observes that "the political activities and attitudes of the imperial Guptas was greatly influenced by their political ideology which was usually a reflection of and conditioned by their religious beliefs."

When we analyse the numismatic history, especially of north India of the Gupta and post-Gupta phase, there is a great paucity of coinage. The same is attributable to the Vākāṭakas also. Shankar Goyal in his article, 'The Myth of the Vākāṭaka Coins' (*The Indian Historical Review*, Vol. XXXIV, No. 2, July, 2007, pp. 1-15, has at length discussed the issue regarding the non-prevalence of Vākāṭaka coinage. The thrust of the writing is to negate the ascription of a few coins to the Vākāṭaka kings made by Ajay Mitra Shastri and others. Shankar Goyal's critical observation is well thought out. He writes, "no credence should be given to such coins unless they are obtained from regular archaeological excavations and their authenticity is proved by detailed investigation." He is quite justified in making such assertions.

Among his other articles related to the numismatic studies which drew my attention is 'Coins of Prabhākaravardhana Pratāpaśīla and Harsha Śīlāditya' (*Journal of the Numismatic Society of India*, LIV, Pts. 1-2, 1992, pp. 65-69). The very nature of coins examined by him created great interest in me to know more about it. The article carries a detailed discussion on the opinions expressed by Alexander Cunningham, Hoernle and Richard Burn. Finally, he settles with the opinion expressed by K.D. Bajpai who has compared the palaeographical features of the Madhuban and Banskhera records of Harsha with the legends seen on the coins. On the whole, Shankar Goyal substantiates the identification of the title Pratāpaśīla with Prabhākaravardhana and of Śīlāditya with Harsha with cogent arguments.

Shankar Goyal has a diversified approach in understanding Indian numismatics. One such is making us to know and understand about the great contributions made by some of the great numismatists, such as, P.L. Gupta, A.S. Altekar, Ajay Mitra Shastri, V.S. Pathak, Lallanji Gopal and S.R. Goyal. He has written on them exhaustively and brought out in full measure their immense contribution in the field.

The doyen among numismatists, P.L. Gupta's contribution has been immeasurable ('On P.L. Gupta's Contribution to Gupta History and Coinage,' *Journal of the Numismatic Society of India*, Vol. LXIV-V, 2002-03, pp. xxx-xxxiii). In this learned article Shankar Goyal has brought out P.L.Gupta's contribution in the areas of both, the Gupta history and their coinage. One thing which is commonly seen in the works of P.L. Gupta is that he has kept in mind both the students and research scholars. His simple and lucid style of writing either history or numismatics assumed the nature of text-books for the students of numismatics and epigraphy.

Shankar Goyal has critically examined in his article many of the views expressed by P.L. Gupta which are interesting and has given his own observations on them.

Another article of Shankar Goyal, written in Hindi, 'Dr. P.L. Gupta aura Guptakālīna Suvarṇa Mudrāyeṅ' forms a part of the felicitation volume brought out in honour of P.L. Gupta entitled *Baḍhate Kadam–Badalte Āyāma*, Varanasi, 1995, pp. 271-78, makes an interesting reading.

The articles authored by Shankar Goyal regarding some of the eminent numismatists constitute not only a well-structured narrative about their contribution, but the way he has analysed their writings makes us to understand their academic profundity personality, their approach towards the subject and their well-documented thought-process. For instance, his article on 'A.S. Altekar and the Bayana Hoard' (*Journal of the Numismatic Society of India*, Vol. LXVII, 2005, pp. 80-84) reflect the above said statement. In this beautiful article, as a good preamble, he has furnished several hoards, right from the Kalighat hoard brought to light in the year 1783 up to Bayana (1946) and also subsequent hoards. Apart from providing a host of information about different hoards and their analysis, he speaks about the great persona of Altekar, "He always keeps an open mind and is prepared to change his opinion when adequate evidence is put forward. For example, he changed his opinion on Kācha coins several times. Similarly, while describing the Chakravikrama type coins of Chandragupta II, he at first stated that the god who is seen theirin bestowing a gift on the king before him is Vishṇu himself, but later, after weighing the evidence put forward by other scholars, he changed his opinion and admitted that the divine figure is that of the Chakra Purusha aspect of Vishṇu."

Another multifaceted personality was V.S. Pathak, a tireless Indologist, who, as a prolific writer, has touched upon various aspects of early Indian history, including numismatics. Shankar Goyal in his article 'V.S. Pathak's Contribution to Numismatic Studies' (*Journal of the Numismatic Society of India*, Vol. LXVIII, 2006, pp. 121-25) has brought out the personality of Pathak in the best possible manner. He begins his writing with various academic positions held by him followed by a list of his works, mainly the books authored by him. Further, he has given a beautiful narration of Pathak's contribution in untangling many of the issues connected with Gupta coinage. He undertook a semantic and etymological study of some numismatic terms, such as, *mudrā*, *rūpa*, *sikkā*, *nishka*, *viśvarūpa*, *śatamāna*, etc. Shankar Goyal sums up the article by stating that "Originality and critical acumen were the hallmarks of Pathak's writings. He showed an enviable capacity to dissect the past scientifically. And that was his *forte*."

Shankar Goyal in his article on 'Ajay Mitra Shastri's Contribution to Ancient Indian Numismatics' (*Journal of the Numismatic Society of India*, Vol. LXVI, 2004, pp. xi- xliv) has given a very detailed account of his contribution. Undoubtedly, Ajay Mitra Shastri's contribution is so immense that it has enriched the study of numismatics manifold. Shankar Goyal recalls in his article regarding his contribution to Audumbara coinage and substantially to the Sātavāhana coinage and also various aspects connected with ancient Indian coins.

Shankar Goyal's approach has been exceptionally good in writing on eminent numismatists and their contributions. Another article from his pen is on the 'Notes on Professor Lallanji Gopal's Contribution to Numismatic Studies', in *Select Papers on Professor Lallanji Gopal*, Varanasi, 2009, pp. 13-28. Perhaps this is one of the lengthiest articles where Shankar Goyal has given a very exhaustive treatment to his works and achievements and his indelible impression in the area of numismatics.

Another paper of Shankar Goyal, which is worth noting here, discusses the huge contribution of S.R. Goyal to numismatic studies (to be shortly published). In this, apart from assessing the works of S.R. Goyal, Shankar Goyal shows how the testimony of coins should be used and evaluated in the reconstruction of ancient Indian history. The paper is also marked, like his other writings, by exhaustiveness, inclusion of uptodate information, logical thinking and his own suggestions and views on many issues.

Thus, Shankar Goyal's writings both in the realm of epigraphy and numismatics make an absorbing and fascinating reading. Irrespective of the subject chosen by him they have received full attention. His thoroughness in approach to the subject placing before us all the available sources and a detailed analysis made by different scholars and his own conclusions are very well brought out in his book and articles. His writings on various aspects of the study of epigraphy and numismatics attract all — numismatists, students and senior scholars.

Chapter Five

Shankar Goyal on the Gupta Age

J.K. SHARMA
Professor of History
Panjab University, Chandigarh

Shankar Goyal's contribution to the history and historiography of the classical age is indeed unique and awesome. He began his long journey into the study of ancient Indian historiography since with his doctoral programme, for which he wrote a thesis, *Main Trends in Indian Historiography Since Independence* (1992). Since then he has written extensively equipped with scholarly insight on various aspects of ancient Indian history and historiography, edited works and a large number of widely acclaimed papers, which also include his Presidential Addresses delivered at the prestigious Epigraphical Society of India, the Indian History Congress, the South Indian History Congress, and forewords, etc. The scholarly and critical content of Shankar Goyal's laudable contribution can be seen from the fact that his edited works contain the papers of contemporary India's celebrated historians like R.S. Sharma, A.K. Narain, Romila Thapar, Irfan Habib, R. Champakalakshmi, Kesavan Veluthat, V.K. Thakur, Kumkum Roy, V.S. Pathak, G.C. Pande, K.D. Bajpai, B.N. Mukherjee, A.M. Shastri and Lallanji Gopal, to name only a few here. Apart from them, eminent scholars from other countries including J. Gonda (Utrecht, Nederland), G.M. Bongard-Levin (Moscow, Russia), A.K. Warder (Toronto, Canada), David N. Lorenzen (El Colegio De Mexico), Alois Wurm (Wien, Austria), Walter M. Spink (Michigan, U.S.A.), Bardwell L. Smith (Minnesota, U.S.A.), Priti Kumar Mitra (Hawaii, Honolulu, U.S.A.), Mubarak Ali (Sindh, Pakistan) and many others have also enriched his edited projects by their valuable contributions. I have observed him growing and acquiring more intellectual insights each time I happen to meet him.[1]

For the historiographical study of the period under review, Shankar Goyal gives much space to the works of S.R. Goyal (henceforth SRG) who is a doyen of ancient Indian history in general, and the Guptas in particular, and whose colossal work *A History of the Imperial Guptas* (Allahabad, 1967)[2] has elevated him to the rank of a well recognised historian, nationally and internationally. This book was incidentally SRG's doctoral thesis, and it is widely acclaimed and used by the researchers, teachers and the students today. Again, it has tended to remove many hitherto existing stereotypes and pre-conceived biases on the Guptas, and has added new dimensions to its studies. Shankar Goyal not only follows SRG, but extends his legacy to open new vistas of study.

Since Shankar Goyal has contributed immensely to the Gupta history, it appears to be a somewhat exceedingly difficult task to cover his wide range of works in a few pages here. Obviously, I am left with only an alternative to select some, and skip others.

SHANKAR GOYAL ON THE CHANGING PERCEPTIONS OF GUPTA HISTORY AND HISTORIOGRAPHY

Shankar Goyal underlines the changing perceptions of the Gupta period due mainly to the alternative interpretations of literary, numismatic and epigraphical (including archaeology) sources. For him, the inherent problem of the literary sources is that they do not reflect the contemporary Gupta scenario completely. The Brāhmī script though deciphered during the first half of the nineteenth century, the problem of the actual reading and interpretation of epigraphs remained and continued even in the twentieth century. The archaeological excavations have enlarged the area of studies further, but their interpretations have originated unending debates.

Shankar Goyal shows great concern that the Gupta historiography could not make much headway during India's colonial period. The Western historians used their own personal preferences in their larger frame of anti-India biases. Thus, V.A. Smith had the fascination of the role of great man in history, so he picked up Samudragupta and Chandragupta II for his studies. The time of the small kings was considered insignificant, and their periods were termed as the 'dark periods'. This has what he has done about the period between the decline of the Kushāṇas and the rise of the Guptas. However, the subsequent researches have made it irrelevant. Same is the case with the Indian scholars, like, R.G. Bhandarkar, H.C. Raychaudhuri, K.P. Jayaswal, R.N. Dandekar, etc., who failed to add anything substantial due mainly to their obsessions. Thus, according to Shankar Goyal, the Gupta historiography remained stagnant by and large.

However, the post-colonial period has reversed the earlier trend, writes Shankar Goyal, as there are produced voluminous works on the Guptas. Simultaneously, it also witnessed the emergence of some new trends, hitherto unknown completely. Shankar Goyal attributes them to the re-interpretation of literary and epigraphical sources, as well as the new light thrown by archaeology. He appreciates the contribution of R.C. Majumder to the historiography of ancient India and the Guptas.[3] He praises him for his originality, frankness and fearlessness, and adds that his inquisitive nature and quest for unearthing more information has added to his stature among the leading scholars. It is mainly because of this fact that his imprint is found on the subsequent researches on the Guptas in particular, and ancient India, in general.

Though A.L. Basham has not written any monograph on the imperial Guptas, his brief discussion on them in his *The Wonder that was India*, and whenever he found the opportunity to speak on them in the forewords to others' works subsequently, he has made the objective assessment of their cultural achievements.[4] However, like his other Western counterparts, he also uses the term 'autocrat' for the ancient Indian kings, which to Shankar Goyal[5] has raised serious questions about his objectivity. Thus, even the most sympathetic Indologist could not shed the Western construct of 'Oriental Despotism' about India.

For Shankar Goyal, the Marxist writings on the Guptas have originated new trends in their historiography, and he appreciates the contribution of the Marxist scholars like R.S. Sharma and Romila Thapar in enriching it with new tools of analysis. What he dislikes about it is the use of theoretical Marxism and the deliberate use of only the selective negative features, but ignoring the positive ones at the same time by others. He finds that an attempt was made to determine the influence of feudal tendencies on the Gupta polity in the pre-Marxist studies of Indian feudalism.[6] Here, he is seen to be endorsing the feudal-federal construct of the Gupta polity, as suggested by SRG.

D.D. Kosambi, the father of ancient Indian Marxist studies, argues that Indian nationalism has revived the Guptas. He finds the origins of Indian feudalism from the Guptas, and for this, he has formulated the two-stage theory, i.e., "feudalism from the above", and "feudalism from the below", and adds further that the *Gītā* provided for it the ideological background.[7] Shankar Goyal comments that the first stage of feudalism corresponds to the traditional view of feudalism as a system of government, more or less.[8] Interestingly, R.S. Sharma, another great Marxist historian accepts only the one-stage theory of the origins of feudalism.

Shankar Goyal notices two strikingly different points in R.S. Sharma's assessment of the Guptas. Thus, on the one hand, he espouses the theories of feudalism and the process of the urban decline from them, he also notices some progress.[9] To quote Shankar Goyal,

> He (R.S. Sharma) gives the impression of not being dogmatic anywhere. Though he is quite critical of the social inequalities and condition of women,

> but he also notes the spheres where their condition seems to have improved. He points out to the decline of trade but appreciates the Gupta achievements in the realm of arts and literature.[10]

However, Sharma's constructs are used generally for various curbs on peasants' movement, slavery, languishing trade, and urban decay, and his ideas on some socio-economic progress have become non-existent in the process, since they cover a comparatively very small space in his works.

RomilaThapar, another leading Marxist historian, is renowned for her brilliance and accurate interpretation of sources she selects for her studies. Shankar Goyal finds her quite reasonable and objective in her analysis of the Guptas.[11] He not only appreciates her but uses her definition of the term 'classical' in his works also. She argues that the textile trade brought richness, and the material culture shows that the degree of comfort was not restricted to the upper classes only.[12] Here, she does not seem to share fully the perception of R.S. Sharma regarding the beginning of urban decay from the Guptas.[13] She does not miss the opportunity of revisiting her previous works, if she wants to insert some fresh ideas into them. This she does for the Mauryas, and the Guptas, and for the latter she gives the title 'Threshold Times : c. AD 300-700' in her revised book.[14] It must be maintained that she has unfolded the correct picture of early India by not indulging in any polemics.

Shankar Goyal's historiographical study of S.R. Goyal's *A History of the Imperial Guptas* (1967) is thorough and analytical. He calls it a "watershed" in the Gupta historiography, "for it suggested new solutions to most major problems of Gupta history forcing the scholars to either accept them or reject them with the result that the outline of Gupta history as was generally accepted till 1967 gradually became modified usually on the lines suggested by S.R. Goyal."[15] SRG surveys the approaches of earlier historians of the Gupta history and suggests that there is a necessity of studying the political history against the background of various factors operating in society.[16] Thus, the political history should not be studied in isolation of other disciplines, as this is the only way to both develop interest in it and save it. It will also help in the growth and better understanding of other disciplines.

It is interesting that SRG does not reject all the identifications and suggestions made by others earlier. But if he accepts some, he works hard to find out still more convincing arguments in its defence. This gives freshness to his views. Thus, he accepts V.S. Pathak's interpretation of the term *Lichchhavi–dauhitra*, and P.L. Gupta's suggestion of the initiation of the Gupta era by Chandragupta II.[17] SRG's identification of the original home of the Guptas in eastern U.P. (Allahabad) has received a wider acceptance. His studies of Samudragupta, Rāmagupta, the Śaka war of Chandragupta II, identification of king Chandra of the Meharauli iron pillar inscription and the role of religious ideology in Guptas' decline — all have created interest in the Gupta political history. He believes in the study of not only "what and when happened" but also "why and how did it happen",[18] since this provides wider opportunities to do justice with the scientific writing of history.

While SRG recognises the important role played by "economic factor in shaping the course of history, he keeps himself free from the dogmatism characterising the writings of some Marxist historians."[19]

SRG lays emphasis on the influence of the pacifist Buddhist ideology as a vital factor for the Guptas' decline, which to Lorenzen, the Mexican Indologist, is somewhat "overdrawn", as the epigraphical sources are quite limited about it. But Shankar Goyal finds some element of truth in SRG's theory, and maintains that the large permanent donations to the huge Buddhist monasteries, such as Nālandā, must have caused financial drain to the Gupta finances.[20] He also writes on the contribution of Vaishṇavism in making the early Guptas exceptionally strong rulers. Simultaneously, Shankar Goyal also expresses disagreement with SRG partially. To quote him,

> Goyal's (SRG) firm location of the beginnings of this process in the early Gupta age is convincing, but to insist on the preponderant role of Buddhist institutions in this process, as Goyal (SRG) tends to do, seems less justified.[21]

Shankar Goyal comments that SRG's new approach to the Guptas and its results have created "a stir in the world of scholarship", and as a consequence, it has received a wider appreciation at the hands of such eminent historians, as A.L. Basham, R.C. Majumdar, David N. Lorenzen, and many others. While Basham calls it as "the best analysis of Gupta history", Majumdar opines that his "claims are based on reasonable grounds", and Lorenzen calls him as "one of the five great historians of early India."[22] Again, many others "hurried either to refute Goyal's conclusions or modify their own in the light of his suggestions, some choosing the easy expedient of not taking note of them. But younger writers have often been deeply impressed and are sometimes carried away. Naturally, "all the solutions... of Gupta history have not been accepted by all, but his basic approach and ideal of historiography do remain unchallenged."[23] Here, Shankar Goyal seems to concede the mixed response of scholars to SRG's conclusions.

SHANKAR GOYAL ON THE HISTORIOGRAPHY OF GUPTA NUMISMATICS

Shankar Goyal is a serious scholar of ancient Indian numismatics also. Apart from writing several papers on the numismatic problems of ancient Indian history, he also published a monograph on its historiography in 1998, and the numismatography of the Gupta empire is included in its chapter VIII.[24] It is a comprehensive and analytical work which critically analyses the works of almost all the numismatists of early India. He traces out the origins of Gupta numismatic studies much before the Gupta inscriptions. He refers to the *Catalogue of the Coins of Ancient India in the Indian Museum, Calcutta*, Vol. I: *The Early Foreign Dynasties and the Guptas* (1906) of V.A. Smith, and the *Catalogue of the Coins of the Gupta Dynasties and of Śaśāṅka, King of Gauḍa* by John Allan (1914). However, since a large number of hoards of Gupta coins came to light subsequently, much headway could not be made.

However, the researches of A.S. Altekar mark the actual beginning of the studies of Gupta numismatics.[25] His *Catalogue* "is a colossus which brought uptodate the material that had cropped up since the publication of Allan's *Catalogue*."[26] Altekar has brought to light a number of types and varieties of coins that continued to remain unknown for a long period. Shankar Goyal focuses on his new reading of King-and-Queen type of coins, which to Altekar were issued jointly. Altekar's tendency of changing his opinion from time to time helped him to incorporate the latest discoveries in his researches. Says Shankar Goyal,

> He always keeps an open mind and is prepared to change his opinion when adequate evidence is put forward.[27]

Shankar Goyal makes a good analysis of the works of P.L. Gupta,[28] a distinguished numismatist. He worked on the coins of Kācha, whom he identified rightly with Bhasma of the *Āryamañjuśrīmūlakalpa* and he also noticed that Purugupta did not issue any coins. He is stated to have taken the study of numismatics further.

Jai Parkash Singh's work, *History and Coinage of Skandagupta Kramāditya* (1976),[29] covers the times of Kumāragupta I and Skandagupta. Shankar Goyal sums up Singh's main arguments on SRG's hypothesis of Kumāragupta I's conquest of south India, thus,

1. The discovery of the Tiger-slayer type coins of Kumāragupta I from the south is not indicative of his conquest beyond the Narmadā. Further, they were not active in circulation there hence they must have gone there with the merchants. But Shankar Goyal considers the suggestion as conjectural and fanciful.
2. Singh refutes SRG's suggestion that the Aśvamedha type of coins of Kumāragupta I were perhaps issued after the completion of successful south Indian campaign. To Singh, it cannot be indicative of such adventure, since it was not necessarily performed after the successful completion of a campaign in ancient India.[30]

It must be maintained here that though Shankar Goyal has dismissed the comments lightly by calling them as fanciful, they seem to be worthy of fresh consideration.

SRG demonstrates his profound knowledge to study the various problems of Gupta numismatics.[31] To Shankar Goyal, he analysed for the first time the methods and techniques of studying various types of data, including numismatic evidence, for the reconstruction of Gupta history. While dealing with numismatic data of the period SRG takes note of the work done by early numismatists, nature of numismatic evidence and internal and external aspects of numismatic evidence. He opines that the find-spots of a few coins, or even of a hoard, is by itself not always a reliable evidence on which to base conclusions regarding the location of the kingdom of the issuer. "But when coins of a particular class turn up year after year at an ancient site more certain conclusions can be drawn." Similarly, when an area yields hoard after hoard, containing the coins of early rulers, that area may be regarded as the early centre of the activities of that royal family. Unfortunately, Shankar Goyal points out, "earlier numismatists, and even a large number of recent historians, have paid sufficient attention neither to the composition nor to the provenance of the hoards of the Gupta gold coins and have not applied the age and area concept to the study of Gupta numismatics while a proper application of this principle is likely to yield very significant results."[32]

On many a numismatic problems SRG sheds new light and suggests new solutions. For example, on the attribution of Chandragupta-Kumāradevī coin-type SRG has argued that these coins were issued either by Chandragupta I or by Samudragupta before he issued the Standard type coins. According to him, the latter alternative seems to be the correct one. On Śrī Vikrama coin of Samudragupta SRG has criticised the generally accepted opinion that the solitary coin giving the *biruda 'Śrīvikrama'* to Samudragupta found in the Bamnala hoard was issued during the reign of Chandragupta II, when the obverse die of the Standard type coins of Samudragupta was inadvertently used with the reverse die of the Archer type of Chandragupta II. It is argued that as no Gupta king used two titles, it cannot be assumed that Samudragupta adopted both the titles *Parākrama* and *Vikrama.* However, SRG has pointed out that Skandagupta assumed the titles *Kramāditya* and *Vikramāditya* both. Further, according to him, mertrology and other numismatic considerations are in favour of regarding this coin as the issue of Samudragupta. Another theory of SRG, which is worth-noting here, is concerned with the coins of Prakāśāditya. In this he has given arguments to prove that Prakāśāditya ruled just after Bhānugupta (known date 510 A.D.). For this he has taken the help of the *Āryamañju-śrīmūlakalpa* which refers to 'Pra' initialled, that is Prakāśāditya as the rebellious son of 'Bha' initialled, that is Bhānugupta.

B.N. Mukherjee has made a tangible contribution to the studies of ancient Indian coins.[33] His book *Coins and Currency System in Gupta Bengal* (1992) gives many a good suggestion about the monetary system in ancient

Bengal. The discovery of a few coins of Samudragupta and Chandragupta II in a hoard during the excavations at Mainamati (Comilla district of Bengal) in a layer of eighth century A.D. perhaps indicates the prevalence of gold coins of the imperial Guptas there even centuries after their rule.

Shankar Goyal argues that Mukherjee's 'Commentary'[34] on H.C. Raychaudhuri's work titled *Political History of Ancient India* (edition 1997) has "not much to commend itself ", as he has not incorporated all the new discoveries and others' viewpoints in it. Secondly, he is unable to show the change from chronological reconstructions to socio-economic concerns in the study of Gupta dynasty.[35] Here, Shankar Goyal's observations are terse and objective.

The inclusion of the work of Ellen M. Raven's *Gupta Gold Coins with a Garuḍa-Banner* (1994)[36] in his chapter by Shankar Goyal shows his sincerity to take notice of the progress made in numismatic researches abroad. He appreciates Raven for her research on hitherto ignored subject and describes it as "a masterpiece of numismatic research," "monumental," and "stupendous". According to Shankar Goyal, "It is only such researches that can give a new direction to numismatic studies."[37] The work of Raven, which is in two volumes and covers cxxvii+490 pages and contains 113 tables, 59 plates, 2 maps and 139 line-drawings in 29 sheets, dwells upon only five gold coin types of the Guptas, for it is only on them that the Garuḍa-banner is depicted. Even the coins of Kācha and Ghaṭotkachagupta which bear Garuḍa-banner have not been included in her study as she could not examine them personally. Ellen M. Raven has identified 14 basic images of Garuḍa and some 150 actual representations. She has also tried to find a pattern behind this variety and trace its chronological evolution. Though she is mainly concerned with gold coin types of the Guptas with Garuḍa-banner, she has also taken into consideration silver, copper and lead coins, including those of other dynasties on which this device occurs. However, since her work is in two volumes, it needed a much more detailed analysis from Shankar Goyal.

Besides the above mentioned works, Shankar Goyal also discusses a few miscellaneous ones, which I skip due to the space constraints.

On the whole, Shankar Goyal has displayed his complete but critical study of the Gupta coins along with their types and varieties. There is a clarity, and hence all numismatists are provided a sufficient space, as far as possible.

SHANKAR GOYAL ON THE POLITICAL IDEOLOGY OF THE EARLY IMPERIAL GUPTAS

Shankar Goyal has not written much on religion, but whatsoever he has written shows his firm grip in interpreting various ticklish religious issues of the Gupta history. In his paper, entitled 'Political Ideology of the Early Imperial Guptas',[38] he makes a serious attempt to prove that war was a recognized institution in ancient India, and the conception of *Chakravartī* was popularised and was given the Vaishṇava orientation in the Gupta period. His presentation focuses on the following issues: (i) It is evident from the ancient thinkers, such as Kauṭilya and Manu, that the war was a recognized institution in ancient India. (ii) Indian theory of imperialism finds its origins as early as the Vedic period. It made popular the conception of *Chakravartī* ideal later. (iii) The Gupta kings linked *Aśvamedha* sacrifice with the Vedic ritual, thereby making it an integral part of Vaishṇavism. (iv) The Vaishṇavite interpretation of *Chakravartī* ideal is almost conclusively established by the unique *Chakravikrama* type of coin of Chandragupta II. Further, it is now unanimously believed that the *Chakra* represents the *Chakrapurusha* (or Vishṇu).[39] (v) This ideology of Samudragupta becomes more explicit from the analysis of the epithets used for him in lines 24 and 25 of the Prayāga *praśasti*. Shankar Goyal adds that he not only claimed *Chakravartī* status by virtue of being a performer of *chirotsanna* (elaborate) Aśvamedha as the Vedic Chakravartīs did, but also claimed this status by projecting himself as "the veriest *Apratiratha* (Vishṇu) moving on the earth".[40] (vi) He develops from the description of Hsuan-tsang, the Chinese pilgrim, about Narasiṁhagupta Bālāditya, the later Gupta king, that perhaps Buddhism had made him weak and timid.[41]

Thus, whereas Vaishṇavism made the early Gupta kings valiant fighters, the later Gupta kings became weak because of their faith in Buddhism. Shankar Goyal develops the ideological differences between the early and later Gupta kings as clearly as possible. But the use of certain explanations in support of early Gupta Vaishṇava leanings do not appear to be wholly convincing. Firstly, the use of words "conclusive" or "unanimous" for the Vaishṇava acceptance of the *Chakravikrama* type coin of Chandragupta II looks somewhat exaggerated, since it remains debatable. Secondly, the importance of Aśvamedha sacrifice is over-assessed, as even in the preceding period doubts were cast over its actual significance.[42] Thirdly, most of Indian ruling dynasties have not produced more than four or five brave kings. Thus, the onus of the entire responsibility of decline on Buddhism is perhaps not logical. Fourthly, and the last, perhaps the Gupta kings claimed the functional equality with gods, but not otherwise.

However, Shankar Goyal has not only quoted the diverse sources for this study, he has collated and interpreted them in their true historical perspective. This paper alone is an index to his dispassionate study and understanding of early Indian religions.

SHANKAR GOYAL ON THE EMERGENCE OF 'MEDIEVAL' FACTOR IN INDIAN ART

One of the significant contributions of Shankar Goyal to the Indological studies is concerned with the art of classical age.[43] In this meticulously researched piece he has shown how in the early post-Gupta centuries the classicism of the Gupta age gradually declined and medieval factor became more and more pronounced in Indian art. Thus, according to Shankar Goyal, the story of the art of the Gupta age which begins with the emergence of classicism and the transformation of the Kushāṇa art into Gupta art comes to a close with the decline of classicism and the emergence of medieval factor in Indian art. Shankar Goyal has divided his chapter into three parts : 1. the nature of Gupta classicism, 2. factors in the transition from classicism to medievalism, and 3. the emergence of medieval trends in Indian art. As is well-known, the art of the Gupta period is generally referred to as the 'classical art' of India and the Gupta age is called the classical or golden age of Indian history. The term 'classical' usually means "an age in which literature, architecture and fine arts reach a high level of excellence to form a standard or model for later times." The Gupta art is 'classical' because of its intrinsic quality of high order, which was shared throughout the country but was never parallelled earlier or later, and which, serving as a veritable index, helps us appreciate the nature of achievements accruing to anterior or posterior artistic practices in the country. Kālidāsa, the greatest poet-dramatist of the age, describes the art of the period as 'fine art'. Apart from acute passion for refinement the Gupta art, specially sculpture, was characterized by several features. In the Gupta sculpture the human figure is used as the vehicle for the transmutation of Nature into art. It is a synthesis between the external form and the inner meaning, like the Kālidāsian imagery of the union of Speech and Thought. Another feature of the Gupta classical art is its wide geographical range. It not only filled the entire country from one end to the other, but also inundated the surrounding regions in a peripheral overflow. Specially, wheresoever the Bhāgavata religion spread its benign influence backed by an impassioned literary appeal, art monuments sprang up in its train as visible reflectors of the popular surcharge. Moreover, the elements of regional moods were integrated in the Gupta art in such a way that the product did seldom lose its homogeneity.[44]

The transformation of the classical heritage into medieval culture did not take place all at once. Says Shankar Goyal,

> It was brought about slowly in the course of several centuries intervening the decline of the Gupta empire and the establishment of the Delhi Sultanate. But the period of about two centuries, roughly from the fall of the Gupta empire (550 A.D.) to the rise of the Pratihāras (c. 750 A.D.), sheds light on the classical and medieval periods both by a sort of *dehalīdīpaka-nyāya* (the maxim that a lamp placed on the threshold illumines both the inside and outside of a room) and thus belongs to both.[45]

Following N.R. Ray and R.S. Sharma, Shankar Goyal[46] has shown that in Europe one of the main factors that led to the transition from classical to middle ages was the immigration and invasions of the barbarian nomads. As in Europe, the pressure of the foreign tribes not only shattered the imperial fabric of India, it also corrupted her classical values, modified her social and economic institutions and generated a sense of pessimism leading to the theory of social decline in the Kali Age which the post-Gupta literature and epigraphs so vividly describe. Other main factors that played a significant role in the transformation of the classical society in Europe as well as India were feudalism and regionalism which increased localism and insularity in economic life.[47] The formation of regional cultural units such as Andhra, Assam, Bengal, Gujarat, Karnataka, Kerala, Maharashtra, Orissa, Rajasthan, Tamilnadu, etc., and the emergence of regional languages and literatures started from sixth-seventh centuries. In the seventh century Yuan Chwang mentions several nationalities. The *Mudrārākshasa* of Viśākhadatta speaks of different regions whose inhabitants differed in customs, clothing and language while the *Kuvalayamālā* (eighth century) notes the existence of 18 major nationalities and describes the anthropological character of 16 peoples, pointing out their psychological features and citing the samples of their languages. Shankar Goyal is of the view that the post-classical Indian society was also greatly disturbed by the new religious thought-currents.[48] "The Paurāṇika Hinduism was divided into a number of cults and sects. Among them were included Śaivism, Vaishṇavism and Śāktism, not to mention a large number of minor sects and sub-sects. ...The popular or conventional form of the Hindu sects was characterized by the worship of numerous deities in temples. They were endowed with grants of land, tolls and taxes. Temple- and monastery-building activities, which acquired momentum in the later Gupta age, reached their climax during the eleventh and twelfth centuries. Great temples and monasteries of this period possessed large estates and enormous wealth, with the result that the priestly class, as in medieval Europe, acquired a powerful hold over the people."[49]

Shankar Goyal argues that the disintegration of the Gupta empire and the rise of feudalism, impact of foreign invaders, regionalism, insularity, growth of Smārta-Paurāṇika religion and Tāntrika tendencies were concomitant with and brought about a change of scene in the sphere of art as well.[50] The rise of feudalism, he asserts,[51] influenced the post-Gupta art in several ways. The ancient religious art at Bharhut, Sāñchī, Karle, Kanheri, Junnar, Amarāvatī, Nāgārjunīkoṇḍa, etc., was patronized mainly by the mercantile and commercial classes, artisan and craft guilds as well as the royal families. "But the art of the period from c. 550 A.D. onwards was supported mainly by the kings of different principalities, feudatories, military chiefs, etc., who alone usually could own and donate land to religious institutions."[52] In the fourth-fifth centuries Vātsyāyana made *nāgarakas* (and not *sāmantas*) the centre of his *Kāmasūtra*. But in the sixth-seventh centuries "the arts patronized by the rich (both the old commercial class and the new feudal lords) reflect aristocratic tastes in their embellishment and in the dignified countenance and elaborate coiffures of both male and female figures. The aristocratic lovers of Badami, Ajanta, Ellora, Deograh, Nachna, etc., indulging in *madhupāna* (drinking of wine) or enjoying music and dance, attended by women with *chauris* or wine-jars, certainly betray the feudal outlook of the age."[53] Further, "the Rajput chiefs of the post-Gupta period, many of whom were Hinduized foreigners or Hinduized tribals, strove hard to glorify themselves. The epigraphic evidence supports the fact that the kings of the leading dynasties from the sixth century onwards performed ceremonial *dānas* such as *hiraṇyagarbha*, *shoḍasha mahādāna*, *saptasāgara mahādāna*, *dharitrīdāna* and even *brahmāṇḍadāna*. The wealth and power bestowed by them made the priests of the period greedy and fond of luxury. This psychology was in perfect consonance with and to a great degree the cause of craze for the sensual indulgence which dominated the literature and art of the period."[54] Furthermore, "the Smārta-Paurāṇika religion of the post-Gupta age was influenced by the magical elements such as *maṇḍalas*, *yantras*, *nyāsas* and *mantras* which soon became widespread. In the fifth-seventh centuries many Brāhmaṇas received lands in Nepal, Assam, Bengal, Orissa, Central India and the Deccan, where Tāntrika texts, shrines and practices appeared about this time. Tāntrikism permeated every sect and religion—Jainism, Buddhism, Śaivism and Vaishṇavism, and from the seventh century onwards continued to hold ground throughout the medieval period."[55]

On the whole, according to Shankar Goyal, for about a thousand years, roughly from about the third century B.C. to the end of sixth century A.D., Indian art admits, despite local variations due to local tastes, to a common denominator at each different stage of its evolution. But now regional spirit began to assert itself.[56] No longer satisfied with the flat-roofed shrines of the Gupta period, new fashions in architecture concerned themselves with the development of the *śikharas* and *maṇḍapas*, and bold architects began to convert the entire mountain blocks into monolithic shrines resembling Kailāsa and Meru. In the realm of sculpture and painting also the post-Gupta centuries witnessed the emergence of a distinct 'medieval' trend with many regional variations. Plasticity of the fully rounded and modelled form had been the most significant characteristic of classical Indian sculpture and painting both. But now movement started towards summarizing the rounded volume in the direction of flat surface and linear angles. Being essentially three dimensional, sculpture resisted for long the intrusion of this medieval trend while painting, which is essentially two dimensional, offered much less resistance. During the early medieval period art movements in the different regions also tended to separate from one another. Concludes Shankar Goyal,

The art scene was gradually seized upon, as if by 'a sort of bankruptcy in

> creativity'. The art expressions tended to become more and more merely gestures without conviction, performance without feeling. Sculptural expressions tended towards non-communicability denuding the sculpture of all the qualities of excellence of the earlier periods : it lost much of the aesthetic charm and became highly mechanized. It was no longer illuminated by the spiritual experience of the sculpture and ceased to be intelligible to the people at large. ...There arose a different approach towards art which is what is referred to as the 'medieval factor' or 'medievalism' in Indian art.[57]

SHANKAR GOYAL ON THE IDEA OF 'CLASSICISM' OF THE GUPTA AGE

Shankar Goyal has written extensively on the nature of 'classicism' of the Gupta age.[58] Explaining the term 'classical', he writes,

> The term 'classical' is derived from the Latin epithet *Classicus*, found in a passage of Anlus Gellius, where a *Scriptor Classicus* is contrasted with a *Scriptor Proletarions*. The metaphor is taken from the division of Roman people into three classes by Servius Tivellius who calls Roman of the first class *Classici*, of the second *Classem* and the last *Proletarii*. Accordingly the epithet 'Classic' is generally applied to an author of the first rank, and more particularly to a Greek or Roman author of that character. Thus the term 'Classic' is a synonym for the choicest products of the literature of ancient Greece and Rome. The high esteem in which Greek and Latin were held at the revival of letters obtained for these authors the name of 'Classics', and when other first rate works are intended, some distinctive name is added, as the English Classics, Spanish Classics or French Classics. The term 'classical', therefore, refers to the literary and other production of the first rate order.[59]

In the European context, Shankar Goyal further writes, "the classical tradition chiefly meant the cultural heritage of Greece and Rome and the Roman concept of Universal Empire and its legacy of law and jurisprudence. This legacy was greatly transformed in the medieval period under the impact of various factors and forces chief of them being the immigration and invasions of the barbarians, growth in the dominance of the Christian Church, feudalism, etc."[60] According to Shankar Goyal, "In India the situation was *mutatis mutandis* the same. Here usually the age of the imperial Guptas is equated with the 'classical age' of India, also called 'golden' because of its great achievements. Its achievements in literature, arts and sciences correspond to the achievements of the Greeks and Romans in these spheres, its concept of the *Chakravartīkshetra* is comparable with the concept of the Universal Empire, the title 'Caesar' adopted by the Roman emperors reminds one of the title 'Vikramāditya' usually adopted by the Gupta emperors and subsequent rulers, the growth of the Smṛti Law corresponds to the development of Roman law and jurisprudence, and so on. Even the factors in the decline of classicism in

India were similar to those of Europe."[61] However he is of the view that

> there is no unanimity about the upper and lower limits of the Indian classical age. Its upper limit is sometimes extended to 750 A.D. and the lower one is so stretched by some as to include the Kushāṇa and sometimes even the Maurya age in it. It is not surprising since in Europe also historians and chroniclers have been using the term 'ancient' as almost synonymous with the age of the Classical or Graeco-Roman civilization. It may, therefore, be reasonably conceded that in India also the age of the imperial Guptas marked the efflorenscence and culmination of earlier tendencies, many of which go back to the Maurya period and that some of its glory continued for about two centuries after the fall of the Gupta empire. However, the age of the mighty Gupta emperors was the focal point of this long period.[62]

Romila Thapar expresses a similar opinion in a recent study through her statement that "the classicism of the Gupta period is not an innovation emanating from Gupta rule but the culmination of a process that began earlier."[63] It is in this sense, argues Shankar Goyal, that this issue should be tackled.

CONCLUSION

To conclude, the range of Shankar Goyal's work on the imperial Guptas is too large and diverse to be assessed in a few pages here. Though he has written on many diverse areas of ancient India, his favourite and preferred area continues to be historiography. Before him, this discipline was virtually in its infancy, and only R.S. Sharma, RomilaThapar, D.N. Jha and V.K. Thakur had contributed marginally. But Shankar Goyal has enriched this virtually left out area by contributing many significant works on ancient Indian historiography. His work on the religious ideology of the imperial Guptas, art and culture is original and immense. His grip on the sources is very strong, and he believes that if all the sources are collated properly, the outcome may automatically be satisfactory.

REFERENCES

1. Some of Shankar Goyal's writings on Gupta history, including his edited and other monographs which also deal with some aspects of Gupta history and historiography, include the following: *The Image of Classical India: Its Changing Colours and Contours*, Jodhpur, 1997; *Aspects of Ancient Indian History and Historiography*, New Delhi, 1993; *Recent Historiography of Ancient India*, Jodhpur, 1997; *Ancient Indian Numismatics: A Historiographical Study*, Jodhpur, 1998; *Marxist Interpretation of Ancient Indian History*, Poona, 2000; *Problems of Ancient Indian History*, Jaipur, 2001; *Contemporary Interpreters of Ancient India*, Jaipur, 2003; *Ancient India: A Multidisciplinary Approach*, Jodhpur, 2006; *175 Years of Vākāṭaka History and Historiography*, Jodhpur, 2009; *King Chandra and the Meharauli Pillar* (ed.), Meerut, 1989; *Reappraising Gupta History for S.R. Goyal* (ed.), New Delhi, 1992; *Indian Art*

of the Gupta Age : From Pre-Classical Roots to the Emergence of Medieval Trends (ed.), Jodhpur, 2000; *Reconstructing Indian History for S.R. Goyal*, Vol. I : *Professor S.R. Goyal: The Profile of a Historian* (ed.), Jaipur, 2003; *Early India : Historical Probings* (ed.), Jodhpur, 2015. Besides this, Shankar Goyal has contributed numerous papers on the classical age in general, and the imperial Guptas in particular.

2. S.R. Goyal, Allahabad, 1967.

3. R.C. Majumdar's edited works include : *The Vākāṭaka-Gupta Age*, Lahore, 1946; *The Classical Age*, Bombay, 1954; *A Comprehensive History of India*, Vol. III, Pt. i, New Delhi, 1981.

4. Cf. A.L. Basham, *The Wonder that was India*, London, 1954; *The Cultural History of India* (ed.), London, 1975; his Foreword to *Economic Life in Northern India in the Gupta Period* of S.K.Maity, Calcutta, 1958; his Foreword to *The Imperial Guptas*, Vol. I, of P.L. Gupta, Varanasi, 1974; his Introduction to *Essays on Gupta Culture*, ed. Bardwell L. Smith, Delhi, 1983.

5. Shankar Goyal, *Recent Historiography of Ancient India*, p. 327.

6. Shankar Goyal, *The Image of Classical India*, p. 94.

7. *Ibid.*, p. 95; also see D.D. Kosambi, *An Introduction to the Study of Indian History*, Bombay, 1956; idem, *The Culture and Civilization of Ancient India in Historical Outline*, London, 1965.

8. *Ibid.*

9. R.S. Sharma, *Ancient India*, New Delhi, 1999, p. 162.

10. Shankar Goyal, *The Image of Classical India*, p. 97.

11. Romila Thapar, *A History of India*, Vol. I, Harmondsworth, 1966, pp. 136-66; also in A.L. Basham's *A Cultural History of India*, ed., pp. 38-50.

12. *Ibid.*, pp. 150-51.

13. Shankar Goyal, *The Image of Classical India*, p. 98.

14. Romila Thapar, *The Penguin History of Early India*, pp. 280-325.

15. Shankar Goyal, *Recent Historiography of Ancient India*, p. 262.

16. *Ibid.*, p. 263.

17. *Ibid.*, p. 264.

18. *Ibid.*, p. 268.

19. *Ibid.*

20. *Ibid.*, p. 271.

21. *Ibid.*, p. 272.

22. *Ibid.*, pp. 272-73.

23. *Ibid.*, p. 273.

24. Shankar Goyal, *Ancient Indian Numismatics*, pp. 152-75.

25. A.S. Altekar, *The Catalogue of the Gupta Gold Coins in the Bayana Hoard*, Bombay, 1954; idem, *Guptakālīna Mudrāyeṅ*, Patna, 1954; idem, *Coinage of the Gupta Empire and Its Imitations*, Patna, 1957.

26. Shankar Goyal, *Ancient Indian Numismatics*, p. 155.

27. *Ibid.*, p. 159.

28. P.L. Gupta, *Gupta Sāmrājya*, Varanasi, 1970; idem, *The Imperial Guptas*, Vol. I, Varanasi, 1974.

29. Varanasi, 1976.

30. *Ibid.*, pp. 7-8.
31. S.R. Goyal, *An Introduction to Gupta Numismatics*, Jodhpur, 1994, pp. 1-40.
32. Shankar Goyal, *Ancient Indian Numismatics*, p. 164.
33. B.N. Mukherjee, *Coins and Currency System in Gupta Bengal*, New Delhi, 1992.
34. B.N.Mukherjee's 'Commentary' on H.C. Raychaudhuri's *Political History of Ancient India*, New Delhi, 1997. It is in 30 pages (pp. 764-94), but it overlooks many aspects of Gupta history, argues Shankar Goyal.
35. Shankar Goyal, *Ancient Indian Numismatics*, pp. 168-70.
36. Groningen, 1994, quoted from Shankar Goyal.
37. Shankar Goyal, *Ancient Indian Numismatics*, pp. 170-72.
38. Shankar Goyal, edited with B.Ch. Chhabra, P.K. Agrawala and Ashvini Agrawal, *Reappraising Gupta History for S.R. Goyal*, New Delhi, 1992, pp. 215-23.
39. *Ibid.*, p. 220.
40. *Ibid.*, p. 223.
41. *Ibid.*, p. 215. Shankar Goyal quotes from Samuel Beal's, *Si-Yü-Ki* or *Buddhist Records of the Western World*, Vol. I, Delhi, 1969, pp. 168-69; cf. also S.R. Goyal, *A History of the Imperial Guptas*, p. 354.
42. The claim of the Bhāraśiva Nāgas to have become a dominant power after the Kushāṇas because they are stated to have performed no less than 10 Aśvameda sacrifices is dismissed on the ground that it could be performed without any actual conquest.
43. Shankar Goyal, 'Transition from Gupta Classicism to Medievalism in Indian Art', his ch. in *Indian Art of the Gupta Age*, eds. S.R. Goyal and Shankar Goyal, Jodhpur, 2000, pp. 208-21; also see, his *Harsha : A Multidisciplinary Political Study*, Jodhpur, 2006, pp. 238-68; idem, *The 'Medieval' Factor and the Age of Harsha: A Cultural Study*, Jodhpur, 2016, pp. 130-43.
44. For a detailed discussion on the nature of Gupta classicism in Indian art, cf. *Indian Art of the Gupta Age*, pp. 208-11.
45. *Ibid.*, p. 214.
46. *Ibid.*; N.R. Ray, 'The 'Medieval' Factor in Indian History', being his Address as the General President of the Twenty-ninth Session of the Indian History Congress, Patiala, 1967, pp. 1-42; R. S. Sharma, 'Problem of Transition from Ancient to Medieval in Indian History', in *Indian Historical Review*, March 1974, Vol. I, No. 1, pp.1-9; idem, *Perspectives in Social and Economic History of Early India*, New Delhi, 1983, Ch. XVI; idem, *Early Medieval Indian Society: A Study in Feudalisation*, Kolkata, 2001, Ch.1; Devangana Desai, 'Art Under Feudalism in India (c. 500-1300 A.D.)', in *Indian Historical Review*, March 1974, Vol. I, No. 1, pp. 10-17; also see, V. K. Thakur, 'Transition from the Ancient to the Medieval Period', in *Problems of Indian Historiography*, ed. D. Devahuti, Delhi, 1979, pp. 79-82; B.N.S. Yadava, 'The Accounts of the Kali Age and the Social Transition from Antiquity to the Middle Ages', in *Feudal Social Formation in Early India*, ed. D.N. Jha, Delhi, 1987, pp. 65-112.
47. *Ibid.*, pp. 215 ff.
48. *Ibid.*, p. 216.
49. *Ibid.*, p. 217.

50. *Ibid.*
51. *Ibid.*
52. *Ibid.*, p. 218.
53. *Ibid.*
54. *Ibid.*
55. *Ibid.*, p. 219.
56. *Ibid.*, pp. 220 ff.
57. *Ibid.*, p. 221.
58. In his *Reappraising Gupta History for S.R. Goyal*, pp. 61-73; cf. also, his *Problems of Ancient Indian History*, pp. 207-26.
59. In *Reappraising Gupta History for S.R. Goyal*, p. 66.
60. *Ibid.*, pp. 66-67.
61. *Ibid.*, p. 67.
62. *Ibid.*
63. Romila Thapar, *The Penguin History of Early India*, p. 281; see, Shankar Goyal, 'An Investigation into the Feudal Nature of the Vākāṭaka Economy : A Study of the Epigraphic Evidence', his General President's Address delivered to the XXXVII Annual Congress of the Epigraphical Society of India, Baroda, published in the *Journal of the Epigraphical Society of India*, Vol. XXXVIII, 2012, pp. 9-10.

Chapter Six

Situating Harsha in the History of Early India by Shankar Goyal

MAHESH VIKRAM SINGH
Professor of History
Kashi Vidyapith, Varanasi

The illustrious journey of publication of researches on the history and age of Harsha by Professor Shankar Goyal starting with *History and Historiography of the Age of Harsha*, Kusumanjali Prakashan, Jodhpur, 1992, and followed by *Harsha : A Multidisciplinary Political Study*, Kusumanjali Book World, Jodhpur, 2006; *The 'Medieval' Factor and the Age of Harsha: A Cultural Study*, Kusumanjali Book World, Jodhpur, 2016; and *Harsha Revisited: A Re-interpretation of Existing Data*, D.K. Publishers Distributors Pvt. Ltd., Delhi, 2018, has now reached to his monograph on the critical study of the life, travels and records of Yuan Chawng with the title *The Significance of Yuan Chwang in the Context of the Seventh Century: A Critical Assessment*, D.K. Publishers Distributors Pvt. Ltd., Delhi, 2018. No wonder if Shankar Goyal has even more in store about Harsha for the world of history but it is now beyond doubt that no researcher on the history of Harsha has taken so much of pain in enlightening us on the subject in such a detail covering almost all the dimensions of the age of Harsha and the sources thereupon that Shankar Goyal has taken to dig out every bit of it so far. Definitely, his researches on the history of Harsha and his age also incorporate his D.Litt. dissertation,but it is all about his ever growing appetite for unlocking the doors of knowledge about this personality and his period which brought out such masterpieces of research on it.

Here we see a historian taking pains in retracing the serious and genuine scholarship of our celebrated historians which are now more and more difficult to find. Shankar Goyal, a worthy son of S.R.Goyal, a worthy father, has been bold enough to probe into many unanswered or unclarified questions of the age of Harsha, right from debating the authenticity and relevance of the sources, both major and minor, and the data stored therein besides situating the whole history of Harsha in the trends and practices of his times. He even goes on to bring to notice some brand new or untapped epigraphic and numismatic records for the matter. Another noteworthy feature of his researches is his boldness in coming out with more logical interpretations and inferences which may sometime appear in the form of hypothesis or may be based on his imaginations in the absence of any concrete data thereabout agreeable or not-agreeable to some, but are worthwhile in connecting the threads of history much away from sheer political gossips.

In the age when political history was losing attention of the scholars for lack of fresh direct sources of information about a king or dynasty or political events, to say battles and wars, administrative framework etc., particularly about the ancient world, and as Shankar Goyal has rightly pointed out that the most damaging criticism levelled against the current form of political history in the West is that it is elitist in content, that it lays too much emphasis on kings and heroes, and that it pays too much attention to political events, military conquests and chronology, he himself dared to dwell on the political history of the Harsha and his times is in itself a challenge he gave to other scholars. Shankar Goyal is quite clear in his thought when he says that the age of 'innocent' writing of political history is over and a new era of 'critical self-consciousness' has begun. And he rightfully stands to this cause by matching his approach with the new demands of understanding political history in the backdrop of whole social, economic, demographic and anthropological settings of the times related as well as to the geo-political concerns of a political development and its impact. This challenge Shankar Goyal had taken as early in 2006 by coming out with his scientific piece of history titled *Harsha : A Multidisciplinary Political Study*. In my own opinion thus the political developments or chronology may even be put under a larger scan of whole civilizational and cultural trends with regard to relations between dominant/leading forces and subservient elements/masses inter-alia leading to the rise or decline and fall of a particular civilization in different eras of history. This very approach I myself tried in my book *India Rediscovered: A New Vision of History and Call of the Age* (Northern Book Centre, New Delhi, 2006). However, Shankar Goyal has quite precisely focused his political history upon a period that of Harsha which marked a clear transition from classical to medieval tendencies in the context of Indian history, not to say that he has not at all attempted any other period of ancient Indian history, as his short but in-depth study on the Vākāṭakas particularly demands scholars' attention for being a piece of serious fruitful research too (may refer to his, *175 Years of Vākāṭaka History and Historiography*, Jodhpur, 2009).

Then comes the problem of dealing with the questions of 'how' and 'why' in the political history or any history for that sake. Since history has been generally attempted with objective of discovering just the 'what' and 'when' aspects of events or developments, this fails to enlighten us any more about the nature of progress of humanity asking for or not any corrections or lessons in our present as well as to the future! Some of our highly noted historians, beginning from D.D. Kosambi, R.S. Sharma, Romila Thapar, D.N. Jha, K.M. Shrimali and many others who followed the line of Marxist interpretation of the understanding of the growth of civilizations have definitely tried to give a frame to the understanding of our history with a view to make it more relevant for the readers, leaders and administrators. Yet it often lacked comprehension of some simultaneous drives and tendencies engaged in the formation of certain culture and its impact. Thus 'how' and 'why' questions become even more pertinent if at all one wishes to give some meaning to the study of history. S.R.Goyal, illustrious father of Shankar Goyal, did indulge in initiating some unbiased study of history dwelling upon the questions of 'how' and 'why' and came out with many of his fresh interpretations and inferences dealing with the whole ancient Indian political history comprehending almost all the available sources as well as opinions of other authorities on the subject. Shankar Goyal has rightly been drawn into the footsteps of his father with all the seriousness and acumen he has at his command. At a time when researches in history and that too in ancient Indian history have, more often than not, fallen prey to whimsical notions in our land, and presentation and reproduction of history has become a game of political and fallacious cultural vendetta, one can never be indifferent to all the energy and efforts of Shankar Goyal in producing and presenting such serious pieces of ancient history, and that too of, at the brink of transition from classical to medieval which is so relevant to understand even our present often hovered by the images and shadows of medieval India.

The attempt of Shankar Goyal to present a historiographical study in the beginning bespeaks of the genuine effort put up by him in studying the subject. This begins with his first ever research work on the subject, *History and Historiography of the Age of Harsha*, published in 1992. He does not confine himself to mere narration of the views of earlier and recent scholars in his field of study, such as V.S. Pathak, B.N. Sharma, D.

Devahuti, K.K. Thaplyal, S.R. Goyal and others, but has quite critically examined the nature and limitations of such researches to underline the necessity for further enquiry and his own interpretation of the events and sources thereof. In dealing with his subject Shankar Goyal quite scientifically goes on to discuss four phases of historiography of the age of Harsha not only in detail but in straightforward manner with his own numerous interpretations. As according to him, the first phase covering the pre-independence period and early years of independence of our nation was confined to 'what' and 'when' questions of history and to the correlation of Chinese and Indian sources. This phase was mainly represented by M.L. Ettinghousen, C.V. Vaidya, K.M. Panikkar, R.K. Mookerji, R.S. Tripathi and G.S. Chatterjee. To the second phase, he says, belong the writings of R.C.Majumdar and others who introduced a thoughtful analysis of the literary information. It is in this very spirit V.S. Pathak has been rightly referred to as suggesting a cautious approach in dealing with the biographical writings of early medieval India which were written with personal motives, interests, bias and prejudices and deserve to be adjudged against established historical data, particularly the archaeological sources. Nevertheless, the traditional trend of presenting history as a plain narrative of events accepting information on their face-value continued side by side in the works of scholars like B.N. Sharma, K.K. Thaplyal and others.

The phase of critical analysis and scientific approach commencing in 1970 was the third phase of this historiography, according to Shankar Goyal. It is found in the writings of D. Devahuti who tried to attempt 'how' and 'why' questions of history rather hesitatingly. Appreciating Devahuti's efforts in this direction Shankar Goyal points out its limitation as well, and questions her over reliance on Chinese sources. He further notices that the feudalistic aspect of Harsha's reign also goes unattended in her work. The fourth phase of the historiography of the age of Harsha is said to have begun with the writings of S.R. Goyal, who has been able to shed new light on a number of issues related to the period of Harsha besides attempting 'how' and 'why' questions of history. Shankar Goyal has given rightful regard to the works of S.R. Goyal about the date of *Harshacharita* of Bāṇa. He obviously becomes a true carrier of this phase of historiography of Harsha and his times.

Shankar Goyal has given much emphasis to the examination of sources about Harsha and his age. As we all feel, very little or nothing is going into the scientific and critical study of the sources of ancient Indian history, either indigenous or foreign, at present, which used to be a passion of many a great Indian and foreign scholars of history like Alexander Cunningham, John Marshall, James Princep, R.G. Bhandarkar, P.V. Kane,

D.D. Kosambi and many others like S.R. Goyal who followed the line once upon a time and which truly enlivened our ancient history for our generation and those to follow. Shankar Goyal is of the firm view that the accounts left by Yuan Chawng and Bāṇa's biography of Harsha, forming the bulk of data about Harsha, should be studied with critical alertness and the information found therein should be accepted only after weighing them in the whole situational context.

Undoubtedly, both of the above mentioned sources, have so comprehensively made the personality and deeds of Harsha a curious feature of the age which might not have come to light otherwise. We may in this context enlist a pertinent comment of Irfan Habib in his foreword to Shankar Goyal's volume entitled, *The 'Medieval' Factor and the Age of Harsha: A Cultural Study*, that "If we exclude Aśoka, the ruler best known to us from ancient India would undoubtedly be Harsha. True, unlike Aśoka's series of inscriptions on rocks and pillars, only three copper plate grants survive from Harsha. But then, we have two contemporary witnesses, totally independent from each orher, who have left accounts of him in writings, each of which forms a class by itself. One is Bāṇa, himself a great name in Sanskrit literature, who wrote *Harshacharita*, the first royal biography in Sanskrit; the other, the Chinese pilgrim Yuan Chawng (Xuan Zhwang), who wrote his great work, *The Records of the Western World*, whose information is supplemented by the *Life* compiled by Hui li." Nevertheless, without undermining the relevance and importance of these sources Shankar Goyal does keep in mind that while Bāṇabhaṭṭa was a court poet, if not a bard, of the Pushyabhūtis brought and bred up in the typical feudal setting of his age offering us the ever first court laurels about a king or dynasty, Yuan Chwang happened to be more obsessed with his own person and personal importance and achievements regarding Mahāyāna, the Great Vehicle, he claimed to have been acknowledged by the important political powers of northern India of his times of travel. Thus it always demand special care in handling these sources while deducing a true picture of Harsha and his times from the point of view of factual history. Though Shankar Goyal had been dealing quite critically with these sources ever from the beginning of his research in this field which has been maturing all through the past decades and he has now come out with even more clarity and details in 2018 with his new title, *Harsha Revisited: A Re-interpretation of Existing Data*.

As about the *Harshacharita* of Bāṇa, Shankar Goyal has tried to critically examine and comprehend all the dimensions of this work along with Bāṇa's own personality and background and his motive of writing such biography. Thus he goes on to deal with personal history of Bāṇa, his relationship with Harsha, date and motive of this writing, its place in

Sanskrit literature, impact of Purāṇa model of his times, its nature as an *ākhyāyikā*, and as forerunner of the biographies of kings (*charita kāvyas*), question about its completeness, Bāṇa's own view of history and question of reliability of the *Harshacharita* as a work of history and finally also a discussion on the reflection of the trends and tendencies of his times. All this puts handling of this major source about Harsha by Shankar Goyal at a high plank. And hence Kumkum Roy has rightly remarked in her foreword to this work of Goyal, "Goyal provides a critical assessment of the claims made in the text in the light of other sources. Readers will find its evaluation as a *kāvya* useful, as it enables us to move beyond considering the text as literally true, even while recognizing its place in literary history."

Coming to the data left by Yuan Chwang, it may be said that he definitely stands out aloft for enlightening us about one of the greatest rulers of early India, Harsha and about his times, viz. the seventh century A.D., more so for being a period of phenomenal transformation of Indian polity and society into a feudal system thereafter. Besides his detail discussions about several dimensions of Yuan Chawng's records in his *Harsha Revisited: A Re-interpretation of Existing Data*, nothing better than Shankar Goyal's exclusive presentation on Yuan Chwang and his life and records with the title, *The Significance of Yuan Chwang in the Context of the Seventh Century: A Critical Assessment* could be expected in the proper line of historical studies with all the scientific temper and reason one is supposed to nurture. This piece of work brings to all of us a big respite for its scientific and critical approach and also for the importance of the era of ancient history it sheds light upon. While the *Records* (*Buddhist Records of the Western World*) of Yuan Chwang have been generally taken at it's face value and very little attempts have been there, just to say D. Devahuti and a few others, to see through it or to read the things in between the lines of his narration and its comparison and corroboration with other contemporary sources and archaeological evidences, it remained a-begging that a more concerted and detail effort should go into bringing out comparably a more truthful picture of the deeds and stature of Harsha as well in the backdrop of the polity and society of his times. How far the *Si-Yü-Ki* or *Buddhist Records of the Western World* by Yuan Chwang and the *Life* of the Master of the Law (i.e., Yuan Chwang) composed by Hui-li and Yen-Ts'ung besides correspondences of Yuan Chwang with Prajñādeva and Jñānaprabha of Mahābodhi and then another work named *She-Kia-Fang-Che* composed by some other Chinese disciple of Yuan Chawng on hearing descriptions about India from the later like Hui-li are in agreement among themselves and how far they can be corroborated, compared and supplemented as well with other Chinese records about India like *Chiu t'ang-shu, T'ang hui-yao,*

Tz'e-fu yüan-kuei and *Wen-hsien t'ung-k'ao* as well as with the information we have from our indigenous sources like *Harshacharita* by Bāṇabhaṭṭa, *Āryamañjuśrīmūlakalpa*, *Rājataraṅgiṇī* of Kalhaṇa, Madhuban, Banskhera and Kurukshetra-Varanasi and other epigraphic and numismatic records of Harsha's deeds, independent epigraphic records from Ganjam plates and Koṅgoda about Śaśāṅka, and those of Bhāskaravarman and Dhruvabhaṭṭa or Dhruvasen II, Aihole inscription of Pulakeśin II always needed to be handled more carefully for the full appreciation of this precious record of Yuan Chwang. The monograph on Yuan Chwang's records about India is an effort to make a critical appraisal of the information given by him in the political, economic, social, religious and cultural backdrop of the seventh century India.

Then Shankar Goyal gives due attention to the plays attributed to king Harsha and their historical value for depicting the culture of its times. He agrees with many other scholars that its real authorship may go to Dhāvaka or Bāṇa himself. Epigraphic and numismatic records available so far have found further critical handling by him. These include three copper plates of Harsha of Saṁvat 22, 23 and 25. He also discusses at some length about the place names mentioned in them and the problem of their identification. In addition to that he brings out a lively discussion on the newly discovered Kurukshetra-Varanasi grant of Harsha of the year 23 along with it's translation and the inscription of the seal. He also takes into account all the numismatic collections so far and presents a discussion on the coins of Pratāpaśīla (Prabhākaravardhana) and Śīlāditya (Harsha).

Shankar Goyal goes on to analyse all the aspects of the life of king Harsha with a rare command. There are a number of questions related to the trustworthiness of the information given in *Harshacharita* and the accounts of Yuan Chawng, and also about the sequence of events which he has tried to answer. Harsha's alleged role in the conspiracy of Rājyavardhana II's murder by Śaśāṅka and its relationship with the politico-religious trends of the time, Bāṇa's effort to present a different picture of Harsha. Yuan Chawng's overenthusiastic description of Harsha's involvement with Mahāyāna Buddhism, Harsha's political melodrama in fetching the Buddha's tooth-relic from Kashmir, his own leanings towards Śaiva cult, the problem of the authorship of the three plays, *Priyadarśikā*, *Nāgānanda* and *Ratnāvalī*, attributed to king Harsha and the possibility of Bāṇa being their actual author, Harsha's strategy of taking over both Thanesar and Kanauj, differentiation between the areas actually ruled by Harsha and the areas which fell under his influence, the protracted nature of Harsha's battle with Pulakeśin II, the feudal-federal nature of the empire and the administration of Harsha and his role in promoting feudalism are some of the major issues discussed by

Shankar Goyal deserve careful consideration. Lastly it is also important to note that Goyal has come forward with all the arguments in the favour of his opinion that king Harsha was also a product of his age, nothing more nothing less, besides being the last in the class of emperors trying to project oneself as a genuine guardian and protector of his subjects and pretending to follow the ideal classical dictum of kingship allowing all the cultural patterns and religious faiths to flourish in his empire and having good relationship with far off rulers of his times.

Coming to the history of Harsha and his age Shankar Goyal begins with tracing the early history of Pushyabhūtis. He has explained the socio-economic and religious background of Sthāṇīśvara (commonly known as Thanesar), the homeland of the Pushyabhūtis. It has been suggested that because of the agricultural and trade facilities in this region the Vaiśya caste could rise to a dominant status here, and as such Yuan Chawng's reference to Harsha as of Vaiśya origin is more acceptable. A debate on the Vaiśya origin of the Pushyabhūtis may however continue, but the suggestion that agricultural and trade base of Thanesar had something to do with the rise of Vaiśya communities to the status of kings calls for a further investigation. Similarly, it is argued that the Śaiva background of the land was a factor in Harsha's devotion to Lord Śiva. Shankar Goyal lays a great emphasis on the politico-religious factor in the murder of Rājyavardhana II, but apart from the reference to the Śaiva leanings of the rulers of the age, any other argument or evidence is lacking in support of this hypothesis. While discussing the political background, he has suggested that Vaishṇavism was a pacifist cult while Śaivism, a more aggressive ideology, could find more adherents among new political powers. This hypothesis, of course needs a thorough investigation before being accepted. However, in my own opinion the growing leaning of most of the rulers of the age towards Śaivism from thereon does indicate a transition in the religio-political scenario of early medieval times which also implies overtaking and overpowering of Buddhist centres and communities of the main land by Śaivite forces. We do have indications of simultaneous and sometimes joint worship of both Buddha, the Parama Saugata, and Rudra in some tribal pockets of central India, precisely the Mahākosala region, and this may at the same time explain Harsha's connection with both Lord Śiva and Mahāyāna Buddhism. As we also find, Buddhism is finally removed from the scene to give place to Śaiva cults and its worshippers in the process of rise/formation of some native resistance against the Turkish invaders a little later to which Buddhists did not seem to be so emboldened (also refer to my paper, 'Sectarian Political Implications of Śaiva Nativism in Ancient India', presented in the 78th Session of the Indian History Congress, Kolkata, 2017). In dealing with the political background of the Pushyabhūtis in general and of Harsha in particular, Shankar Goyal while referring to the factors responsible for the decline and fall of the imperial Guptas, has emphasized mainly upon the rise of feudalism and the involvement of the later imperial Guptas with Buddhism and also that of the earlier imperial Guptas with Vaishṇavism.

Further, referring to the geo-political shift, Shankar Goyal has suggested that a shift in the political centre of gravity was to occur from Magadha to Prayāga (the seat of power of the imperial Guptas, as suggested by S.R.Goyal and supported by many others) and then to Kanauj, finally settling down in Delhi at a further later stage for various reasons of freshly upcoming regional powers in the eastern, western, central and southern India as well as for the vacuum created with the displacement of imperial Guptas in the Gangetic zone, including also a continuous stream of invasions from north-western frontiers at a little later stage, I would wish to add! And to me, it appears also to be a reversal of shifting of nucleus of politico-cultural activities in early times when it was moving from north-west, i.e. Punjab, to Hastinapur-Kurukshetra-Indraprastha and then towards Kosala and Magadha.

How the Pushyabhūtis acquired an independent status during the time of Prabhākaravardhana from that of a humble feudatory of the Maukharis, and what were their relations with the contemporary powers are some of the important topics attended quite meticulously by Shankar Goyal. The marriage of Rājyaśrī with the Maukhari king Grahavarman and the shelter given to the two brothers Kumāragupta and Mādhavagupta have been described as political factors helping the rise of Pushyabhūti power. In the case of Harsha's accession to the thrones of Thanesar and Kanauj Shankar Goyal has followed the suggestions of R.C. Majumdar, V.S. Patahk, D. Devahuti and S.R. Goyal by rejecting the plain version of Bāṇa. Going beyond the arguments of all the above mentioned scholars he has tried to prove further that Rājyavardhana II had all the desire and ability to rule and he did rule for some time before being murdered during his expedition against the Later Guptas, adding as well that Harsha might have been a party to that conspiracy.

In describing the wars and conquests of Harsha Shankar Goyal has evaluated the power of the contemporary neighbouring states in comparison with that of Harsha. The war with Chālukya Pulakeśin II was not just a test of power but a protracted struggle. Shankar Goyal has been quite methodical in explaining the extent of Harsha's empire. The area under his direct rule has been distinguished from the areas of the kings accepting Harsha's suzerainty, his sphere of influence, regions ruled by independent friendly states and the areas which were independent but 'a natural prey' for the conqueror. Another noteworthy feature of this aspect is Harsha's relations with China and Iran.

The feudal structure and its impact on different aspects of life during the times of Harsha forms one of the most important feature of his studies and the area of analysis for Shankar Goyal which pushed him to publish another monograph on Harsha with the title, *The 'Medieval' Factor and the Age of Harsha: A Cultural Study* in 2016. This master craft of Shankar Goyal has been praised by some high authorities in the field of Indian history. Irfan Habib in his foreword to this monograph of Goyal observes, "What distinguishes the present volume is the author's effort to survey the nature of state, society and culture (including court culture) in the age of Harsha. It is a work of both synthesis, taking into account the works of scholars such as R.S. Sharma, B.N.S. Yadava, Romila Thapar and others, and of exploration, based on the author's own extensive study of the sources of the period." Irfan Habib goes on to add, "To put it simply, Dr. Shankar Goyal argues that while the picture of India in the seventh century did correspond broadly to that of Europe after the decline of the Roman Empire, yet owing to important variations, such as the presence of caste system in India, Indian feudalism—for which he seems often to prefer the term 'medieval'—was different in important respects from its European counterpart. He sees similarities in the emergence of political decentralisation, sub-infeudation of land rights, and regionalization of culture, while acknowledging a major point of differences in the absence of serfdom in India, balanced, so to speak, by an increasing rigour in the caste system." Similarly, Romila Thapar commenting upon this work says, "Shankar Goyal's book *The 'Medieval' Factor and the Age of Harsha: A Cultural Study* focuses on the age of Harsha as a watershed between the end of the ancient period and the coming of the medieval, subsequent to Harsha. Goyal uses the idea of a watershed in a very meaningful way to discuss elements of change that made the transition possible and recognizable. The span he covers is wide and the history is discussed with impressive detail. By examining changes in society, economy, religion and art, he shows the gradual evolution to medieval society. The many facets that he covers are well-integrated. 'Medieval' is a difficult term to define, but all credit to him that he defines it in the context of those times and does so with clarity." For Shankar Goyal it has been worthwhile to explain how far narrations about Harsha and the contemporary society could be related to or was a reflection of the feudal context of the time. Because it is now amply established that the Indian feudalism beginning as early as from the post-Mauryan times has already taken its roots by the time of the Later Guptas and it became one of the major factors in the decline and disintegration of the Gupta empire. Hence, scaling the personality of Harsha as the last great king of ancient India and evaluating his relations with and his influence upon his contemporary political powers as well as the impact of his religious and cultural deeds could never be done in isolation in terms of just his personal merits or demerits. Instead, all this has to be situated in the feudal structuring of the Indian economy and polity along with its social, religious and cultural implications. This, of course, includes the nature of political and military ambitions and objectives of Harsha, his religious and cultural leanings and all his fanciful feats which have been largely referred to by most of the modern historians as his great achievements relying much upon *Harshacharita* of Bāṇabhaṭṭa and *Records* and *Life* of Yuan Chwang. Shankar Goyal traces medieval tendencies in India from the fall of the Gupta empire. Foreign invasions and feudalism were the two major factors which brought about this change. And it is from the period of Harsha that the feudal structure became more pronounced. Goyal compares Indian feudalism with that of Europe, and tries to delineate the impact of feudalism on the social, economic and political life of the era. It has been important to bring to notice by Goyal Bāṇa's disapproval of the feudal political tendencies, the nature of warfare of his age and his disbelief in the divinity of the ruler. Commenting upon the work of Shankar Goyal, Kumkum Roy says, "Shankar Goyal provides an account of society, economy and cultural developments during the reign of Harsha, defining it as a crucial period in the transition to the medieval. He takes into consideration earlier scholarship on the theme and develops his arguments relying on a range of sources. Working broadly within the paradigm of Indian feudalism, Goyal provides a vivid and detailed description that will prove valuable for both the specialists and the more curious lay reader. His discussion based on Bāṇabhaṭṭa's work is particularly interesting as it provides scope for a critical evaluation of contemporary political and cultural practices, as well as of the narrative strategies adopted by one of the most renowned Sanskrit authors of the early medieval period."

Referring to the self-sufficient and local tendencies Shankar Goyal remarks, "guilds appear to have become mostly fossilized into occupational sub-castes which retained some form of social control over members but did not do much in the sphere of economic cooperation." One of the major feudal characters of the economy is reflected in Yuan Chwang's admiration of great grants to the Brāhmaṇas and other religious recluses and institutions as well as to the administrative retinue in the form of land or village grants. Though all it was said in the praise of Harsha but Yuan Chwang's descriptions are more than a testimony also of the feudal character of kingship more concerned with fanfare and show business than genuine build up of infrastructure for the economic growth and general prosperity of the people. From all what Yuan Chwang has narrated about allocations from the royal exchequer, nature of Harsha's military expeditions and the great religious assembly at Kanauj and also the quinquennial grants and gifting at Prayāga it is amply displayed that it all were more an extravaganza and personal aggrandizement on the part of the emperor telling much upon the state treasury and implying, of course, serious economic distress at the end. Shankar Goyal also refers to the decline of cities and the changing patterns of urban and rural life, ambivalence in the form of 'Kali Crisis' as symptoms of medievalism.

Further, Shankar Goyal's observation about the feudalization of education leading towards the end of the era of *gurukulas* and the rise of monastic and temple education in the form of schools or 'universities' with regular grants from the kings now allowing more and more influence of the latter upon it, and by implication, I wish to add, the priestly class of the society very well tied up with the former, is much commendable. The impact of feudalism and that of regional medieval tendencies upon the literature and languages, art and religion have also been taken note of carefully. In his effort to explain changes in the social domain Shankar Goyal has quite cogently referred to the growing rigidity of the caste system, the proliferation of castes, new social mobility in the form of general occupational freedom granted to the Brāhmaṇas and other castes, etc. He has by and large accepted the views of R.S. Sharma, B.N.S. Yadava, D.N. Jha and other such scholars in this regard. Referring to the notices of Yuan Chwang, Shankar Goyal observes that though not concerned to explain the changing social patterns under the Indian feudalism in its technical terms, Yuan Chawng has definitely referred to the growing stagnation and confinement of social statuses of the people of India with the practice of intra-caste marriages and abstention from inter-dining with the peoples of different castes that particularly with lower castes, and also to the communities who were considered outcasts not allowed to interact directly with the so-called persons belonging to upper castes. Goyal goes on to observe further that on the other hand, Yuan Chwang has also mentioned about the upward social mobility in the political domain, as he while saying that though the rulers belonged to the Kshatriya caste only there could be persons of any caste rising to the status of kingship, as was the case with the Pushyabhūtis itself and a Śūdra king in Sindh. Then he also gives indication of the growing merger of the Vaiśya community with the Śūdras, as both are said to have engaged in agriculture, a feature which has been generally understood by many a scholars in terms of increasing rights of the Śūdras in the growing feudal scenario. The writer of the present article however feels that it was instead a phenomenon of downgrading of many of the Vaiśya communities to the status of the Śūdras whereas, most of Śūdra communities had come down to be treated as outcasts or untouchables ('Social Status of Artisans in the Early Period of

Indian History', paper presented and published, *Proceedings of the Indian History Congress*, 51st Session, Calcutta, 1990; may also see my book, *India Rediscovered: A New Vision of History and Call of the Age*, New Delhi, 2006).

Shankar Goyal has also taken rightful pain in explaining the administrative structure of the age of Harsha in feudalistic terms. He deals quite elaborately with 'sāmanta-system' and 'feudal-federal' structure of the empire of Harsha. But he keeps restraint in dealing with the administrative units, revenue system and the law and justice, the inter-relationship or transfer of authorities to the sāmanatas or the local lords perhaps for the paucity of data in this regard. Nonetheless, the feudalistic composition of the militia has been described in some detail.

Immediate disintegration or break-up of the empire after the death of Harsha is another interesting subject which captures the attention of any scholar dealing with the subject. So Shankar Goyal giving due share to this aspect observes that though Harsha ruled for about forty years but he could not give attention to or made efforts for the consolidation of his empire, in spite of the fact that he did not have to face any serious threat to it after his accession to the throne of Thanesar and Kanauj. It was, of course, the weakness of the feudal-federal system which led to the break-up of Harsha's empire. In addition, Goyal has his own speculation about the lesser social acceptability of the Vaiśya origin of the Pushyabhūtis which does not sound so valid in the absence of any clear data indicating the same. However, one may agree to such other speculations attributed to the fall of Harsha's empire soon after him which list Harsha's absence from the capital for a long time due to his quinquennial assemblies and yatras, his indifference to the construction of defensive forts/posts, lack of any north-western frontier policy and the erosion of economic base of the empire through emptying of the treasury in religious charities.

Assessing the personality of Harsha as a man, a ruler, a politician and a religious figure Shankar Goyal keeps a very close eye to the whole of his behaviour and deeds. He is of the opinion that Harsha was quite involved with politics of his times and he was in fact the child of his era and certainly not its maker. As a king, he is not acceptable as the last great Hindu king of ancient times. He did not show any administrative acumen or innovative skill which was required for the consolidation of his empire. Nor did he take interest in public welfare schemes apart from his loudly spoken charities which are said to have done more with a personal motive. The narrative of Harsha's personal virtues may also be regarded as partial and exaggerated, and the dramas attributed to him are considered to have been composed by others and most probably by Bāṇa. Goyal has also gone on to find some conspiracy in the murder of Rājyavardhana II of which Harsha has also been considered a party to that plot, and also that the search for Rājyaśrī being conducted with a political motive so as to gain the throne of Kanauj and Thanesar, brings the whole personality of Harsha under a big scanner. And in this sense Shankar Goyal looks at Harsha as also a plotter rather than a person of undaunted identity.

Harsha's endeavours to recover the tooth-relic of Buddha from the king of Kashmir, devotion shown to the statue of Avalokiteśvara at Kanauj and the importance given to Yuan Chawng and Mahāyāna Buddhism have all been regarded as aspects of the policy of appeasement towards the people of Kanauj who have been assumed as mainly the followers of Mahāyāna Buddhism. The account available in the *Life* about the Hīnayānis' plot against the life of Yuan Chawng in the Kanauj assembly has been favoured as against the version given in the *Records*, according to which it was the disgruntled Brāhmaṇas who tried to kill Harsha (not Yuan Chawng) on the occasion due to excessive favour shown to Yuan Chawng by the emperor himself. The story found in the *Life* has been preferred by Shankar Goyal just because he considers that there could not have been any reason for the Brāhmaṇas to have remained annoyed with the king because Harsha's engagement with Buddhism was only superficial and temporary, as he remained a worshipper of Lord Śiva right till the end of his life, and even at the Prayāga quinquennial assembly he bestowed charities on to the Brāhmaṇas for a larger number of days than upon the followers of other faiths. This and some other contentions of Shankar Goyal ought to negate the general notion about Harsha as a Buddhist. It is, however, questionable how could a king like Harsha, remaining more associated with the Hindu faith, lead an expedition against Kashmir just to recover the tooth-relic of Lord Buddha, and also summon a great assembly of religions at his capital just to appease his Kanaujian subjects presumed to be of Buddhist leanings ! In my own opinion Harsha's connection with Buddhism cannot be diluted just by discrediting Yuan Chawng's reports as overenthusiastic. And even if Harsha is said to have remained a worshipper of Lord Śiva throughout his life, his involvement with Buddhism of his times was quite pronounced. If the assembly at Kanauj indicates a drift from his early attachment to the orthodox Brāhmaṇical faith, there could also be a plot of his murder by the impatient Brāhmaṇas who had been enjoying the privileges of superior attention thereto, as reported in the *Records*! To us it appears that whatever might have been the original belief of Harsha, like Aśoka, he too found greater merit in Buddhism in the later years of his reign, and tried to bring about a rapport between different hostile faiths/sects on the one hand, and to suppress divisive or disintegrating social tendencies of orthodox Brāhmaṇism on the other. But he perhaps also went beyond his limitations ignoring the reactionary tendencies of his age which also resulted into the break-up of his empire soon after his death. If the Chinese reports of a Chinese invasion immediately after the death of Harsha has any historical value, it can be compared with the invasion of the Indo-Greeks at the close of the Mauryan rule, as both these invading forces had connection with the Buddhists of their times and both were repelled by the native formations in their own right. This and some other possible questions invite further research into the subject.

Taking an overview of all the works of Shankar Goyal on Harsha and his age one can never be indifferent to all the skill and labour put into researching about the subject covering all the dimensions of this study. His claim of dealing with the 'how' and 'why' questions of Harsha's age and his search for a harmonious pattern may be considered to have been well established in most of the cases. While D. Devahuti is said to have restrained herself from 'not going far enough' in her analysis of things, Shankar Goyal on the contrary seems to be burdened with a number of hypotheses which have sometimes demanded overstretching the interpretation of available data. He closely follows S.R. Goyal on many occasions and goes on to expand latter's views further. No doubt, Shankar Goyal presents a more realistic picture of Harsha's personality and deeds, and does not hesitate in rejecting generally accepted notions wherever he find reasons to counter them with all his sense and skill of history writing.

Thus Shankar Goyal has been rendering great service to the study of ancient Indian history, and particularly of the period of Harsha, considered to be the last phase of ancient India and beginning of the medieval trends. He deserves all the commendations for bringing out no less than five monographs and numerous articles of his critical studies until now on various aspects of the subject with a proper scientific zeal of history to the benefit of research and researchers in this era and area which no other Indian scholar has done to this extent so far. Let me lastly quote R. Champakalakshmi in this regard, "Shankar Goyal makes a serious attempt to give a new direction to study the history and culture of the age of Harsha against feudal atmosphere of the period. He rightly argues that age of Harsha is the focal point of change from ancient to medieval. His conclusions are sound and deserve very careful consideration."

REFERENCES

Ārya Mañjuśrī Mūla Kalpa, ed. and trans. by K.P. Jayaswal as *An Imperial History of India*, Lahore, 1934.

Banskhera Copper Plate of Harsha, *Epigraphia Indica*, IV, 1896-97, pp. 208-11.

Beal, S., *Si-Yü-Ki* or *Buddhist Records of the Western World*, Delhi, 1969.

—, *The Life of Hiuen-Tsiang*, New Delhi, 1973.

—, *Chinese Accounts of India*, Vol. II, Calcutta, n.d.
Devahuti, D., *Harsha : A Political Study*, 2nd edn., Oxford University Press, New Delhi, 1983; 1st edn., Oxford, 1970.
—, ed., *The Unknown Hsüan-tsang*, New Delhi, 2001.
Goyal, Shankar, *History and Historiography of the Age of Harsha*, Jodhpur, 1992.
—, *Harsha : A Multidisciplinary Political Study*, Jodhpur, 2006.
—, *Ancient India : A Multidisciplinary Approach*, Jodhpur, 2006.
—, *175 Years of Vākāṭaka History and Historiography*, Jodhpur, 2009.
—, *The 'Medieval' Factor and the Age of Harsha : A Cultural Study*, Jodhpur, 2016.
—, *Harsha Revisited : A Re-interpretation of Existing Data*, New Delhi, 2018.
—, *The Significance of Yuan Chwang in the Context of the Seventh Country : A Critical Assessment*, Delhi, 2018.
—, '*Harshacharita* as a Source of History', in the *Papers from the Aligarh Historians Society*, ed. Irfan Habib, 69th Session, Indian History Congress, Kannur University, Kannur, 2008, pp. 122-52.
—, 'Yuan Chwang's India and the Problem of the Extent of Harsha's Empire and Sphere of His Influence', in the *Papers from the Aligarh Historians Society*, ed. Irfan Habib, 77th Session, Indian History Congress, Kerala University, Thiruvananthapuram, 2016, pp. 104-16.
—, 'Harsha : A Retrospective', Presidential Address, Section I : Ancient India, 78th Session, Jadavpur University, Kolkata, 28-30 December, 2017, published in the *Proceedings of the Indian History Congress*, 78th Session, Jadavpur University, Kolkata, 2017, Delhi, 2018, pp. 27-41.
Goyal, S.R., *Harsha and Buddhism*, Meerut, 1986.
—, *Harsha Śīlāditya*, Meerut, 1986.
—, *A History of Indian Buddhism*, Meerut, 1987.
Habib, Irfan, ed., *India — Studies in the History of an Idea*, New Delhi, 2005.
Harshacharita of Bāṇa, ed. Kasinath Pandurang Parab, 5th edn., Bombay, 1925.
—, ed. P.V. Kane, 2nd edn., Delhi, 1965.
—, tr. E.B. Cowell and F.W. Thomas, 2nd edn., Delhi, 1968.
—, ed. Jagannath Pathak, 6th edn., Varanasi, 1998.
Kādambarī of Bāṇa, ed. P.V. Kane, Bombay, 1920.
—, tr. C.M. Ridding, London, 1896; Indian repr., Bombay, 1960.
Kurukshetra-Varanasi Copper Plate Inscription of Harsha, *East and West*, Vol. 57, 1-4, 2007, pp. 193-203 ; *Epigraphia Indica*, XLIII, i, 2011-12, pp. 40-51.
Madhuban Copper Plate Inscription of Harsha, *Epigraphia Indica*, I, 1892, pp. 67-75.
Majumdar, R.C., *Readings in Political History of India*, ed. S.P. Gupta, Delhi, 1976.
Majumdar, R.C. and Pusalker, A.D., eds., *The Classical Age*, Bombay, 1954.
Nāgānanda of Harsha, tr. P. Boyd, London, 1872.
—, ed. R.D. Karmarkar, Poona, 1919.
Pathak, V.S., *Ancient Historians of India*, Bombay, 1966.
Priyadarśikā of Harsha, ed. Jivanand Vidyasagar, Calcutta, 1874.
—, tr. G.D. Nariman, A.V. William Jackson and C.J. Ogden, New York, 1923.

Ratnāvalī of Harsha, ed. K.M. Joglekar, Hedvi, 1907.
—, ed. and tr. C.R. Devadhar and N.G. Suru, 2nd edn., Poona, 1954.
Ray, N.R., 'The 'Medieval' Factor in Indian History', being his Address of the General President of the 29th Session of the Indian History Congress, Patiala, 1967.
Sen, Surendranath, *India through Chinese Eyes*, Madras, 1956.
Sharma, R.S., *Śūdras in Ancient India*, Delhi, 1958.
—, *Indian Feudalism*, Calcutta, 1965.
—, *Early Medieval Indian Society : A Study in Feudalisation*, Kolkata, 2001.
—, 'Problem of Transition from Ancient to Medieval in Indian History', in *The Indian Historical Review*, New Delhi, Vol. 1, No. 1, March 1974, pp. 1-9.
She-Kia-Fang-Che, ed. P.C. Bagchi, Calcutta, 1959.
Singh, Mahesh Vikram, *India Rediscovered : A New Vision of History and Call of the Age*, New Delhi, 2006.
Thapar, Romila, *The Penguin History of Early India*, New Delhi, 2003.
—, *The Past Before Us : Historical Traditions of Early North India*, New Delhi, 2013.
Watters, T., *On Yuan Chwang's Travels in India*, Delhi, 1961.

Chapter Seven

Shankar Goyal's Contribution to Medieval/Modern History and Historiography of Rajasthan

L.S. RATHORE
Former Vice-Chancellor
Jai Narain Vyas University, Jodhpur

Shankar Goyal, M.A., Ph.D., D.Litt., was Professor of History, Jai Narain Vyas University, Jodhpur (Rajasthan). He retired in 2019. Born in 1959, he has emerged as a recognized authority of the historiography of ancient India and medieval/modern Rajasthan. Apart from publishing over 150 research articles in reputed journals and standard works, Professor Goyal has also authored / edited about forty significant works so far, dealing with some aspects of ancient Indian history and the historiography of medieval/modern Rajasthan, including *Recent Historiography of Ancient India, Harsha: A Multidisciplinary Political Study* and *Origin and Growth of History Writing in Rajasthan* (in three volumes). His books and many articles brought him recognition from scholars such as Professors R. N. Dandekar, G.C. Pande, R. S. Sharma, Irfan Habib, Romila Thapar, R. Champakalakshmi, Shireen Moosvi, Kumkum Roy, A. M. Shastri, V.S. Pathak, Lallanji Gopal, N.N. Bhattacharyya, V.N. Misra, M.K. Dhavalikar, K.V. Raman, Bardwell L. Smith (Minnesota, U.S.A.), Walter M. Spink (Michigan, U.S.A.), Maurizio Taddei (Napoli, Italy) and P. K. Mitra (Rajshahi, Bangladesh).

Of late Shankar Goyal has been very prolific and in recent years has published a large number of research articles and three significant works on medieval/modern historiography of Rajasthan.[1] He possesses a remarkable capacity, talent and acumen in exploring virgin fields and new avenues in the field of research in history. His work *Origin and Growth of History Writing in Rajasthan*, Volume I : *Khyats and Allied Works of Historical Genre*[2] is a clear testimony of his original thinking. It is a pioneering work, highlighting selective Khyats and other sources of medieval Rajput history, where Goyal has shown a certain novelty value in his approach, analysis and evaluation.[3]

The Khyats are considered as significant sources for the proper understanding of Rajput history of medieval Rajasthan. The simple meaning of Khyat is that it is mainly a bardic historical prose literature. The Khyats were mostly written under the patronage of the rulers who were keen to perpetuate the memory of their exploits in various fields. The Khyats were written on the basis of past memories, speculations, traditions, personal records and experiences of the writers. They provide a detailed account of the histories of rulers, chiefs, nobles and other dignitaries of the period; their achievements, historical events, military strength and battles. They give wide information on various aspects of the life of rulers and their queens, the genealogies and successions, the palace intrigues and family feuds, and the fairs and festivals. They are more or less accurate and correct, despite imperfections of dates and chronology. They help in discovering vital information and reliable facts about the medieval Rajput history, despite slight exaggeration of local patriotism and exaltation of the rulers. They depict a broad framework of the history of medieval Rajasthan, though it may not be a complete one. Because they reflect the actual course of happenings in medieval Rajasthan, they are undoubtedly regarded as a valuable source of Rajput history. Shankar Goyal in his magnificent work has examined six prominent Khyats, namely, *Muhnot Nainsi ri Khyat* (ch. 2), *Bankidas ri Khyat* (ch. 3), *Dayaldas ri Khyat* (ch. 4), *Jodhpur Rajya ki Khyat* of Ai Dan Khidia (ch. 5), *Marwar ri Khyat* of Tilok Chand Joshi (ch. 6), and *Jaisalmer ri Khyat* of Ajit Singh Mehta (ch. 7). His narration, comments and evaluation of these Khyats is critical, dispassionate and precise which enhances the worth of his work. In addition to the Khyats which constitute the primary source, Goyal has also mentioned other auxiliary sources of the medieval Rajput history, namely, Vat (Bat), Vachanika, Davavait, Hal, Ahawal, Haqiqat, Vamshavali, Pattawali, Pidhiyawali, Vigat, Tahakikat, etc. Of these, he considers Vigats, Vamshavalis and Vats as important branches of historical literature (ch. 1).

Shankar Goyal's work is very well documented. The factors which led to the decline of Khyat literature have been carefully discussed. The main factors emphasized by him are : the lack of historical accuracy, not enough connected historical account of the period, rise of new forces of change, neglect of social upheavals and economic dissatisfaction, the end of the medieval traditions of chivalry and heroism and the like. These factors have been woven together by Goyal in a skilled manner (ch. 8).

Though Goyal is a well-known authority on ancient Indian history and historiography, by writing this work, I believe, he has successfully carved out a niche for himself in the field of Rajasthan studies. His book is of utmost importance both for the scholars and researchers of the history of Rajasthan. It is a unique contribution, perhaps the only one of its kind. The presentation of the historical material is systematic, the narration is reliable and the analysis is objective. Based on facts, the work is logical, well organized and coherent; its contents are clear and easy to understand. The description of Khyats as basic source of history has been given in such a delightful manner that the general readers can also derive pleasure and enjoyment by reading the book.

It would be desirable here to quote the views of some historians on the quality of Shankar Goyal's work.[4] A well known scholar Hukam Singh Bhati, former Director, Rajasthani Shodh Samsthan, Chopasani, Jodhpur, and Pratap Shodh Pratishthan, Udaipur, states that Shankar Goyal's *Khyats and Allied Works of Historical Genre* is an 'extremely invaluable work' and an example of 'constructive research'. He writes, "As far as I know his work is the first study of Khyat literature of Rajasthan to be written in English language. He has brought together the results of earlier researches on the subject, and has added much that is his own, studying the original sources afresh in a truly critical and analytical spirit to produce a clear and concise account of the important Khyats which will be of great value and help to all students, researchers and teachers of the universities of Rajasthan who wish to make a specialized study of its literature, and to all others who are seriously interested in the past of this glorious land. ... All in all, a definite contribution to the history of Rajasthan." Another historian K. S. Gupta, Professor of History (retd.), Mohanlal Sukhadia University, Udaipur, and National Fellow, Indian Council of Historical Research, New Delhi, is of the view that Shankar Goyal has done a great service for students, teachers and researchers of the history of Rajasthan in bringing to light Khyat literature in English. Evaluating Goyal's work on Khyats, Gupta says, "His *Khyats and Allied Works of Historical Genre* is definitely the first and only account of its kind, at once critical, scholarly and uptodate. No scholar wishing to work on the subject can afford to ignore his book. ... It will create a new awareness and stimulate the interest of all those interested in the history and culture of Rajasthan. Professor Goyal has laid the scholarly world under deep debt by writing this extremely useful book." Similarly, V.S. Bhatnagar, Professor of History (retd.), University of Rajasthan, Jaipur, observes that "Goyal's *Khyats and Allied Works of Historical Genre* is a neatly brought out, compact and comprehensive work on the Khyats, Vats, Vachanikas, etc. ... The rich Bibliography adds to the value of the work." According to B.L. Bhadani, Professor of History (retd.), Aligarh Muslim University,

Aligarh, "...By writing this book in English, Professor Shankar Goyal has done a great service of the academic world." Another savant T. K. Mathur, Professor of History (retd.), Department of History, M.D.S. University, Ajmer, says that "The refreshing approach of Shankar Goyal have rightly put the works of Khyat writers in a novel perspective. All scholars seeking to work on the subject will have to reckon with his work which they would find most useful." The last opinion, I quote, is that of S.N. Dube, Professor of History (retd.), University of Rajasthan, Jaipur. He writes, "The saga of the valorous land of Rajasthan, known for its chivalry and sacrifices, was sung graphically in ballads and bardic tales since times immemorial. An outcrop of the traditional accounts was the emergence in medieval times of a genre of peculiar writings which, with the sifting of layers of romantic and panegyric coats, can be of great use for the fascinating history of the region. Professor Shankar Goyal's present venture, I am sure, would provide a fresh impetus in that direction."

Needless to say, Shankar Goyal's book *Khyats and Allied Works of Historical Genre* has been rated high both in quality and contents by the eminent historians working on Rajasthan. It is a definite and true contribution in the field and that there is no doubt about it. Had Goyal not written any other book, this single work on Khyat literature would have been enough to put him in the front rank of eminent historians of Rajput history of medieval Rajasthan.

Shankar Goyal's book *Origin and Growth of History Writing in Rajasthan*, Volume II : *Historians and Historiography in Modern Rajasthan* [5] is another unique and fascinating work on the history of Rajasthan. The uniqueness of the work lies in the fact that the author correctly demarcates the various stages or traditions that have dominated the historiography of modern Rajasthan. For this he has chosen eleven representative historians of his choice, namely, James Tod, Shyamaldas, G.H. Ojha, V.N. Reu, Dasharatha Sharma, S. R. Goyal, G.N. Sharma, R.P. Vyas, L.S. Rathore, G.S.L. Devra and Sobhag Mathur in his work because they have appeared to him as the pioneers in different traditions of the history of Rajasthan. The first tradition in the historiography of modern Rajasthan started in the nineteenth century with the *Annals and Antiquities of Rajasthan* written by Tod. With its appearance history writing in Rajasthan acquired a distinct identity. This chapter of Shankar Goyal is exceptionally good. Tod's invaluable contribution lies in the laying of the foundation of the systematic study of the land. He was one of those Western historians who may be regarded, of course with some reservations, as pro-India and that too at a time when such specimens of Western historians were quite rare. The historiography of Rajasthan, from the period of Tod to the dawn of Indian independence, reflected the trend of writing the chronological histories of the dynasties. The historians, such as, Tod, Shyamaldas and Ojha, etc., belong to this tradition. The second tradition emerged from the middle of the twentieth century when the chronological tradition became weak, and a new trend that emerged saw the history of Rajasthan against the perspective of national history. V.N. Reu was probably the first historian who corrected the history of Marwar region with the history of various other Indian regions. But his historiography was greatly conditioned by the fact that he enjoyed the patronage of the Jodhpur *Darbar*. The third tradition in the historiography of Rajasthan developed in the later half of the twentieth century where the emphasis has been on the regional political unity of Rajasthan within the larger perspective of India's national unity, and on the need of the study of the life of common people as against the earlier importance given on the royal and feudal classes. Dasharatha Sharma was mainly instrumental in giving emphasis on this trend. From his *Rajasthan through the Ages*, Volume I, it is the personality of the whole of Rajasthan which emerges, of course as an integral part of India, not of any particular region like Mewar or Marwar. The other significant exponent of this tradition was S.R. Goyal, the father of Shankar Goyal, whose contribution to this trend had been abiding. He viewed the history of Rajasthan of the pre-Pratihara period as the history of a region of India, as a part of the whole, often giving many novel suggestions. Before S.R. Goyal no historian of worth worked so extensively on the history of Rajasthan of the pre-Pratihara period. Even Dasharatha Sharma devoted only about twenty pages of the early historical period of this region while other historians concentrated their attention on the early medieval, medieval and modern Rajasthan. Along with this tradition, a few more trends developed simultaneously in the later half of the twentieth century. One tradition, the fourth one, is that of blending together the chronological trend of writing the history of Rajasthan with that of national unity perspective. G.N. Sharma and R.P. Vyas belonged to this category. Sharma imbibed the historical approach of early historians, such as, Shyamaldas, Ojha and Reu, and was also in tune with the history writing of the generation of Dasharatha Sharma, etc. Vyas emphasized on the study of social and economic history rather than continuing to work on political history, and the deeds of the king, but he did not follow this approach himself in his *Adhunika Rajasthan ka Brihata Itihasa*, in two volumes, and wrote chapters on social, economic, administrative and religious aspects without showing any interaction between them. This criticism of Vyas is a clear testimony of Goyal's logical thinking. The fifth stage is poetic compositions about historical characters. The best example of this tradition is L.S. Rathore. The author describes at length Rathore's attitude to poetry and history both. In the sixth stage the emphasis is given to the study of culture of Rajasthan. G.S.L. Devra's contribution in this field is of special significance. And the last tradition in the historiography of modern Rajasthan is the emphasis given on the nature of freedom struggle in the erstwhile princely states of Rajasthan. Sobhag Mathur has shown great interest in this trend.

As I have mentioned earlier, the beauty of Shankar Goyal's work *Historians and Historiography in Modern Rajasthan* lies in the fact that he has very ably classified the various traditions in the historiography of Rajasthan and has demonstrated their characteristics in a critical and dispassionate manner. The work is scholarly and authentic, interesting and novel, and excellent and impressive. By this work, I feel, Shankar Goyal has clearly demonstrated his ability, knowledge and skill in writing the historiography of modern Rajasthan, and can be categorized as one of the most brilliant historians in the field.

The story of history writing in modern and contemporary Rajasthan further continues in Shankar Goyal's *Origin and Growth of History Writing in Rajasthan*, Volume III : *Historians and Historiography in Contemporary Rajasthan*, which includes some more historians who have contributed immensely to enrich the history and culture of Rajasthan and are regarded as pioneers in their respective fields of study. These include M. S. Jain, K.S. Gupta, V.S. Bhatnagar, S.P. Gupta, Dilbagh Singh, T.K. Mathur, Vinita Parihar and Shankar Goyal. Jain's comprehensive work on modern Rajasthan, entitled *Rajasthan through the Ages*, Volume III, Bikaner, 1996, took a view of specific regions as well as the whole state with one eye on the wider context of British imperial policies strengthened by his sound understanding of history of modern India. His analysis elucidates the connectedness of events and processes to get to the bottom of the intricate mechanism of historical experience. K.S. Gupta has been a prolific writer which is a testimony to his prowess as a researcher. Some of his major works include *Mewar and the Maratha Relations* (New Delhi, 1971) and *Selections from Banera Archives* (in three volumes, Udaipur, 1967, 1971 and 1974). The work *Mewar and the Maratha Relations* is by any standard the 'flagship' among the publications of Gupta. He is a first rate historian of economic history. Whereas scholars in other parts of the country stressed on the land revenue systems, trade patterns, monetary systems, etc., K. S. Gupta highlighted the pricing policy of essentials. V.S. Bhatnagar's academic contribution is phenomenal. His monumental work is *Life and Times of Sawai Jai Singh* (New Delhi, 1974). He gives each and every detail of the work done and role played by Jai Singh. He also translated a Prakrit text of 1455 A.D. in English which came out under the title *Kanhadade Prabandha* by Padmanabha (New Delhi, 1991). He deserves our appreciation for translating this important epic. He has translated all the four cantos in an accurate and precise manner. Moreover, his notes and comments have enhanced the value of the work which also demonstrates his mastery over the subject. S. P. Gupta should easily find a place among the more prominent historians of Rajasthan. His works particularly provide an excellent base work for the researchers who are working on the economy of Amber/Jaipur. He had introduced *arhsatta*, a treasured source, and other documents related to the history of Amber. Whereas Gupta is a pioneer in documenting the nature of agrarian production system in eastern Rajasthan where, on the basis of various kinds of primary, village-level documents, he has offered a vivid description of production relations and functioning of land revenue administration, Dilbagh Singh in his monograph *State, Landlords and Peasants : Rajasthan in the Eighteenth Century* (New Delhi, 1990) extended his investigations into the functioning of the land revenue administration and pointed out the role of caste considerations in the extraction of surplus. He highlighted the importance of social hierarchies in the functioning of medieval political formations. His explorations about the role of moneylenders, the Mahajans, have been fundamental in understanding the complex relationship between the exploited and the exploiters. T.K. Mathur's *Feudal Polity in Mewar* (Jaipur, 1987) is an attempt to study the nature and role of the feudal set-up in the Rajput states. He tried to move away from the existing works of earlier scholars who attempted to study feudalism merely as the political role of the nobility in relation to the monarchy. He researched extensively and thoroughly the various archival and non-archival sources and has gone a step further to study feudalism as an institution. Vinita Parihar has been deeply involved in the study of the history and culture of modern Rajasthan and contributed immensely in this field. Her *Society in Transition* (Jaipur, 1989) seeks to examine and explore the form, nature and pattern of the society of Marwar in the nineteenth century. Another work of Parihar entitled *Rajasthan men Uttardai Shasan ke Liye Sangharsh* (Jaipur, 2002) is devoted exclusively to the history of *Prajamandal* movements in Rajasthan. She traces the journey of the establishment of responsible government under the banner of *Prajamandal* movements. The beauty of her style lies, *inter alia*, in quoting the original sources wherever possible and the views of other writers on the subject and analysing them dispassionately before arriving at her own conclusions which are generally well-based. Shankar Goyal's *Origin and Growth of History Writing in Rajasthan*, Volume I : *Khyats and Allied Works of Historical Genre* (New Delhi, 2017) is a pioneering work analysing selective Khyats and other sources of the medieval Rajput history. In his other book *Origin and Growth of History Writing in Rajasthan*, Volume II : *Historians and Historiography in Modern Rajasthan* (Delhi, 2018) he, for the first time, demarcates the various stages that have influenced the history writing of modern Rajasthan. In his *Origin and Growth of History Writing in Rajasthan*, Volume III : *Historians and Historiography in Contemporary Rajasthan* (Delhi, 2019) he further examines the contributions of some contemporary historians of Rajasthan.

Shankar Goyal has also edited two volumes in Hindi titled *Rajasthan Bharati*, Volume I : *Bharatiya Itihasa ko Rajasthan ka Avadana*, and Volume II: *Bharatiya Samskriti ko Rajasthan ka Avadana*, jointly with Sobhag Mathur.[6] These two volumes have been dedicated to Professor S.R. Goyal, an eminent historian, who had been Professor and Head, Department of History, Jai Narain Vyas University, Jodhpur, and retired in the year 1992. Volume I of *Rajasthan Bharati* deals with Rajasthan's contribution to Indian history. Apart from forty-five pages devoted to Professor S.R. Goyal's works and his contribution to history, the book contains sixteen articles by scholars which depict important characteristics of the history of Rajasthan. The editors have taken due care to show the glorious deeds of the history of Rajasthan which have added lusture to the history of India. Volume II of *Rajasthan Bharati* demonstrates that the cultural values of the history of Rajasthan form an illuminating part of Indian history. The book contains twenty-one interesting articles that show that despite its limited sources, Rajasthan's contribution to Indian culture has been highly magnificent. The cultural values for which Indian history is known, such as, patriotism, bravery, self-respect, secularism, patronage to arts, literature, music, architecture, etc., have all emanated from the land of Rajasthan. Rajasthan is the seedbed of Indian history and culture and this theme has been demonstrated in an attractive and scholarly manner by the editors of *Rajasthan Bharati*. The work is of great significance for the students of history who wish to know Rajasthan's contribution to the history and culture of India.

Shankar Goyal has himself contributed substantially in *Rajasthan Bharati*. Apart from writing on S. R. Goyal's approach to history (pp. 19-28) in Part I of both these works, in Part II of Volume I he writes an important paper on the historicity of Samyogita, the heroine of *Prithvirajaraso* (pp. 27-32), and refutes the arguments of Dasharatha Sharma who concedes that the tradition is unanimous in recognising her existence and there is nothing illogical and irrational about it. In Part II of Volume II he throws light on the works of Brahmagupta, a sixth century mathematician and astronomer, who is called *Bhillamalakacharya* (pp. 11-15). These research articles of Goyal in Hindi language are really thoughtful.

Another important edited work of Shankar Goyal is *Rajasthan : From Prehistory to the Independence Era*.[7] Dedicated to Professor S.R. Goyal, as Volume IV of *Reconstructing Indian History for S.R. Goyal*, the festschrift contains thirty-four articles on various aspects of the history of Rajasthan written by scholars of repute, such as, Professors V.N. Misra, S.N. Rajaguru, B.D. Chattopadhyaya, G.N. Sharma, K.S.Gupta, V.K. Vashishtha, M.R. Singh, T.K. Mathur, R.P. Vyas, D.C. Shukla, F.K. Kapil, and a host of others. The work seeks to re-study the history and culture of Rajasthan in the light of new material which is being constantly discovered and in the light of new interpretations which have bacome imperative due to the changing historiographical attitudes. Shankar Goyal also contributes two research papers in this work on different aspects of the historiography of Rajasthan. His paper on James Tod (pp. 225-32) is particularly well thought of, methodical and illuminating.

In one of the keynote addresses delivered at the ICHR National Seminar on 'The Revolt of 1857 and the Anti-British Rebellions that Preceded It' held at the World University Service Centre in Chennai on July 30-31, 2007, Shankar Goyal discusses the nature and character of the mutiny of 1857 and the role played by Rajasthan. According to him, the movement of 1857 was not a war fought for the independence of India. He argues that 1. Till the middle of the nineteenth century the concept of India as a nation and also the ideal of national self-determination had not emerged in this country. 2. As regards the situation in Rajasthan, it is obvious that the rulers of its princely states remained wholly loyal to the British. 3. As regards the *jagirdars*, they saw the mutiny mostly, if not in every case, from the angle of ruler-feudal relationship and utilized the opportunity provided by it to revive the feudal power against the authority of the rulers. They were only rarely inspired by larger patriotic sentiments. 4. So far as the common man in concerned, he was more directly concerned with the oppressive behaviour of the *jagirdars* and the ruler of the state in which he lived. The policies of the British affected him but only indirectly and through the state ruler and *jagirdars*. For him all these three—the British, state ruler and local *jagirdars* — were oppressors but he usually had a soft corner for the state ruler and local *jagirdars* because of the tribal and caste affiliations; in the case of the British he did not have this bond of affinity. In view of these facts Goyal believes that the mutiny of 1857 cannot be regarded as a national movement in the context of Rajasthan also.[8]

All in all, Professor Shankar Goyal's research output and works on medieval/modern historiography of Rajasthan have been stupendous, brilliant and scholarly. His works reveal originality and quality both. He has emerged as a historian of outstanding ability, talent and knowledge. His specialization in the historiography of Rajasthan is unrivalled, and on the basis of his contribution in the said field, he is undoubtedly one of the most eminent scholars of history and historiographical literature of Rajasthan.

REFERENCES

1. Incidently Shankar Goyal published his first research paper on the history of Rajasthan as a student of High School in early 1974 in *Shodha Patrika*. But here I seek to evaluate his books only, not his articles published in journals and other standard works.
2. New Delhi, 2017.
3. Also see my Introduction to this work (pp. ix-xi).
4. All quoted in Goyal's work.
5. Delhi, 2018.
6. Jodhpur, 1995.
7. Jaipur, 2003.
8. The revised and updated version of this address appeared in the *Proceedings of the Rajasthan History Congress*, Volume XXX, Udaipur, December 2015, pp. 297-317.

Chapter Eight

Shankar Goyal's Studies on the History of Deccan and South India

A. CHANDRASEKARAN
Professor Emeritus, Department of Indian History
University of Madras, Chennai

A scholar who has made a significant mark in the field of ancient Indian history, attempting investigation in other periods of history and on other regions of India is quite a laudable effort. His expertise in the studies of other regions and on different aspects in different periods will undoubtedly throw light and help the historians to delve more deep into the subject. Professor Shankar Goyal has been attempting such a commendable work in the field of south Indian history for several years which is really a huge contribution from him. His book *Studies in the History of the Deccan and South India* (Jodhpur, 2009) is extremely useful not only to the students of the history of Vākāṭakas but also to those of south Indian history and culture. The Vākāṭaka period has been his special field of study, of course apart from the age of Harsha, a great north Indian monarch, and this book bears the stamp of his critical acumen. However, here I am concerned with his major papers and lectures, including his endowment lectures and presidential addresses, which were delivered in different conferences held in various cities of south India and in other parts of the country in the last two decades or so. I must admit that I have the privilege of listening to his lectures and addresses and reading many of his research articles and found them extraordinarily brilliant and original, laden with many new ideas and suggestions.

In the Loyola College Endowment Lecture titled 'The Vākāṭakas in the History of the Deccan : A Fresh Appraisal in the Light of Recent

Discoveries and New Interpretations' (published in the *Proceedings of the Twenty-sixth Annual Session of the South Indian History Congress*, Bangalore, 2006, pp. 689-702), Shankar Goyal makes a serious attempt to give a new direction to the political history of the Vākāṭakas. His approach in this essay is basically different. It is concerned not merely with 'what' and 'when' questions of the age of Vākāṭakas; it raises 'how' and 'why' questions as well regarding the political events and developments of the period. It also delineates and critically examines various phases and trends through which the historiography of the Vākāṭakas has passed. Shankar Goyal is of the view that the historians who attempted studies on the Vākāṭakas were greatly benefited by modern epigraphical researches. Earlier it was believed that the Vākāṭakas were a dynasty of Yavanas or Greeks. The period during which they flourished also remained uncertain for a long time. Later J. Dubreuil and H. Heras threw more light on the Vākāṭakas and the former had said that the one that had the greatest influence on the civilization of the whole of the Deccan was unquestionably the illustrious dynasty of the Vākāṭakas. Shankar Goyal put forth the arguments of K.P. Jayaswal, S.K. Aiyangar, D.C. Sircar, A.S. Altekar, R.C. Majumdar and K.A. Nilakanta Sastri on the Vākāṭakas and their rule in the Deccan. V.A. Smith's view in respect of the post-Maurya pre-Gupta centuries has also been analysed. V. V. Mirashi's political and cultural history of the Vākāṭaka dynasty is also taken by him for examination. Shankar Goyal again refers to the work of S.R. Goyal entitled *A History of the Imperial Guptas* in which a critical examination of the Gupta-Vākāṭaka relations was made. After Mirashi's writings in 1963, many new Vākāṭaka inscriptions have come to light. But in this essay Shankar Goyal points out that no revised and detailed political history of the dynasty has been published. Even the account of Vākāṭaka history given by A.M. Shastri is brief. Shankar Goyal also comments on the work of K.M. Shrimali on the Vākāṭakas in which Shrimali for the first time explains the serfdom, tribal origin of the Vākāṭakas and the process of Sanskritization channels. Thus, Shankar Goyal attempts an analysis of the Vākāṭaka rule in the Deccan and examines the major works of historians on the subject — K.M. Shrimali, A.M. Shastri and S.R. Goyal. (For further details, see his *175 Years of Vākāṭaka History and Historiography*, Jodhpur, 2009; idem, 'Vākāṭaka Historiography: The Old and the New', published in the *Proceedings of the Indian History Congress*, Delhi, 2009-10, Kolkata, 2010, pp. 101-17).

In his very extensive Presidential Address entitled 'An Investigation into the Feudal Nature of the Vākāṭaka Economy: A Study of the Epigraphic Evidence', delivered to the XXXVII Annual Congress of the Epigraphical Society of India held at Baroda (*Journal of the Epigraphical Society of India*, Vol. XXXVIII, 2012, pp. 1-38), an analysis is made by Shankar Goyal on the different aspects of the feudal nature of the Vākāṭaka economy in the Deccan. Shankar Goyal points out that the Vākāṭakas were placed on a footing of near equality, though the Gupta rulers continued to remain their overlords. He opines that there was an increase in the number and prestige of the subordinate kings and there were not much of complexities of feudal system in the later part of the Gupta period. Quoting R.S. Sharma that the post-Mauryan changes in economy and society had brought out the tremendous impact of the land grants beginning with the period of the Sātavāhanas he proves that the feudal elements in economy and society had already become prevalent, though not dominant, in the period of the imperial Guptas. Shankar Goyal asserts that the process of strong feudalization of the state apparatus was set in motion by the practice of making grants of lands to the Brāhmaṇas from the first century A.D. onwards. He carefully traces the features in the Vākāṭaka economy in the light of their inscriptions which are indeed feudal in nature. He notes that there is a non-existence or non-availability or paucity of coins in respect of the Vākāṭaka rule. Coins in precious metals were obviously needed for higher trade and land transactions. Shankar Goyal says that the inscriptions of the Vākāṭakas refer to such transactions and silver coins must have existed in their kingdom. It is said that the Gupta gold and silver coins have been reported in some sites in the Vākāṭaka territories. The coins of other dynasties were also in circulation in Vākāṭaka kingdom. This leads to say that the rule of the Vākāṭakas in parts of central India and northern Deccan exhibits the growth of small village settlements and relative decline of urban economy and this is well brought out by Shankar Goyal. Further, after perusing through vital texts and materials, he emphatically says that the pressure on land was not much in the Vākāṭaka kingdom which could result in the obvious growth of agriculture based rural settlements. Shankar Goyal elaborates the information with the evidences from inscriptions. He narrates various instances from them and proves the existence of the feudal structure in the Vākāṭaka territories. He also brings out the general pattern of privileges and obligations of donees found in the Vākāṭaka inscriptions and points out that the Vākāṭakas kept the ownership of land in their own hands. It is also stated that a greater number of the settlements mentioned in the Vākāṭaka inscriptions belong to the category of rural settlements which is also supported by K.M. Shrimali. Shankar Goyal also argues that there was a decline of urban settlements in the Vākāṭaka territories and further states from inscriptional evidences that the relative decline of trade and traders in the Vidarbha region might have given momentum to the growth of rural settlements in the Vākāṭaka kingdom. While concluding his Presidential Address, Shankar Goyal states that "the two and a half centuries of the

Vākāṭaka ascendancy in parts of central India and the northern Deccan with its non-monetary, small-scale village settlements and relatively declining urban economy presents a *milieu* in which elements of feudalism are found and it should not be construed that every feature of feudalism should be noticeable in the Vākāṭaka territories."

Professor Shankar Goyal has a notable trait in analyzing the religious aspects of south India. While making a study on the 'Bhakti Movement in South India' in his Presidential Address delivered to the Cultural History Section of the South Indian History Congress at Tirunelveli in 2009 (*Proceedings of the Twenty-ninth Annual Session of the South Indian History Congress*, pp. 370-79), he moves cautiously to explain the nuances of the intrinsic values of the compositions of the hymns of Śaivaite Nāyanmārs and Vaishṇavite Āḷwārs. He correctly observes that harmony and tolerance characterized the relations among different religious sects and a change came over in the Tamil region in about the third century A.D. and people began to entertain fears that whole land would be converted to Jainism and Buddhism. As a result, Shankar Goyal avers, gifted saints of Śaivism and Vaishṇavism traversed the country singing, dancing, and debating all through their way and manifesting devotional aspects in their soul-stirring hymns. He rightly agrees with the view of K. R. Srinivasa Iyengar that these saints left behind them an imperishable legacy of devotional poetry which has rarely been equaled anywhere in quantity and quality.

Shankar Goyal also duly points out that the collection and preservation of the devotional songs of the Śaiva and Vaishṇava saints is to be attributed to the labours of two religious leaders Nambi Āṇḍār Nambi and Nāthamuni. The Bhakti movement reached its peak in the seventh century A.D. and Shankar Goyal appreciates the hymns of the Nāyanmārs and says that these songs are full of noble sentiments of devotion. He correctly estimates that they emphasize the majesty and grandeur of God and the feeling of submission, self-abnegation and surrender to God and this revival of Śaivism was a great stride in the direction of the Bhakti movement in south India. He exactly pinpoints that these Tamil saints of the Bhakti movement created a firm foundation of Tamil mysticism and Bhakti philosophy and made no distinction of caste, creed or sex in the cause of devotion.

As a diligent practitioner of history, Shankar Goyal has read in depth the complete lives of the Nāyanmārs and Āḷwārs of south India before investigating into their devotional literary works to understand their conception of bhakti marked by humility, penitence and repentance. He shows similar patterns in examining the traits of Āḷwārs who were looked upon as wise seers who exercised spiritual sovereignty over the hearts of men. He feels that their bhakti was certainly more intense than the bhakti advocated in *Bhagavadgītā*. He observes that they may not have succeeded in making much positive contribution to philosophical thought, but their revelation of a depth of fervor produced by the idea of deity as incarnating himself out of love for his creatures and desiring in return their whole-hearted devotion is worth noting. He feels that he has really enjoyed the poetical and spiritual fervor of the compositions of the Āḷwārs.

While narrating about Āṇḍāl or Godā who thirsted for the divine and poured forth her divine love into some of the finest poetry she wrote, Shankar Goyal remarks that the devotion of Āṇḍāl shows *mādhurya bhakti* in the most intense form like that of the gopīs of the *Bhāgavata* and of Mīrā of Rajasthan. He goes to the extent of saying that the Āḷwārs have transmuted their bhakti into *Śṛṇgāra* taking their cue from Godā. Quoting profusely from the views of R. Champakalakshmi, M.G.S. Narayanan, Kesavan Veluthat and others, Shankar Goyal states that the hymns of the Nāyanmārs and Āḷwārs reveal that the general nature of their bhakti was similar, that is, of dispassion in relation to the world and intense longing for personal union with God. He brings out the great similarity between the Upanishadic teachings and the hymns of bhakti saints. He also agrees rightly that the Bhakti movement was a protest against orthodox Vedic Brāhmaṇism and asserts that the hymns of Nāyanmārs and Āḷwārs made bhakti a well-established ideal for all and sundry and thus spells out an earnest message of personal religion to all the people.

In his Presidential Address entitled 'The Madras School of Ancient Indian Historians' delivered in the Historiography Section of the Twenty-third Session of the Tamil Nadu History Congress, held in Salem, Tamil Nadu, which was published in the *Proceedings Volume* of 2016, pp. 445-65, Shankar Goyal attempts to evaluate the historical writings of the Madras school of ancient Indian historians. He limits his study to a few prominent historians to focus more on political history in relation with socio-economic, religious and cultural changes.

Expressing his views on the historical works of S. Krishnaswami Aiyangar on a wide range of subjects, like, *Ancient India*, *South Indian History and Culture*, *Some Contributions of South India to Indian Culture*, *South India and Her Muhammadan Invaders*, *The Evolution of Hindu Administrative Institutions in South India* and *History of Tirupati*, Shankar Goyal considers that these works are of great importance for understanding the history of the peninsular India in its proper perspective. He avers that Aiyangar's contributions to south Indian history and culture is tremendous and there is no field from the earliest times to the British period where his suggestions can be ignored even now.

Shankar Goyal also comments on the fixation of chronology by

Aiyangar, particularly the Sangam literature in pre-Pallava period, referable to the early centuries of the Christian era and the date of the Kaḷabhra interregnum in south Indian history from 300 A.D. onwards to 700 A.D. The maritime relations between the Cholas and the Śailendra empire in Malaya and Sumatra, the heroic efforts of Kākatīyas and Hoysalas and their feudal chieftains to save south India from the effects of Muslim invasions and some more facts brought out by Aiyangar are aptly pointed out by Shankar Goyal. Further, he says that Aiyangar's contribution to the history of Vijayanagar is very significant and he is known for the new methods that he introduced in interpreting the history of Vijayanagar.

Shankar Goyal believes that Aiyangar possessed not a scrappy knowledge which most people get by reading incorrect translations of the original texts and Aiyangar's proficiency in Sanskrit was an asset to him. He also praises the involvement of Aiyangar with the journals, like, *Indian Antiquary* and *Journal of Indian History* and says his contributions in all these are worth serious perusal. He pays encomiums to him by saying, Aiyangar's career had been an inspiring example to many and deserves to be cherished as examples of devotion to scholarship.

While giving a detailed account of the works of K.A. Nilakanta Sastri, Shankar Goyal considers him as one of the distinguished scholars of ancient Indian history and archaeology , who also produced excellent students who have made a significant mark in their respective positions as academicians and educational administrators. Shankar Goyal classifies the complete works of Sastri into five categories as: (1) His major works whose dominant trait is political, (2) Works on cultural and social history, (3) Edited works, (4) Works on methodology, and (5) Some minor writings and stray historical articles. The earliest work to come out from the pen of Sastri, namely, *The Pāṇḍyan Kingdom*, and his subsequent writings, *The Cōḷas*, *Foreign Notices of South India* and the works on *Further Sources of Vijayanagar History* and *South Indian Influences in South East Asian Countries* were great contributions and are also models of historical writings in which original sources have been critically examined and fully utilized. This opinion of Goyal is the testimony to his candid understanding of the south Indian politics and culture and his deep interest in them. He further says that Sastri's works on south India builds up the broad outlines of the history of the peninsular India and brings out the multicoloured and fascinating cultural life and cultural movements of the people of south India. He appreciates Sastri's belief in the uniqueness of historical situations and his attitude in changing his opinion or altering his conclusion if newly discovered dependable data warranted such a change. Shankar Goyal feels that simple, clear and lucid style of Sastri's historical writings with polished language and depth of feeling avoiding highly ornamental and complex sentences add charm and freshness to his writings and asserts that he is to be credited with the writing of a full-scale connected history of south India from prehistoric times to the fall of Vijayanagar empire in the seventeenth century A.D. He also holds the view that Sastri had a laudable aim to discover the rich cultural heritage of south India that lay hidden for a long time. (On this, also see Shankar Goyal, 'Professor K.A. Nilakanta Sastri's Approach to History', in *Proceedings of the Twenty-fifth Annual Session of the South Indian History Congress*, Madurai, 2005, pp. 694-99; idem, 'Historiography of Professor K.A. Nilakanta Sastri', *Journal of Indian History and Culture*, XII, 2005, pp. 36-50)

Another historian of repute from south India, T.V. Mahalingam is, as aptly remarked by Shankar Goyal, an eminent historian who had greatly contributed to south Indian history. He rightly feels that his works, such as, *Administration and Social Life under Vijayanagar*, *Economic Life in the Vijayanagar Empire*, *Bāṇas in South Indian History*, *South Indian Polity* and many more add much strength to south Indian historiography. His collection and cataloguing of records and Mackenzie manuscripts have been pointed out by Shankar Goyal which are of some value to the south Indian history. He also lauds the other important work of Mahalingam on the Pallavas entitled *Inscriptions of the Pallavas* which is described by many as a source book throwing light on many aspects of the early medieval south Indian history, polity, society and economy. Shankar Goyal's appreciation on the preparation of a series of ten volumes entitled *Topographical List of Inscriptions in the Tamil Nadu and Kerala States up to A.D.1300* by T.V. Mahalingam as a monumental work containing information from more than 15,000 inscriptions, lithic records and copper plates listed and arranged in proper manner has drawn our attention to this remarkable endeavour. He also praises its value for serious researchers as a work which presents various facets of political, social, economic, religious and cultural life of the people in different regions in the ancient and early medieval period of history and further states that these materials can be fruitfully used for reconstructing several unknown aspects of south Indian history and polity. Further, he also commends that Mahalingam's information on Upanishadic evidences add new dimensions to south Indian history but laments that Mahalingam also followed the 'traditional' approach of earlier historians who wrote countless monographs on the history of India. (Cf., for details, Shankar Goyal, 'Some Notes on T.V. Mahalingam as a Historian', *Proceedings of the Twenty-fourth Annual Session of the South Indian History Congress*, Poondi, 2014, pp. 734-38).

In his Valedictory Address 'Need of an Integral View of the Political History of South India', delivered at the XXII Annual Session of the South Indian History Congress, held at Thiruvananthapuram, Kerala, February 25-27, 2002 (published in the *Proceedings of the Twenty-second Annual Session of the South Indian History Congress*, pp. 515-17), Shankar Goyal has argued that now there is an immediate need to study the political history of south India from the holistic or integral point of view in which cultural and political aspects of life are treated as various aspects of an organic whole, for the narrative part dominating in most of the recent works on political history treats it as if it has no relation with the socio-economic, religious and cultural changes. According to Shankar Goyal, the periods of south Indian history of which an integral picture of political history may be attempted include those of the Chālukyas of Vātāpi, Pallavas, Chōlas and the Vijayanagar empire. Some significant works dealing with their sources and various aspects of their history were published in the latter half of the last century by S. Krishnaswami Aiyangar, K.A.N. Sastri and T.V. Mahalingam. But as they were engrossed in the 'reconstruction' of political history and various aspects of cultural history they did not find sufficient time to produce an integral view of political history.

On the whole, according to Shankar Goyal, "there is no denying the fact that being the pioneering effort, the works of Aiyangar, Sastri and Mahaligam provided the much needed and reliable chronological framework to study south Indian history. But the fact remains that the period in which all of them worked, many other historians of the country were producing their works from altogether new angles—Marxist and integral. Had Sastri and Mahalingam taken up the history of south India from the integral standpoint, with their remarkable knowledge of the subject and grasp of source-materials, their works would have become trend-setters for the succeeding generation of historians."

In a significant article titled 'Buddhism in Early South Indian History', published in the *Proceedings of the South Indian History Congress*, Tiruchirappalli, 2003, pp. 539-42, Shankar Goyal discusses the spread of Buddhism in Tamil land and its impact on literature, more particularly the *Maṇimekhalai*, in which we find clear evidence of the popularity of Mahāyāna Buddhism. As is well-known, the *Maṇimekhalai* is one of the five great epics in Tamil. Its author Sittalāisātan or Sattanār, a grain merchant of Madurai and an erudite scholar of Tamil, Sanskrit and Pali, has been variously placed between second to sixth century A.D. Like the stories of the Greek epics *Iliad* and *Odyssey*, the stories of the *Śilappadikāram* and *Maṇimekhalai* are connected, i.e., the story of *Maṇimekhalai* continues the thread where the *Śilappadikāram* stops. There are thirty chapters (*cantos*) in the *Maṇimekhalai* which all speak about the life-history of Maṇimekhalai, the daughter of Kovalan and Mādhavī. While narrating the nunnery life of Maṇimekhalai, the heroine of the epic, it also expounds the Buddhistic philosophy. Shankar Goyal gives reasons to believe that in the *Maṇimekhalai* all the important tenets of Mahāyānism are reflected. Obviously when this epic was composed Mahāyānism had become very popular in the Far South.

In another well reasoned paper titled 'Harsha's Relations with the Deccan and Far South', published in the *Proceedings of the Twenty-second Annual Session of the South Indian History Congress*, Thiruvananthapuram, 2002, pp. 135-37, Shankar Goyal critically examined Harsha's relationship with Pulakeśin II, the Chālukya emperor of Vātāpi. So far many scholars have been assuming that Pulakeśin II had fought and defeated Harsha either between 610 and 612 or sometime before 634 A.D., the date of Aihole record. But after examining all the evidences, literary and epigraphical, Shankar Goyal has convincingly shown that "the struggle between these two great monarchs was going on even in 640 A.D. when Yuan Chwang visited Maharashtra." He concludes, "His (Yuan Chwang's) testimony proves that the Harsha-Pulakeśin conflict recorded in the Aihole inscription was not decisive. This struggle was a protracted one and was going on in 640, for in his record of the journey made in 640 Yuan Chwang explicitly says that at the time of his visit Harsha had 'not yet conquered' Pulakeśin. It, therefore, follows that the conflict which took place before 634 was only one of the numerous battles fought by them. It is, thus, quite possible that the conflict between the two also occurred before the battle recorded in the Aihole *praśasti* of 634, for which no evidence is now available. This analysis renders the question of the date of the Harsha-Pulakeśin war mentioned in the Aihole *praśasti* quite irrelevant. We can safely say that the conflict recorded in the Aihole *praśasti* was in the nature of a battle, not of a war. That is, the Aihole *praśasti* records only one phase of the long-drawn war between Pulakeśin and Harsha, and not the whole war."

On the opinion of some scholars that Harsha carried his victorious arms to the Far South also, Shankar Goyal emphasized that the evidence of a seventh century inscription composed in old Kannaḍa, found near Gaddemane village in Shimoga district of Karnataka, does not prove that the king Śila-āditya mentioned in it is identical with Harsha. Here, as Shankar Goyal points out, even the name of Harsha is not given. Similarly, the evidence of a stanza by Mayūra, supposed to be Bāṇa's father-in-law (or son-in-law), making a reference to the conquest by Harsha of the countries of Kuntala, Choḷa, Madhyadeśa and Kāñchī, is too weak to substantiate the theory of Harsha's invasion of the deep south. Shankar Goyal argues that "Had Harsha been able to conquer these southern regions he would had become the emperor of almost the entire Indian sub-continent. Making Harsha the Lord of such a vast empire should require substantial positive evidence which is not forthcoming."

Again in the Deccan history, Shankar Goyal in his article, 'Chandragupta II's Relations with the Vākāṭakas during the Regency of Prabhāvatīguptā', published in the *Proceedings of the Twenty-fourth Annual Session of the South Indian History Congress*, Calicut, 2004, pp. 128-32, explains the political influence of Chandragupta II on the Vākāṭakas during the regency of Prabhāvatīguptā which information is based on the Pune and Rithpur copper plates. He states that this evidence of the documents should be testified with a critical scrutiny. He discusses the box-headed characters and nail-headed characters found in the copper plates which give information regarding grants made during the rule of the Vākāṭakas. It is found from the evidences that the Guptas had matrimonial alliance with the Vākāṭaka rulers. Chandragupta II gave his daughter Prabhāvatīguptā in marriage to Rudrasena II, the Vākāṭaka ruler, and a few historians, such as, P.L. Gupta and A.S. Altekar argue that the Gupta rulers extended influence on the Vākāṭaka court and its politics. But on the basis of genealogy, religion and the Deccan traditions, Shankar Goyal assertively explains with adequate evidences that some sort of Gupta influence on the Vākāṭakas during the minority of the sons of Rudrasena II might have been possible but not to that great extent as it is suggested by some historians.

In continuation to this, Shankar Goyal presented a paper at the 16th World Sanskrit Conference, 2015, Sanskrit Studies Centre, Silpakorn University, Bangkok, Thailand, on the recently discovered Ramtek Prabhāvatīguptā Memorial Fragmentary Stone Inscription which is of great value for the Vākāṭaka-Gupta history (published in the *Epigraphic Studies*, Select Papers from the Panel on Epigraphy, ed. D.P. Dubey, New Delhi, 2018, pp. 129-37). According to Shankar Goyal, the testimony of the extant portions of this highly fragmentary record clarify and elaborate numerous points of the Gupta-Vākāṭaka relations and the history of the Deccan. Firstly, it makes it clear that Chandragputa indeed looked after the Vākāṭaka administration during the minority of Prabhāvatīguptā's sons. Secondly, it also shows that he was believed to have been a *tri-samudra-nātha* (the lord of the three oceans), a claim which on the one hand, indicates that for sometime he exercised at least nominal suzerainty over the Vākāṭaka kingdom including almost whole of the Deccan and, on the other, tends to strengthen the testimony of the Meharauli record regarding the warlike activities of Chandra (generally identified with Chandragupta II) in south India. The record also mentions some person who is described as bearing the entire burden of the great kingdom which was difficult to bear and as the beast of burden. He was obviously Chandragupta II who is believed to have looked after the Vākāṭaka kingdom after the death of his son-in-law Rudrasena II.

But Shankar Goyal argues that the only military achievement of

Chandragupta II was his Śaka conquest in western India, while this inscription refers to his being "the lord of the three oceans". "Does it mean a fresh conquest of south India by Chandragupta II or does it mean only a reference to his father Samudragupta's conquests of the southern seas?", he asks. In Shankar Goyal's view, "this record does not prove that Chandragupta II achieved some significant and fresh success in the south as a literal translation would lead us to believe." To him it sounds more logical that *tri-samudra-nātha* and all other such descriptions applied also to Samudragupta, Kumāragupta I and Skandagupta are merely conventional descriptions without much historical significance. However, the same cannot be said about the title *tri samudra-toya-pīta-vāhana* which is applied to Gautamīputra Sātakarṇī, for he controlled a considerable portion of the southern peninsula. As regards the Vākāṭakas, there is absolutely no direct hint of Chandragupta II's hegemony over them. This inscription has absolutely nothing to say about any sort of military or administrative support to the Vākāṭakas rendered by Chandragupta II. It only concedes the overlordship of Chandragupta II in southern peninsula only *in theory*. Even the numerous inscriptions of Chandragupta II and his successors do not inform about such an eventuality. Therefore, Shankar Goyal is right when he warns us for not indulging in wild speculations based on conjectural restoration of the now lost text in the Ramtek inscription.

In a methodical and precise article titled 'A Comment on Hans T. Bakker's Suggestion on the Vākāṭakas' (*Proceedings of the Thirty-second Annual Session of the South Indian History Congress*, Chennai, 2012, pp. 839-42), Shankar Goyal states that due to the recent discoveries of numerous Vākāṭaka inscriptions many amazing publications have been made by scholars, such as, K.M. Shrimali, A.M. Shastri and S.R. Goyal and more recently by Hans T. Bakker. What is interesting to note, Shankar Goyal writes, is the fact that all these scholars have not only worked on those areas of Vākāṭaka history which had been overlooked by their predecessors but have also extended researches different from each other: Shrimali discusses the economy of the Vākāṭakas for the first time and focuses on its agrarian structure on the basis of epigraphic evidence. Shastri makes the best use of all the source-material to prepare the stage for a more balanced historical outline. Goyal's approach is not "what happend?" but "why did it happen ?", not found in other works on the Vākāṭakas. Bakker uses all the evidence and earlier works at his disposal to study art, religion and culture during Vākāṭaka times.

In brief, according to Hans T. Bakker, it is no longer productive to concentrate exclusively on one branch of the Vākāṭakas by ignoring or marginalizing the evidence with regard to the other branch. The kings of Vatsagulma and Nandivardhana made up one family and their history is that of one family for all it is worth: divorce and rapprochement, dominance and submission, peaceful coexistence marred by fits of rivalry, occasionally erupting into downright civil war. Not only is the political history of both houses interlocked, but so are their religion and culture. For Bakker the art of Ajanta can no longer be detached from the artistic achievements of the eastern Vākāṭakas. Bakker has also shown that from the middle of the sixties the kingdom of the Vākāṭakas has come to be seen as pivotal in the history of India, being essential for our understanding of the development of its art, religion and culture; as such it is on a par with the Gupta world, of which it can no longer be considered to be merely a province.

Here Shankar Goyal does not reject altogether the significance of Bakker's thesis that the kingdom of the Vākāṭakas is to be seen, 'on a par with the Gupta world'; but to him it appears to be somewhat exaggerated preposition. As is well-known, Shankar Goyal further points out, most historians have accepted the importance of the Vākāṭaka age in Central India and the Deccan within the Gupta empire. Even Hans Bakker has categorically stated that "at the crossroads of the Indo-Aryan north and Dravidian south, the northern culture of the Gupta kingdom reached the Deccan and developed a character of its own. The major religions of the times, Buddhism, Bhāgavatism and Maheśvarism, all had important settlements in the Vākāṭaka kingdom; constructions in stone, brick or rock testify to the high standards of the arts reached in Central India by the middle of the 5th century."

Shankar Goyal argues that the prosperity of the Vākāṭaka kingdom, as seen by Bakker, presents two contradictory aspects. On the one hand, almost total absence of the Vākāṭaka coins, certainly of their gold and silver coins, gives the impression that the Vākāṭaka economy was extremely poor. On the other, the development of Hindu temples on and around the Rāmagiri (Ramtek hill) and the Buddhist caves in Ajanta do testify to the prosperity of the Vākāṭaka kingdom. This contradiction, Shankar Goyal remarks, may be resolved if we believe that the Vākāṭakas were under the political and cultural influence of the Guptas and the caves and temples which are the only proofs of this prosperity were the result of their relationship—direct or indirect—with the Guptas. However, he asserts that the cultural history of the imperial Guptas and the Vākāṭakas and the monuments of their period cannot be so precisely dated since it merges at both ends in the continuous development of earlier and later periods. "Be that as it may", Shankar Goyal concludes, "the fact that the artistic activities of the Vākāṭaka kingdom were the result of the Gupta influence necessitates some rethinking on Hans Bakker's hypothesis that the Vākāṭakas were on a par with the imperial Guptas."

Thus, Shankar Goyal makes a very good analysis in the studies on the history of Deccan and south India. His in-depth studies on the various aspects of the regions of the Deccan and south India, sources — primary and secondary — and on the distinguished scholars of these regions pave the way for future researchers to further investigate many issues yet left untouched. These works only confirm the general belief that Shankar Goyal's researches establish a singular tradition of historical research in its own right.

REFERENCES

Bakker, Hans T., *The Vākāṭakas : An Essay in Hindu Iconology*. Groningen, 1997.

— (ed.), *The Vākāṭaka Heritage : Indian Culture at the Crossroads*. Groningen, 2004.

Bailey, G.M. and Kesarcodi-Watson, I. (eds.), *Bhakti Studies*. New Delhi, 1992.

Champakalakshmi, R., 'Historiography of South India — New Directions', her Presidential Address to the Historiography Section. In the *Proceedings of the South Indian History Congress*, VII Annual Session, Madras, 1987.

—, 'From Devotion and Dissent to Dominance : The Bhakti of the Tamil Āḷvārs and Nāyanārs'. In *Religious Movements in South Asia : 600-1800*, ed. David N. Lorenzen, New Delhi, 2006, pp. 54 ff.

Chhabra, B.Ch., Agrawala, P.K., Agrawal, Ashvini and Goyal, Shankar (eds.), *Reappraising Gupta History for S.R. Goyal*. New Delhi, 1992.

Dikshitar, V.R. Ramachandra, *The Śilappadikāram*. Oxford, 1939.

Gopinatha Rao, *Sir Subrahmanya Ayyar Lectures on the History of Śrī Vaiṣṇavas*. Madras, 1923.

Goyal, Shankar, *Recent Historiography of Ancient India*. Jodhpur, 1997.

—, *The Image of Classical India*. Jodhpur, 1997.

—, *175 Years of Vākāṭaka History and Historiography*. Jodhpur, 2009.

—, *Studies in the History of Deccan and South India*. Jodhpur, 2009.

Goyal, S.R., *A History of the Imperial Guptas*. Allahabad, 1967.

—, *Gupta aura Vākāṭaka Sāmrājyoṅ kā Yuga*. Meerut, 1988.

—, *The Imperial Guptas : A Multidisciplinary Political Study*. Jodhpur, 2005.

—, *A History of the Vākāṭaka-Gupta Relations*. Jodhpur, 2006.

—, *Fundamentals of Paurāṇika Hinduism*. Jodhpur, 2009.

Goyal, S.R. and Goyal, Shankar (eds.), *Indian Art of the Gupta Age*. Jodhpur, 2000.

Gupta, S.P. (ed.), *Aspects of India's History and Culture*. New Delhi, 1973.

Hooper, J.S.M., *The Hymns of the Āḷvārs*. Oxford, 1929.

Joshi, Munish Chandra, Gupta, S.K. and Goyal, Shankar (eds.), *King Chandra and the Meharauli Pillar*. Meerut, 1989.

Kandaswamy, S.N., *Buddhism as Expounded in Maṇimēkalai*. Annamalainagar, 1978.

Majumdar, R.C. and Altekar, A.S. (eds.), *A New History of the Indian People*, Vol. VI : *The Vākāṭaka-Gupta Age (Circa 200-550 A.D.)*. Lahore, 1946.

Majumdar, R.C. and Pusalker, A.D. (eds.), *The Classical Age*. Bombay, 1954.

Narayana Ayyar, C.V., *Origin and Early History of Śaivism in South India.* Madras, 1936.

Narayanan, M.G.S. and Kesavan, Veluthat, 'Bhakti Movement in South India'. In *Indian Movements : Some Aspects of Dissent, Protest and Reform*, ed. S.C. Malik, Simla, 1978, pp. 33-66.

Sastri, K.A.N., *Development of Religion in South India.* Madras, 1963.

—, *A History of South India.* Madras, 1966.

Shastri, A.M. (ed.), *The Age of the Vākāṭakas.* New Delhi, 1992.

—, *Vākāṭakas : Sources and History.* New Delhi, 1997.

Shrimali, K.M., *Agrarian Structure in Central India and the Northern Deccan (c. A.D. 300-500) : A Study of Vākāṭaka Inscriptions.* New Delhi, 1987.

—, 'Religions in Complex Societies : The Myth of the 'Dark Age' '. In *Religion in Indian History*, ed. Irfan Habib, New Delhi, 2007, pp. 36-70.

Spink, Walter M., 'The Vākāṭaka Caves at Ajanta and Their Successors'. In *Reappraising Gupta History for S. R. Goyal*, eds. B. Ch. Chhabra et al, New Delhi, 1992, pp. 247-62.

Subrahmanian, N., *Tamilian Historiography.* Madurai, 1988.

Thapar, Romila, *A History of India*, Vol. I. New Delhi, 1966.

—, *The Penguin History of Early India.* New Delhi, 2003.

Yazdani, G. (ed.), *Early History of the Deccan.* Oxford, 1960.

Chapter Nine

Shankar Goyal on the Problems of the Decline of Political Theory and Political History

NAGENDRA SINGH BHATI
Department of Political Science
Jai Narain Vyas University, Jodhpur

Politics, history and philosophy are closely related subjects. Politics in due course of time becomes history. For any meaningful research in political history, dimensions of the past, present and future cannot be ignored. History is the guide of politics and philosophy is its durable base. It is only through the broad understanding of politics and philosophy that one can view history properly and in right perspective. It in only through the reliance on history that the genuine foundation of vigorous political science can be laid. It is almost indubitable to asseverate the necessity of historical study as a basis and ground work for an understanding of political institutions. History provides political theorists in a great measure the raw materials and adorable data. To fully comprehend political science in its fundamental relations, one must study it historically, and to interpret history in its true significance one must study that politically. As studies they are, therefore, mutually contributing and supplementary. "Politics is vulgar", said John Seeley, "when not liberalized by history; and history fades into mere literature when it loses sight of its relation to politics." "History without political science", he said, "has no fruit; and political science without history has no root." This root-and-fruit aphorism contains more truth than most of us have been in a position to discover. According to Michael Oakeshott, "Politics uprooted from history becomes "a second rate form of human activity, neither an art nor a science, at once corrupting the soul and fatiguing to the mind." Political science thus is drivel, dull and meaningless unless it is supported by the dignity and transcendence of historical experiences. Estranged and amputated from history, political studies would be ephemeral and routine, offering meager satisfactions. History and political science as such should be regarded as working partners in the achievement of what is, in large measure, a common reflective task in the building of a 'decent society'.

Professor Shankar Goyal is one of the well known authorities not only of ancient Indian history but also general history of India and the world. He has done research work on a broad range of subjects, including political history, historiography, feudalism, epigraphy, numismatics, art, etc. He is of course a scholar of history but has been deeply involved with other related disciplines, particularly political science. In his works there is a true mixture of history and politics and his writings show close relationship of history and political science. His edited work *History and Politics: Essays in Honour of Professor P.S. Bhati* (Jodhpur, 2015) reflects his ideas on contemporary political theory. In his 'Editorial' to this book (pp. xvii-xx) he is responsive to the problem of decline of political theory. While discussing this question, he points out that "Now, in the Western world the problem of the decline of political history is being solved by transforming the very concept of political history. The dictum of Jacques Pirenne that "the true aim of historical research is a knowledge of the factors that control men living in society" will perhaps be acceptable, at least on a tentative basis, to the majority of present-day Western scholars for their investigations. This definition implies that the different aspects of history cannot be studied in isolation from one another but only as facets of an integrated reality. ... Thus, it is apparent that political history in the West is staging a comeback by borrowing the methods, spirit, theoretical approach and materials of the very social sciences, such as political science, which are pushing it into the background." This is the essence of what is nowadays called the integral approach to political history and Professor Shankar Goyal not only supports it fully but it has also found reflection in his own works.

Shankar Goyal has written a long 'Introduction' on Professor P.S. Bhati's contribution to the study of politics and history in this book in which, besides writing about the contribution of Bhati, he has given his own ideas and thought on the decline of political theory and political history. This painstakingly research piece is one of his major contributions in the field. Commenting on Bhati's book entitled *The Normative Traditions in Political Theory* (Jodhpur, 1998), he writes, "The classical theories furnish the foundations of nearly all the work which is being done today in the field of politics. What is now required is synthesis, the building of bridges from theory to theory." (p. xxiv). He hopes that a comparative review of the classical theories in the context of this problem, and of the modern studies which build on them, may bring us some way on the road to such a goal. Many contemporary political thinkers such as Eugene J. Meehan, Andrew Hacker, Fred M. Frohock, Bernard Crick and many more have pleaded for a close cooperation between the normative and empirical political theories. All these thinkers enumerate the utility of both the traditional and contemporary concepts of political theory and say that there are few bridges between the two concepts of political theory. All these thinkers, according to Goyal, are impressive because they see, or choose to see, that the task of reintegration, or the creation of a new political synthesis, is the main riddle confronting political theory today. Supporting the normative tradition in political theory and history, Goyal further writes that the ghosts of Plato, Hobbes, Hegel and Marx would continue to haunt the panquets that toast the future. The decorous normative tradition and chaste political values are central to the understanding of politics, and through it alone, one could hope to restrain to the 'idiot masses' who have made over to the power elites and their 'crackpot realism' the final destiny of mankind. With the restoration of vestal and prude political values alone, the blessed moments would supervene and the heavenly days befall political theory.

Commenting on the article entitled 'Political Ideas of Michael Oakeshott', written by Bhati (*IJPS*, Vol. 3, No. 2 and Vol. 4, No. 1, January, 1980, pp. 254-64), Shankar Goyal observes that Oakeshott is one of the foremost and leading political thinkers of our times who not only continues to support the traditional philosophical political theory but is sincere and impressive in his criticism of the empirical-analytical approaches. He stands out in the history of modern normative philosophy as the creator of a system. His major contribution has been to recover political theory as a tradition of enquiry and regain for political science the possibility of a critical, theoretical analysis. (pp. xxvi-xxvii).

On Bhati's article 'Rise and Decline of Behavioural Revolution in Political Science' (*IJPS*, Vol. 8, July, 1984, pp. 106-21), Shankar Goyal remarks that nowadays there is more criticism of behaviouralism than support to it. The traditional political scientists have always criticized this tendency. According to them, the behaviouralism and the post-behaviouralism have not been successful in establishing explanatory laws, as compared to the older and the well known generalizations arrived at in the traditional political theory. Of course, there are supporters of behaviouralism nowadays as well. There is a conflict between tradition and modernity. The present-day necessity is to reconcile them. (p. xxviii). Commenting on Bhati's article 'Post- Behavioural Revolution in Contemporary Political Theory' (*IJPS*, Vol. 10, December, 1986, pp. 102-09), Goyal states that the post-behaviouralism is a movement, that is, an aggregate of people, and also an intellectual tendency. It tries to push political science in new directions. (p. xxix).

Shankar Goyal has put forward scholarly arguments in support of P.S. Bhati's paper 'The Normative Tradition in Political Theory' (*IJPS*, Vol. 12, December, 1988, pp. 79-106). While elaborating his ideas in detail he traces the normative tradition beginning from Greek political thinkers to Karl Marx. According to Goyal, the normative political theory has a complicated arrangement, sensitive frontiers and includes qualitative ideas, which can be best understood by studying the many ways that its recognized masters have practised it. No philosopher and no historical age may be regarded to have defined it conclusively. For the student of history, normative theory provides an "indispensable key", for the student of contemporary public affairs and the inquirer who wishes to peep into the future, it provides an "equally valuable guide". To modern behavioural thinkers, it is necessary to remember that history may not repeat itself, but , in every age there is a large carry-over of the past political thinking and a heavy seeding of ideas that bear fruit in years to come. (pp. xxx-xxxiv).

Shankar Goyal critically examines the causes of decline and revival of normative political theory while discussing Bhati's article 'The Decline of Normative Political Theory and Its Revival' (*IJPS*, Vol. 13, December, 1989, pp. 66-82). He asserts that the causes for decline (if it is correct?) of normative political theory are the formidable growth in the volume of behavioural studies and improvement in the techniques they employ, imperfections of traditional political theory and its mode of inquiry, its historical approach and technological revolution. But, according to Goyal, political theory is not dead, it is up again with rejuvenation and renewed vigour. It is up again because increased interest taken by contemporary political theorists in: (1) a critical, theoretical analysis of politics; (2) combining the realms of fact-finding systematic knowledge and theory-building on the one hand, and the sphere of social policy, political problems and ideological issues on the other; and (3) the reassessment of key political concepts. On the whole, concludes Goyal, political theory cannot hope to develop in the absence of a philosophic framework and the most important dividing line between political theories running along the value committed. Value-free axis seems to be a passing fad. (pp. xxxv-xxxvi).

Commenting on Bhati's article entitled 'The Old and New in Contemporary Political Theory' (*IJPS*, Vol. 14, December, 1990, pp. 44-58), Shankar Goyal argues that the most probable way out for the political theory ought to be to conserve its reflexive, appreciative or traditional character, rooted in prescriptive values, stimulative convictions and macro-generalizations, arrived at by historical observations. A real political theory must be rooted in ethics, philosophy, history, economics and related fields. A Political theory would be rootless without philosophy. Similarly, political theory owes much to history. It is through history that political theory can be used to recreate life, to understand the political phenomenon, to show the creative manifestations and reveal the movements of political life. Thus, it is doubtless that political theory remains unproductive without being conjoined with the study of history, philosophy and economics in depth. Political theory, therefore, ought to be rooted in value premises, and factual knowledge ought to supplement its dimensions. (pp. xxxvi-xxxvii).

All these arguments show that Shankar Goyal has a deep and thorough knowledge on the problems of the decline of political theory and political history. He intelligently reconciles political theory and history which is very important for the scholars of the contemporary period. It is only through history and philosophy, Goyal feels, that political science can retain its creative and radiant traditions, and thereby can become a perceptive and versatile science providing a comforting solace to the bewildered citizens of the technological age. Surely, these ideas and thought of Shankar Goyal on the problems of political theory and political history cannot be questioned.

Chapter Ten

India as a Multicultural Society : Shankar Goyal's View

SHARAD RAJIMWALE
Professor, Department of English
Jai Narain Vyas University, Jodhpur

India has ever been an enigma to the world. Its diversity has dazzled the scholars and its opulent cultures got romanticized in the travel accounts of foreign visitors. But what puzzled them most is the fact that despite such variety of cultures, faiths and languages, it remains a single unified entity. Whether it was ever in the past a 'nation' in the sense in which we understand it today may be debated over ad infinitum, but what surprises the world is that its multiplicity of cultures and religions, racial diversity and linguistic plurality became its strength that caused it to hold together, for in the long run it turned out to be its true identity. It has also been a land of a number of empires and principalities, rising and falling, fighting with one another, intriguing, scheming, speaking unfamiliar languages and sometimes following different faiths; yet ultimately they were proud to be called Indian.

There has always been a peculiar fluidity at the base of all the divergent features of its socio-political life and linguistic variety which despite geographical barriers tended to keep them linked to such an extent that later scholars were compelled to formulate it in the now well-known phrase, "unity in diversity". Pandit Jawaharlal Nehru expresses his wonder in these words, "Astonishing thought: that any culture or civilization should have this continuity for five or six thousand years or more; and not in a static, unchanging sense for India was changing and progressing all the time." (Nehru 1982). In recent days there has appeared a whole corpus of studies in different fields such as history, political science, sociology, cultural studies and so on, aimed at conducting serious research in this phenomenon of diversity, and understanding whether the unity claimed by certain sections is truly a significant factor or merely a romantic illusion.

Professor Shankar Goyal's book entitled, *Prachina Bharatiya Itihasa aura Samskriti, Naye Sandarbha aura Ayam*, published in 2001 by Book Enclave, Jaipur, embodies such an attempt to understand the emergence of multicultural matrix of Indian society. The present work is part one of the two part opus. It is divided into four chapters, each of which is further divided into various sections.

The first part of the book launches into a detailed presentation of the historical predispositions which coloured the opinions of the early Europeans, particularly British scholars as well as their followers in the sub-continent. Starting with Rudyard Kipling and Lord Macaulay to Katherine Mayo and Arthur Koestler, Professor Shankar Goyal lays out before us the central preoccupations of the Western narrative, laden with what Edward Said has described in *Orientalism* as "the pivotal source of the inaccuracy of cultural representations that form the foundation of Western thought and perception of Eastern world." (Said 1995). Several postmodern scholars like Bordeau, Fanon, Aijaz Ahmed and Foucault gave importance to the fact that exclusionary representation has been key to the colonialist project of maintaining its supremacy over Eastern world. Shankar Goyal has enumerated some of the tropes that the Western scholars floated, to be later taken up by the scholars of the East too like 'uncivilized', 'barbarous', 'docile', 'effeminate', 'primitive', 'semi-dormant', 'lazy' as defining features of the colonized people which continued to be perpetuated and further stereotyped by novelists, poets, travelogue writers, memoirists, and so on. Bill Ashcroft, Gareth Griffiths and Helen Tiffin see this process intrinsically bound with the development of the "ideological climate" "where it leads to the naturalizing values (e.g. civilization, humanity,etc.) which, conversely, established 'savagery', 'primitive', as their antitheses and the object of a reforming zeal." (Ashcroft et al 2002). It was necessary for them to construct such an ideological atmosphere, for then it would be convenient to prominently project the "white man's burden" image to which Shankar Goyal refers here which is to civilize the subject people. For the European settlers created an intense dislike in the hearts of the educated natives for their own culture and social-ethical norms for the propagation of which such a class of natives was created. We glimpse this in the pronouncements of certain leading minds of the country who openly expressed gratitude to their rulers for the beneficial influences of "one of the most generous and enlightened nations of the world" (Roy 1823) in undertaking to educate the countrymen in the "arts and sciences of modern Europe". (*Ibid.*). A peculiarly servile tone of address marks these effusions of full-throated admiration for the West. However, what Shankar Goyal misses is the fact that orientation of the growing educated Indians was not always so appallingly tilted; they began to think independently and in many cases English education and language became instrumental in generating a staunch nationalistic consciousness as the examples of Henry Derozio, the Dutt family and the Tagore family show. The tool of English modes of thinking by which English administrators wished to enslave the minds of new Indian generation boomeranged on them as it awakened the Indian pride in its ancient culture and civilization, like the heat of a fire unknowingly stoked into life.

For the better part of this section, Shankar Goyal focuses our attention on the proliferating Western modes of research which over decades produced different schools of thought, ranging from Marxist to extreme nationalistic to liberal-democratic as seen in the works of D.D. Kosambi, R.S. Sharma, R.C. Majumdar, Romila Thapar, Irfan Habib, Satish Chandra, D.N. Jha, Meenakshi Jain, S.A. Dange, Pandit Jawaharlal Nehru, William Dalrymple, etc. Critical of Western biases and interpretative methods, most of the Indian scholars struck an independent line of investigation in order to unravel the deliberately concealed truths. Even in the nineteenth century, intellectuals like Romesh Chunder Dutt, Dadabhai Naoroji, Gopal Krishna Gokhale and Mahadev Govind Ranade had initiated a courageous indictment of the British maladministration that led to the recurring economic crises and resulted in famines and other forms of man-made misery. Their speeches and writings analyzed the exploitative machinery which facilitated "the drainage of wealth from India through home charges payable to Britain and unregulated exports, the absence of protection for India's infant industries, and the negative implications of even construction efforts like railways, which deprived many providers of traditional transport services and facilitated the import of British manufactured goods." (Internet). More than S.A. Dange's book mentioned by Shankar Goyal, it is the work of Debiprasad Chattopadhyaya, K. Damodaran, Gangadhar Adhikari, K.N. Panikkar, Amalendu De, Rajni Palme Dutt, Hiren Mukherji, and P.C. Joshi that provided the shape and direction to the Marxist interpretation of Indian history and society. He also mentions Nirad C. Choudhary which sounds a jarring note as his fame is more in the field of literature than history or cultural studies. Like V.S. Naipaul and Khushwant Singh, Nirad babu has earned some sort of negative reputation for making spiteful and malicious observations on Indian society, mainly based on personal experiences rather than verifiable facts. Besides, he is a well-known anglophile and by his own assertions an inveterate admirer of things English.

Shankar Goyal undertakes to explain the terms "culture" and "civilization" in some detail. In the modern and postmodern contexts it is necessary to be clear about what these two terms exactly mean when we are dealing with the history of the country. A lot of confusion has arisen about the use of these terms in recent years teeming with political disturbances. "Culture" became the rallying slogan behind the sudden rise of Nazi power in 1930s. The notion of culture can easily arouse mass emotions as we are witnessing today. Shankar Goyal makes use of the definitions put forward by such eminent scholars in the past as Malinowski, Arnold Toynbee and MacIver in order to find a common ground for establishing what culture connotes. He rightly distinguishes it from the term "civilization" which usually refers to material attainments and then goes on to underline that the two sides may not necessarily have much to share. In the old fashioned way, culture is seen to refer to abstract markers like ideas, beliefs and concepts. Raymond Williams' *Keywords* defines culture "as a process of individual enrichment, as when we say that someone is "cultured" (in 1605, Francis Bacon wrote about the "culture and manurance of minds"), culture as group's "particular way of life", as when we talk about French culture, company culture, or multiculturalism." (Rothman 2014). There is much discussion of this multifaceted term and the implications of its multiple uses. In the case of developing societies like those of the Middle East and South East Asia, one may notice a lag between the level of civilizational attainments and the slow-moving value systems inherited by the people from historical past. It is an intricate issue, as in the case of India where many cultural entities flourished over centuries and left their mark on one another.

The second part of Shankar Goyal's book discusses the issue of India's growth as a nation and takes up the difficult exercise of clarifying the concept of 'nation'. Here also opinions are divided into those who follow Western thinking and those who believe in exploring indigenous sources. According to the former, the concept of nation originated in the west where particular societies formed some sort of homogeneous entities sharing racial, cultural and religious commonalty. Quoting both old British and Indian historians, Shankar Goyal seeks to offer a picture of India's unique national life wherein several states upholding their sovereign existence clashed with each other and expanded or reduced in size their empires in perpetual military expeditions. If loyalty to one's soil or geographical domain and political sovereignty is what we mean by patriotism, then certainly we have been a land of many nations, for men were punished for treason and rewarded for sacrifices to their ideals. Those who support the idea of India as a nation refuse to accept the Western notion, insisting that the various states such as Magadha, Avanti, Anga, Vijayanagar, etc. share a common cultural-spiritual heritage which binds them into a larger " Bharatavarsha". If we accept the Western idea of nation then even in Western countries internecine separatist identity conflicts dotted their history. They have also been plagued by religious and racial problems, perhaps far bloodier than witnessed by us. It has already been mentioned how Hitler capitalized on the passions of racial superiority by rousing mass feelings of the lost supremacy of Germans. That myth created more lies, persecution of non-Germans, concentration camps and finally spelled the doom of the entire nation. Shankar Goyal's disquisition takes into consideration a number of factors which make a collection of people eligible to be termed a nation, such as possessing a definite geographical area within which they live together, sharing common cultural traits, beliefs and patterns of life and an urge to remain united. However, a more potential factor is a single political system governing such a collection. What makes the birth of a nation and its continuation possible is cohesion among its people however diversified they may be. This is a more liberal and inclusive definition as it allows for different kinds of diversity with adequate room for their growth and prosperity.

Examples of both types are available where a nation has been the home of a single racial stock and a single cultural-religious pursuit like Nepal and Bhutan. But it cannot be regarded as a defining tenet as it does not guarantee that people of a single racial stock or ideological and religio-cultural following may agree to form a nation. German is the official language of both Austria and Belgium, yet the two are separate nations. In Belgium French and Dutch are official languages, yet its people do not want to be identified with France or Holland. Ideologically, Poland, Hungary and Cuba were communist countries (Cuba continues to remain communist), yet language-wise, culturally and racially they are quite different.

In section five of the chapter two Shankar Goyal's statement that the greater the cultural unity, the easier it becomes for people to come together as a nation (pp. 22 ff.) is not absolutely convincing as in the case of Arabic and Persian cultures large chunks of population form separate nations like Saudi Arabia, Qatar and Jordan (of Arabic racial stock), North and South Korea, Peoples' Republic of China and Nationalist China. The reasons in different cases are apparently different. African countries present still more intriguing picture of the Negroid race being fragmented into numerous ethnic and tribal groups, some of which follow Islam, some Christianity, many of which speak various languages like French, Belgian, Spanish, Arabic, English besides their native languages. The case of the West Indian countries is a highly interesting one, some of which attained freedom in the 1960s. With their independent flags, parliaments and constitutions, Trinidad and Tobago, Barbados, Jamaica and Antigua are separate countries, appearing as such in the U.N. and Olympic Games. But in international cricket tournaments all these countries join to form an eleven member team known as the team of the West Indies! Gary Sobers is a West Indian player but a Barbados national; Alvin Kallicharan is a West Indian cricketer but a national of Guyana; similarly Michael Holding is West Indian bowler but a national of Jamaica. Perhaps a Jamaican or a Barbadian watching a cricket match cheers for a West Indies hitting a four irrespective of the fact that he is neither from Jamaica nor from Barbados but a born Guyana or Trinidad national! But in the Olympic Games he may behave differently identifying the performer as belonging to his particular country. Their nationalistic feelings in cricket competition are of a different character from those in the Olympic Games! Somewhere in Shankar Goyal's lengthy disquisition ideas of 'nation' and 'nationalism' appear to coalesce and feeling of loyalty to one's nation gets upper hand in portraying the concept of nation. As his concluding remarks show, it is this 'feeling' of unity, 'this urge' to hold together by the thread of common language and culture that facilitates the sense of being a nation. This may be a crucial factor in movements for separatist political recognition; such identities are not significant in formation of a nation.

The debate over whether India has ever been a nation opens out various ways of probing the issue. It also begs the question whether 'nation' in the Western sense can be regarded as equivalent of the Sanskrit term '*rashtra*'. Whatever the polemical standpoints, one feels that the Western idea of 'nation' appears to sum it up more adequately and accurately than does the more nuanced word '*rashtra*'.

Shankar Goyal opens in chapter three the discussion about India's heterogeneous social fabric which accommodates various racial stocks, ranging from the Aryan and Dravidian to Mongoloid, Austric and Negroid at the broader level. Within each fold can be identified further layers of diversified formations, and social ethnic, cultural, and religious orders. He makes use of such well-known authorities' views as N. Mujumdar, Chamberlain and Gunther to emphasize that false notion of racial superiority has been the bane of many an ambitious military campaign. In the past, racist view of militarism had been given importance with the support of preposterous claims of 'scientific' and 'genetic' researches in order to legitimize its oppressive systems. Even in our days there are large numbers of followers of this thought actively engaged in mobilizing passions in favour of certain religious and political interests. In truth, believers in superiority of Aryan race have always been busy trying to prove that the race is either divinely blessed or it can be scientifically proved that it is a better endowed stock. This, in their opinion explains these peoples' greater achievements and rewards them with authority to rule over others. As a logical corollary, this inherent element of superior gifts justifies their treatment of other (inferior) races and faiths as well as the exclusivist and restrictive systems that are constructed around them. This is the ideological position which the Nazi state of Hitler took in weaning out the Jews and non-Aryan people in creating ghettos and concentration camps for them, and maligning their faiths and beliefs. As Shankar Goyal points out it was the British historians, Arnold Toynbee and G.M. Trevelyan who highlighted the fact that it is not possible to conceive of a single race solely forming a nation. Contribution of other races is equally important.

India offers an extraordinary example of the accommodative process of nation building where many races and beliefs come into contact to influence one another from the earliest known years of history. As Pandit Jawaharlal Nehru remarks in *The Discovery of India*, "The diversity of India is tremendous; it is obvious; it lies on the surface and anybody can see it. It concerns itself with physical appearances as well as with certain mental habits and traits. There is little in common, to outward seeming, between the Pathan of the North-West and the Tamil in the Far South ... It is fascinating to find how the Bengalis, the Punjabis, the Marathas, the Gujaratis, the Tamils, the Andhras, the Pathans, the Kashmiris, the Rajputs the Oriyas, the Sindhis, and the central block comprising the Hindustani-speaking people have retained their peculiar characteristics for hundreds of years, have still more or less the same virtues and failings of which old tradition or record tells us, and yet have been throughout these ages distinctively Indian, with the same national heritage and the same set of moral and mental qualities. There was something living and dynamic about this heritage which showed itself in ways of living and a philosophical attitude to life and its problems ... Foreign influences poured in and often influenced that culture and were absorbed. Disruptive tendencies have risen immediately to an attempt to find synthesis. Some kind of a dream unity has occupied the mind of India since the dawn of civilization. That unity was not conceived as something imposed from outside, standardization of externals or even of beliefs. It was something deeper and, within its fold, the widest tolerance of belief and custom was practiced and every variety acknowledged and even encouraged." (Nehru 1982). Shankar Goyal has done well to emphasize how all aspects of Indian cultural and religious life have been the outcome of influences from diverse cultures and civilizations. This has created a uniquely catholic and open-minded character of the society here. More importantly, it created in Hindu theology a tendency to assimilate certain congenial elements from other faiths and their practices. In the pre-Vedic era there flourished a mighty non-Aryan civilization which was conquered by the Aryans in their ambitious march into the sub-continent. In this long process of conquest Vedic religious and social philosophy imbibed and absorbed from diverse other sources those deities, icons, practices, customs and sacraments that later on became an integral part of the Vedic and Hindu culture. This process set in motion the core dynamism of Hindu culture, namely its splendid resilience, inclusivity and broad catholicity. Explaining it in detail, S. Radhakrishnan delivered a series of lectures in Manchester College, Oxford in 1926 which were later on published in the form of a book entitled *A Hindu View of Life*. At one place the great philosopher-statesman remarks, "Hinduism is wholly free from the strange obsession of the Semitic faiths that the acceptance of a particular religious metaphysic is necessary for salvation, and non-acceptance thereof is a heinous sin meriting eternal punishment in hell. Here and there outbursts of sectarian fanaticism are found recorded in the literature of the Hindus, which indicate the first effects of the conflicts of the different groups brought together into one fold; but the note of Hinduism is one of respect and goodwill for other creeds." (Radahakrishnan 1926).

It is not surprising that non-violence and mutual love occupy central place in spiritual life view and has been preached by the seers and gurus of all religious and metaphysical followings. Despite the counter offensive of hatred and 'otherness' launched by fanatics and adherents of extreme conservatism, the core element of love and unity always proved strong enough to withstand such onslaughts. Swami Vivekananda conveyed a word of caution quite often in his speeches and letters. "The real spiritual man is broad everywhere. His love forces him to be so. Those to whom religion is a trade are forced to become narrow and mischievous by their introduction into religion of the competitive fighting and selfish methods of the world." (Vivekananda's letter to Dharmapala, U.S.A. 1894).

Though Shankar Goyal has not dwelt at length on this aspect of the country's dominant religion which originated in broad philosophical apprehension of man's relation with his world and cosmos, it must be emphasized that our syncretic culture evolved out of this theological vigour ready to assimilate many strands of thought and articles of faith. Religion has always been a great shaping force in our society. While in ancient times and in the ages following them it governed our life and social habits, politics and culture, in more secular and scientific times of the present era it is repeatedly invoked as a weapon to bring a typical racial consciousness of purity, which motivates some sections of our society. That is why it has become all the more important to know the true nature of the development of our religious base and culture.

In this respect Shankar Goyal's small book makes timely appearance. It brings out the central point that at all levels, diversity and heterogeneity form the kernel of our culture. Search for a 'pure' race, caste, language or religious attitude is simply pointless. When the Aryans found a more opulent civilization already flourishing before their appearance on the scene from which they gathered useful elements and concepts to build up their own particular philosophy, the dye of the pluralistic character of India's spiritual-religious composition was cast. Shankar Goyal has admirably analyzed this in the chapter under discussion. Somewhere he mentions the famous philosopher-historian Debiprasad Chattopadhyaya whose work *Lokayata* offers a wealth of evidence to establish how the multiple non-Aryan faith and religions influenced the early stages of the formation of Hinduism and its ritualistic paraphernalia. Recently Asko Parpola, the Finnish Sindhologist and Indologist in his book *The Roots of Hinduism* (Oxford University Press, 2015), arduously worked out an elaborate picture of how the Hindu or Indian culture was the result of two diverse cultural formations. "Indo-Aryans and Dravidians have merged millennia ago to form the roots of Hinduism and sustain the continuity of Indian historical tradition till the present day." (Parpola 2015).

Shankar Goyal further discusses the linguistic variety that enriches the life of the sub-continent and the wealth of literary traditions contained in those languages. Despite the fact that all major languages and their dialects originate from the two completely different language families, the Indo-Aryan and the Dravidian, much linguistic assimilation at the phonetic, morphological and syntactic levels have taken place. Dravidian languages in the south show large scale borrowings from the Aryan languages and the vice versa. It is wrong to say that such a phenomenon of quite different languages coexisting together and significantly influencing the structure of languages is unique to India; English language is a fine example of the conglomerate character of a language comprising elements from such diverse sources as Greek, Latin, German, Yiddish, Hindi, Russian, Frisian, Scandinavian and sundry other families. Perhaps it is difficult to define the 'true' character of English with any degree of clarity. It is a process that produces amazing results. One is reminded of the title of A.L. Basham's book *The Wonder that was India.* The wonder is not that it has a glorious civilization and culture, and an old religious-philosophical heritage that is still alive and palpitating. The wonder is that its diversity and heterogeneity often seems incongruous and discrepant, and yet it continues to cherish these attributes as its life force, keeping united and making room for the prosperous development of all those disparate identities and distinct entities in one Indian nation. For those who still feel puzzled over how a nation can progress with its baggage of pluralistic, diversified composition need to look at this country with an unbiased view for it appears to articulate the following definition of multiculturalism in tangible terms: " ... multiculturalism refers to situations in which people who hold 'different' habits, customs, traditions, languages and/or religions live alongside each other in the same social space, willingly to maintain relevant aspects of their own difference and to have it publicly recognized. Usually the term involves a positive evaluation of cultural diversity and the institutional commitment to its preservation." (Colombo 2014)

REFERENCES

1. Pandit Jawaharlal Nehru, *The Discovery of India*, New Delhi, Oxford University Press, 1982, pp. 61 ff.

2. Edward Said, *Orientalism*, New Delhi, Penguin Books, 2001.

3. Bill Ashcroft, Gareth Griffiths and Helen Tiffin, *The Empire Writes Back*, London, Routledge, 2002, pp. 3 ff.

4. Raymond Williams, *Keywords*. https:// pubpaged.unh.edu/ndml3/ 880williams.htm.

5. Raja Ram Mohan Roy's letter to Lord Amherst, https://oxfordfirstissue.com

6. S. Radhakrishnan, *The Hindu View of Life*, New York, George Allen and Unwin Ltd., 1949, pp. 45 ff.

7. Debiprasad Chattopadhyaya, *Lokayata*, New Delhi, Peoples' Publishing House, 1978.

8. Joshua Rothman, 'The Meaning of Culture', *New Yorker*, Dec. 26, 2014.

9. *Letters of Swami Vivekananda*, Calcutta, Advaita Ashrama, 1995.

10. A.L. Basham, *The Wonder that was India*, London, Picador Macmillan Ltd., 2004.

11.'Why is India a Nation?' Sankrant Sanu , www.https://sankrantsanu.org

12. www.https://open.ac.ukresearchproject

13. Colombo Enzo, 'Multiculturalisms', University of Milan, Italy, sociopedia.isa 2014, pp. 1 ff.

14. Asko Parpola, *The Roots of Hinduism, The Early Aryans and the Indus Civilization*, London, Oxford University Press, 2015.

To be published shortly :

Situating Indian History for Shankar Goyal

Edited with an Introduction by

RADHIKA SESHAN

The present volume is an anthology of essays by such eminent scholars as Professors Romila Thapar, R. Champakalakshmi, Irfan Habib, Shireen Moosvi, Saiyid Zaheer Husain Jafri, Kumkum Roy, Bhairabi Prasad Sahu, Ishrat Alam, Udai Prakash Arora, Nayanjot Lahiri, P. Shanmugam, Radhika Seshan, Susmita Basu Majumdar, Suchandra Ghosh and R. Mahalakshmi, in honour of Professor Shankar Goyal, a dedicated historian and a teacher of history, to felicitate him on his long and productive career.

Ranging from the early historic period to contemporary reconstructions of historical events, the chronological span covered by these essays is remarkable. So is their spatial range—with a special focus on several unique regions of the subcontinent as well as on links with the wider world. These provide the framework for broad surveys as well as in-depth studies, using a range of sources—textual, epigraphic, numismatic, and archaeological. The thematic sweep is also noteworthy—historiographical debates, discussions on diverse societies and economies, on kings as well as ordinary people, and on a range of religious and cultural practices, analyzed from a variety of perspectives. The historical insights that emerge are likely to stand the test of time.